1998 Best Newspaper Writing

WINNERS: THE AMERICAN SOCIETY OF NEWSPAPER EDITORS COMPETITION

EDITED BY CHRISTOPHER SCANLAN

The Poynter Institute
and
Bonus Books, Inc.

02   01   00   99   98   5   4   3   2   1

International Standard Book Number:
International Standard Serial Number:

The Poynter Institute for Media Studies
801 Third Street South
St. Petersburg, Florida 33701

Bonus Books, Inc.
160 East Illinois Street
Chicago, Illinois 60611

Book design and production by Billie M. Keirstead
Cover illustration by Phillip Gary Design, St. Petersburg, Florida

Photos for cover illustration were provided by Chuck Zoeller of
The Associated Press and are used with permission. Photo Credits:
AP photographers Jerome Delay (Princess Diana crash scene), Nati
Harnik (Tel Aviv bombing), and Marty Lederhandler (AT&T exec-
utives); AP stinger Keith Srakocic (KKK rally); pool photographers
Victoria Arocho (Louise Woodward) and David J. Phillip (Grand
Forks, N.D., flood). Photo of Angela Brown, North County High
School, by Baltimore *Sun* photographer Nanine Hartzenbusch.
Photos of ASNE award winners and finalists were provided by their
newspapers.

Printed in the United States of America

This book is dedicated to the memory of
Herb Caen, Murray Kempton, Mike Royko,
and Nancy Jane Woodhull, whose voices
were stilled the year these stories
were written, and to the next generation
of men and women in journalism.

About this series

JUNE 1998

My introduction to the ASNE Distinguished Writing Awards involved a trip across Manhattan at 80 mph in a car driven by a madman in search of tuxedo studs.

The madman was Richard Ben Cramer, a writer whose performance on deadline in covering the Middle East was risk-taking, fearless, and brilliant. As his line editor, I was privileged to accompany Cramer to the banquet in New York where he, Tom Oliphant, Mary Ellen Corbett, and Everett Allen were being honored.

Cramer was, as usual, fighting deadline. Minutes before we were due at the black-tie dinner, Cramer still was in his apartment putting on a borrowed tuxedo. It fit, but he'd neglected to borrow the studs needed to hold the shirtfront together.

Once again Cramer was risk-taking and fearless on deadline...though I wouldn't say brilliant unless by brilliant we mean capable of hurtling his car crosstown at speeds I could not imagine being able to achieve in Manhattan. I confess that sometimes I just closed my eyes as we careened from one of his acquaintances to another in Hell's Kitchen or Greenwich Village, until he managed to dredge up a set of studs from a *Newsweek* editor and get us to the banquet just in time not to miss the meal.

I had forgotten until recently that my affection for this award and appreciation for what it can mean to writers in a newsroom dates to the very inception of the award in 1979. I can attest that ASNE's recognition of Cramer helped to accomplish what the founders of this award wanted. In my old newsroom at *The Philadelphia Inquirer,* Cramer became a role model for fine writing, and continues to be one two decades later.

At the instance of five storied editors—Gene Roberts, John McMullan, David Lawrence, Larry Jinks, and Jim Batten—the honor paid to Cramer's 1978 writing was instrumental in persuading Knight Ridder to deploy eight foreign correspondents, a commitment that the corporation funds to this day.

There is a central reason that this award has become so coveted: Distinguished writers have been determined by distinguished judges. The first panel was composed of Tom Winship in the chair, Jim Batten, Judith Brown, Ed Cony, John Emmerich, Kay Fanning, Phil Geyelin, Jim Hoge, Max McCrohon, Claude Sitton, and Bill Thomas.

Each year, top American journalists have gathered at Poynter to examine the nominations for the Distinguished Writing Awards and, since 1995, for the Jesse Laventhol Prizes for Deadline News Reporting. The latter were endowed by David A. Laventhol, editor-at-large of the Times Mirror Co., to honor his late father, a veteran Philadelphia newspaperman.

The categories of awards this year are deadline news reporting by an individual, deadline news reporting by a team, non-deadline writing, commentary, editorial writing, and criticism. The 1998 ASNE Writing Awards Board was chaired by Gregory E. Favre, executive editor of *The Sacramento Bee.* The other judges were:

Gilbert Bailon, *The Dallas Morning News.*
Joann Byrd, *Seattle Post-Intelligencer.*
Robert H. Giles, Media Studies Center, New York.
Tonnie Katz, *The Orange County Register.*
William B. Ketter, *The Patriot Ledger,* Quincy, Mass.
Frosty Landon, retired, Roanoke, Va.
Carolyn Lee, *The New York Times.*
Wanda Lloyd, *The Greenville* (S.C.) *News.*
Ron Martin, *Atlanta Journal and Constitution.*
Diane McFarlin, *Sarasota* (Fla.) *Herald-Tribune.*
Rena M. Pederson, *The Dallas Morning News.*
Sandra Rowe, *The Oregonian,* Portland, Ore.
Matthew V. Storin, *The Boston Globe.*
Paul Tash, *St. Petersburg* (Fla.) *Times.*
Gil Thelen, *Tampa* (Fla.) *Tribune.*
Howard Tyner, *Chicago Tribune.*

The high level these awards have maintained is due to other key figures. They include Gene Giancarlo and Lee Stinnett of ASNE, who have so efficiently organized the daunting task of selecting the prizeworthy writing. They include Don Baldwin, the first director of what became The Poynter Institute, and Bob Haiman, who as Poynter's president had the joy of participating in 13 of these volumes of fine writing. They include Poynter faculty who have lovingly edited and published *Best Newspaper Writing*: Karen Brown Dunlap, Chip Scanlan, Don Fry, and Billie Keirstead. They include unsung heroines who have coordinated with ASNE on behalf of Poynter: Joyce Olson, Bobbi Alsina, Nancy Stewart, and especially Priscilla Ely.

And they include two individuals who deserve particular thanks and admiration:

Gene Patterson, the retired editor of the *St. Petersburg Times,* invented these awards and invested in them a special purpose, arranging for them to be bestowed in a way that did not merely honor individual achievement but that guided others in understanding how to achieve. As you'll see in this volume, there are invaluable tips from the writers whose work is celebrated.

And Roy Peter Clark has been inspiring prizeworthy performances ever since Gene Patterson commissioned Roy to study newspaper writing and then to try to fix it. At ASNE's 1978 convention, Roy said this:

"The newsroom is a fertile area for encouraging good writers. The main problem is not in individuals, in my experience, but in the institution itself. How do you free writers and editors to do their best work? How do you build into the newspaper an atmosphere conducive to good writing? How do you create an environment in which good writing is recognized and rewarded?"

Two decades later, good writing, distinguished writing, is recognized and rewarded. It's no coincidence that Gene Patterson and Roy Clark are themselves distinguished writers. Please salute them for having given root to something so valuable that we continue, two decades later, to commit ourselves to nurturing it.

James N. Naughton, President
The Poynter Institute

Acknowledgments

This book reflects the efforts and contributions of many people and organizations, chief among them The American Society of Newspaper Editors, especially Lee Stinnett, executive director, and Gregory E. Favre, executive editor of *The Sacramento Bee,* who chaired the writing awards committee. A special thanks to ASNE president Sandra Rowe for her support. Chuck Zoeller of The Associated Press continued to generously provide the news photos used on the cover.

This volume has been especially enriched by my Poynter colleagues. Faculty members Roy Peter Clark, Aly Colón, Karen Brown Dunlap, and Keith Woods each conducted interviews. Researcher/Archivist David Shedden provided his always comprehensive bibliography. Vicki Krueger, an experienced copy editor, wrote the Writers' Workshop sections and proofread the manuscript. Billie Keirstead, publications director, produced this book on a journalism deadline. They were aided by Priscilla Ely, Martin Gregor, Nancy Stewart, and Joyce Olson of the Institute staff.

Readers benefit most of all from the stories and lessons about reporting and writing shared by the winners and finalists of this year's Distinguished Writing and Jesse Laventhol Awards. *Best Newspaper Writing 1998* is their book.

Contents

Helping make natural-born writers: A 20-year journey

Are good writers born or made?

Coming from an editor interested in improving the quality of writing at her newspaper, the question sounded plaintive. Like many an editor and reporter, she wanted to know what produced great writing. Was it a mysterious brew of intellect and ego that a writer either had or didn't have, or was it a skill that could be learned?

In 1979, the publication of the first volume of *Best Newspaper Writing* came down squarely on the nurture side of the perennial debate.

Twenty years later, *Best Newspaper Writing* remains unique on the crowded shelves of journalistic prizes. It celebrates good writing by publishing the winning entries of the annual competition sponsored by the American Society of Newspaper Editors. And by exploring the way the stories were written, in interviews with the winners and essays by finalists, it remains committed to the idea that writing is a craft whose lessons can be shared, described, and, with time and diligence, mastered.

Writing, like most creative endeavors, is often shrouded in myth or clouded by discussions of rituals. (E.B. White started his writing day with a martini, Poet Laureate Rita Dove composes by the light of two candles, one writer uses No. 2 pencils, another swears by WordPerfect, and so on.)

But mystification doesn't help writers who want to write better. What we need to know are the lessons of good reporting and writing that the reporters, columnists, editorial writers, and critics share in these pages.

1998 BEST NEWSPAPER WRITING

The topsy-turvy world of telecommunications was one of the biggest business stories of 1997. John J. Keller of *The Wall Street Journal* won the Jesse Laventhol Award for individual deadline reporting with stories that went behind the scenes of mergers, shake-ups, and boardroom soap operas, and gauged their impact on customers, shareholders, and employees. A day af-

ter he broke the news that AT&T's new president was
out, he filed a richly detailed story:

The former chairman of R.R. Donnelley &
Sons blew into AT&T like a cool autumn wind
last November. Knowing well [board chairman]
Mr. Allen's reputation for being aloof with AT&T
employees, middle managers and Wall Street, the
new president played to all three constituencies.
He urged the rank and file to e-mail him about
their concerns. He could warmly greet the lowliest subordinate with an arm around the shoulder.
He called the executive suite in AT&T's plush
Basking Ridge, N.J. offices "Carpet Land" and
ordered the executive dining room closed, forcing
senior managers to use the company cafeteria as
everyone else did.

When a Ku Klux Klan rally and counter-protests
tested a city's resolve to protect freedom of speech and
itself from the virus of hate, the staff of the *Pittsburgh
Post-Gazette* produced narrative writing on deadline
that won the Laventhol team reporting prize. From
watching and listening posts across the city, the team
did it by bringing readers directly to the scene as in this
battle of words between a young pro-Klan woman and
a group of anti-Klan protesters who confronted her:

"Y'all get the hell out of here!" shouts Elmer
Hyatt, a black man from Wilkinsburg.
"I'm allowed to stand here if I want to, right?
Why should we get out?" [Laura] Finney says.
Angry words go back and forth and Finney
turns around to discover that her cohorts have
melted away into the crowd.
"You know what I'd like to know?" George
Spratley, a North Side man, asks Finney. "What
are you going to do when you go to heaven and
you find out God is a black man?"
"I guess I'll go to hell," Finney says.

Ken Fuson of the Baltimore *Sun* is a writer known
for his ability to touch the reader's heart as well as
mind. He won the non-deadline writing prize with a
six-part serial narrative that told the coming-of-age tale

of a group of blue-collar high school kids staging a production of the musical *West Side Story* and, in the process, learning the difference between drama and real life:

> One by one, execution style, the victims enter the classroom. They clutch sheets of music and wads of tissue.
> *I've got a sinus infection.*
> *I have a sore throat. I can't go any higher.*
> *I think I'm sick.*
> "We've all got the drama flu," one girl explains.
> This is audition week. Student ability will be judged in three areas—acting, dancing and singing. How well they do determines the role they will get. The acting and dancing tryouts are fun, but most would rather find a fresh pimple on prom night than sing alone in public.

When a flooding river brought ice, water, and then fires that destroyed a North Dakota town and its newspaper, editor Mike Jacobs of the *Grand Forks Herald* wrote editorials that comforted and challenged a devastated community. Even as his own newsroom was burning, he wrote these words:

> Our notions about ourselves must also have changed. Thousands of us found the strength of character to help selflessly, even heroically. As our homes were destroyed, we reminded each other that "It's only stuff," and that "So many others have it so much worse."
> We must have wondered, all of us, whether any community anywhere had ever suffered so much and yet we know that others have. Miraculously, we have been spared loss of life. Marvelously, we have found friendships we didn't know about, as strangers came to offer labor, called to offer shelter, reached out to offer strength. Could it have been so in any other town? Yes, perhaps. But never on such a scale in our hometown. And it is in that spirit, from that indomitable strength, that our hometown will go forward. It is going to be a difficult time. Let us begin this morning.

Justin Davidson of *Newsday* and Stephen Hunter of *The Washington Post* share the honors for arts criticism. Davidson brings a music lover's passion, a composer's insight, and a reporter's eye to reviews of opera, Beethoven, and Sibelius that enable readers to see a performance as well as to hear it. After you read this lead, close your eyes and imagine it:

> The pianist Evgeny Kissin propelled himself stiffly onto the stage of Avery Fisher Hall on Thursday, looking rather as if his joints needed oiling. He dutifully bent his mouth into a labored and momentary smile, gave a quick jerk of his torso in lieu of a bow, and then sat at the piano where, in an instant, all his discomfort melted into power and control.
>
> Watching the awkward young pianist plunge into music was like seeing a seal slip into water, and in the 40 mesmerizing minutes that followed, Kissin gave one of the most lissome and lyrical performances of Beethoven's Piano Concerto No. 5 that I have ever heard.

Steve Hunter's reviews are often better than the movies he writes about. He combines encyclopedic knowledge and savage wit that target the essence of the year's best and worst films.

> Little-known fact about Stalinist Russia, 1926, courtesy of *Anastasia:* There was no food but there was a surprising abundance of Maybelline eyeliner.
>
> How else to explain the almond definition of Anastasia's vaguely Orientalized eyes in this beautiful idiot of an animated movie? She doesn't look like a Russian princess at all, but more like a teenage Cher.
>
> Though it's from 20th Century Fox, *Anastasia* shows us a very Disney Russian Revolution. So Disney that, oops, they forgot the Communists.

You get the news from these and the other stories in this volume, the news of the day, the story of our times, and a bonus: humor and sorrow, poetry and prose, compassion, argument, explanation, understanding, and insight. In their stories behind the stories, this year's winners and finalists also teach an enduring and hopeful message to anyone struggling to write: Good writers may be born, but with hard work and steady devotion to their craft, they can also be made, if not great, certainly better.

A NOTE ABOUT THIS EDITION

In February 1998, The Writing Awards Committee of ASNE selected Patricia Smith, a metro columnist for *The Boston Globe,* as the winner of the Distinguished Writing Award for commentary/column writing. She was also chosen as a finalist for the Pulitzer Prize. On June 18, *The Boston Globe* reported that it had asked for and received Smith's resignation after she admitted fabricating people and quotations in four of her columns. Subsequently, the *Globe* asked ASNE to rescind the award and the editors' association agreed. As a result, the columns by Smith that were initially honored do not appear in this book. Commentary/column writing is represented in *Best Newspaper Writing 1998* by the three finalists chosen by the ASNE judges.

This marks the first time in the award's 20-year history that a winning writer has been stripped of the award. Sadly, it is not the first instance of fabrication by a journalist; in fact the Smith case was one of several highly publicized instances of unethical behavior by journalists that surfaced in the spring of 1998.

A fuller description of the Patricia Smith case and the issues it raises for journalists appears in the Commentary section of this book.

The discussions with the ASNE winners in this book are based on tape-recorded telephone interviews conducted by myself and my Poynter Institute colleagues Roy Peter Clark, Aly Colón, Karen Brown Dunlap, and Keith Woods. For reasons of clarity or pacing, we reorganized some questions and answers, and in some cases, inserted additional questions. The edited transcripts were reviewed for accuracy and, in some cases, revised slightly by the subjects.

Christopher Scanlan
June 1998

1998 Best Newspaper Writing

Ken Fuson
Non-Deadline Writing

In winning the ASNE award, Ken Fuson forfeits his chance to be forever known as "the Susan Lucci of American Journalism."

Fuson, 41, was a finalist for the award three times. Those near-misses joined the Ernie Pyle award (finalist twice), the Livingston Award for Young Journalists (finalist three times), and the Pulitzer Prize (never a finalist), a litany of frustration and futility believed unmatched in American letters.

A native of Granger, Iowa, (population 600), Fuson landed his first newspaper job when he was a sophomore in high school and walked into the offices of the Northeast Dallas *County Record* (Woodward Enterprise edition) and asked if he could cover sports. This led to an ugly incident with members of the 0-14 Woodward-

Granger girls' basketball team, who objected to Fuson's describing them as "scrappy."

Fuson attended the University of Missouri, majoring in journalism, where he faced a life-changing decision: Take his finals, thus making four years of school pay off with a degree, or interview Vincent Bugliosi, the author of *Helter Skelter.* Showing the sort of foresight that has long marked his career, Fuson skipped the finals. He is awaiting an honorary degree.

In college, Fuson worked one summer on the *St. Louis Post-Dispatch,* where he interviewed a woman who saved a dog's life by giving it mouth-to-mouth resuscitation. After college, he worked three years at the *Columbia* (Mo.) *Daily Tribune,* once beginning an interview with Dawn Wells—Mary Ann on *Gilligan's Island*—by asking her to marry him. (She declined.)

In 1981, Fuson realized a lifelong dream and returned to Iowa to work for *The Des Moines Register,* where he won the National Headliner Award for feature writing in 1996 and captured three Outstanding Achievement in Writing Awards in the annual Best of Gannett contest.

Fuson has been with the Baltimore *Sun* since the fall of 1996. He has written for *GQ* and *Esquire,* and his profile of Green Bay Packers quarterback Brett Favre was included in the *Best American Sports Writing* anthology.

Fuson and his wife, Amy, have two sons, Jesse, 12, and Max, 7. He also has a stepson, Jared Reese, 20.

"A Stage in Their Lives" also won first place in the University of Missouri Lifestyle Reporting awards.

—Ken Fuson

A stage in their lives, Part 1

JUNE 1, 1997

What a show: love, fear, lost dreams, broken hearts. Here's your ticket to the making of a high school musical. The real action takes place offstage—in the drama known as growing up.

Spellbound she sits, her mother on one side, her boyfriend on the other, as another young woman performs the role that will someday be hers.

Since she was little, Angie Guido has dreamed of standing on stage, playing the Puerto Rican girl who falls in love with the Polish boy named Tony.

Maria.

She will be Maria in *West Side Story.*

Say it loud and there's music playing.

"That's me, Mom," she said.

Say it soft and it's almost like praying.

It won't be long, Angie thinks as she delights in a touring company production of *West Side Story* at the Lyric Opera House in Baltimore. She and 20 members of the Drama Club from North County High School in Anne Arundel County attend the December show with a few parents. This is a prelude; there is expectant talk they will stage the same show for their spring musical.

Someday soon, Angie hopes, she will own the role that is rightfully hers. She has been a loyal drama club soldier, serving on committees, singing in the chorus when she yearned for a solo, watching lead roles slip away because she didn't look the part. But Maria is short, as she is, and dark, as she is, and more than that, Angie is a senior. This will be her last spring musical. Her last chance to shine.

But on the very next night, in that very same theater, another girl from North County High sits spellbound, her mother on one side, her best friend on the other.

She, too, is captivated by the Puerto Rican girl with the pretty voice.

She, too, wonders: *What if that were me?*

Two months later, in the middle of February, two dozen students gather in a dark and cavernous auditorium at North County High School to plan the spring musical.

You don't know them. Not yet.

Find a seat—there, in the middle, close to the stage—and watch.

You will meet two girls. One will have her dream come true, the other won't, and the experience will change them both.

You will meet a boy who can't sing but refuses to quit trying.

You will meet another boy, the leading man, who falls for one of the leading ladies. But so will someone else.

You will meet a girl who wants to be a star, then chooses a new destiny.

Come to the practices. Laugh at their goofy jokes. Encourage them when they flub their lines.

Soon you will know them.

And you will know this:

The high school musical is a rite of passage that will shape—and reveal—the adults they will soon be.

And nothing ever produced on stage can possibly match the drama of growing up.

* * *

As he walks to the drama club meeting, Wayne Shipley is worried. He doesn't have a cast chosen. He doesn't have scripts ordered. He doesn't even know what show he's directing—and February is half gone. Opening night is less than eight weeks away.

The 900-seat auditorium roils with after-school mischief. A boy and girl snuggle. Two boys wage a pretend sword fight on stage. Other students animatedly relive the highlights of their just-completed one-act play festival.

"Hey, Ship!" a boy yells.

Mr. Shipley cuts an imposing figure as he stands before the drama club. At 53, he is tall, mostly bald, partial to blue jeans and cowboy boots. He has the strength and thickness of a former middle linebacker and two potent weapons: a gentle smile that calms the most paralyzing case of stage fright, and a terrorizing stare that automatically persuades teen-age boys this would be a smart time to shut up.

"We are behind schedule, which is obvious," he says before leaving. "Let's get with it, guys."

After 30 years of teaching, Mr. Shipley is retiring; this will be his last musical. The students, who adore him, know he has long dreamed of directing *West Side Story* but has always deemed it too challenging. This year, it's the students who doubt. The touring company's powerful performance at the Lyric last December left many intimidated. How can they possibly do the acting, singing and dancing demanded—especially when they are a week behind?

"Quiet, everybody."

A senior walks to the front. She has a radiant smile and a faint limp.

"Quiet!"

Presenting Starr Lucas, 18, the drama club president and the reason Mr. Shipley feels safe leaving two dozen teen-agers alone in a dark auditorium.

"Starr was named appropriately," he says.

Somehow this girl with the dark blond ponytail and ruby red lipstick became lost in a time warp. Starr is straight off the Berkeley campus, circa 1967: hip-hugging, bell-bottom blue jeans, tie-dyed shirts, a patch on her book bag that says WAR IS NOT HEALTHY FOR CHILDREN AND OTHER LIVING THINGS. She drives a blue Volkswagen Beetle with smiley face decals on the windows and says things like, "I'm waiting for a better generation."

A free spirit without the flightiness, Starr owns a crowded résumé—class president four straight years; member of the National Honor Society for two years; president of the Thespians, the drama honor society, for three years. She calls herself the Drama Queen.

This year, for the first time in her abundant high school career, Starr will not appear on stage, a prospect that both excites and saddens her. She will be the student director of the spring musical.

If there is a spring musical.

"Let's get to work," Starr says. "What do we want to do?"

A Chorus Line?

No.

42nd Street?

No.

The Wizard of Oz?

"Oh, puh-leeze," says Eli Senter, a junior. "If anyone votes for that, I will personally cut their throats."

When Mr. Shipley feels playful, he affectionately refers to the drama club by another name—"Drama Geek Sissies." It's a pre-emptive strike. He knows many North County High students view theater types as loud, weird and effeminate.

Eli wears the Drama Geek Sissy label like a sailor's tattoo. He is 17, 116 pounds (with clothes), all bony angles and pointed opinions. Never in Eli's life has a drama teacher had to encourage him to project his voice.

Ask him about the drama club's reputation among the rest of the student body, and he sneers, "I prefer not to talk about the podunks and morons who don't understand art or the theater."

His high school sits like a factory atop a hill in the northern tip of Anne Arundel County, drawing students from Linthicum, Ferndale and Brooklyn Park. Five minutes away, planes take off from Baltimore-Washington International Airport.

North County High is a blue-collar school in a suburban county; the neighborhood homes are older and middle-class, with basketball hoops in the driveways and swing sets in the back yards. Surrounding the school are four softball and baseball fields, a football field, a track and several practice fields. Generally, Mr. Shipley says, drama is tolerated as a fine alternative for those poor souls unblessed in athletics. Students who do both are exceptions.

The debate continues.

Seven Brides for Seven Brothers?

No.

"Can we go over *The Sound of Music?*" asks Alanna Clements, a senior.

Everyone groans.

"Wait a minute," she protests. "There's a lot of parts and not all of them sing. We could get little kids for the little-kid parts."

"Little kids have parents and little kids' parents suck," Eli says.

Eli wins, Alanna loses. Next case.

"Let's have a very serious talk about *West Side Story*," Eli says. "I want to do this play. Mr. Shipley wants to do it."

"*West Side Story* is too good for us to do poorly," another boy says. "I think we would do it poorly. Our female to male ratio is about—"

"Twenty to one," Michele Miller says.

Of the 1,700 students at North County, perhaps 70 have performed in a fall play, the one-acts or the spring musical. About 30 belong to the drama club, and most are girls. Girls head most of the committees. Girls do most of the organizational work. Girls raise most of the money.

But they don't get most of the parts.

Michele Miller knows there are two great female roles in *West Side Story*—Maria and Anita—and not much else. Because so few boys try out, most land a decent role, while competition is fierce among the girls. Some relegated to the chorus would have a leading role if they were boys.

"If you can sing, you'll be in it," she says. "And everyone else isn't going to get anything."

A senior, Michele loves to act, but hates to sing. She and several other girls prefer *Anything Goes,* the Cole Porter comedy set on a cruise ship.

The lines are drawn.

Eli: "There's a couple of really big scenes for girls in *West Side Story.*"

Michele: "I can visualize a boat with more people on it than a gang."

Eli: "There's no happy medium here, Michele."

She flicks her hands in the air, dismissing him.

"Let's just vote."

Their job this afternoon is to reduce the field to two. They vote in secret, writing on slips of notebook paper.

Starr sits on the floor and counts.

Anything Goes—13.

West Side Story—11.

The Sound of Music—4.

Michele wins, Eli loses. Next case.

But Eli knows he will get another chance. The final decision will come next week, after the dreaded vocal audition. Just thinking about it pains him.

"I can't sing."

When she was 2, Angie Guido sat in the pediatrician's office and heard a familiar song playing over the Muzak system.

"That's Pavawatti," she announced.

The startled doctor looked at her mother.

"Did she say what I think she said?"

Angie has always loved music. Now Rosemary Guido shares her daughter's high hopes for the spring musical. Angie has talked about *West Side Story* since she was a freshman and heard that Mr. Shipley wanted to produce it.

"In her mind, she became Maria," Rosemary says.

Like most of the students, Angie handicaps the competition. If *West Side Story* is picked, her friend Anna Schoenfelder will get a lead role—probably Anita. Mr. Shipley loves Anna. Everyone does.

That leaves the role of Maria. Who else but Angie can play her?

Just one other girl: Angela Brown.

"Mom, she's got a beautiful voice," Angie says, "but I'm a senior."

All things being equal, Mr. Shipley favors the seniors. Angela Brown is a junior. She'll have next year to shine.

None of this matters if Angie Guido blows her vocal audition. She has chosen one of her favorite songs— "On My Own" from *Les Misérables*. She's sure she will nail it.

Just like Angie Guido, there's another girl who can see it all. The white dress. The school gym. The bridal shop. She envisions herself in the final scene, cradling Tony's lifeless body, pointing the gun at the gang members and asking, "How many can I kill, Chino? How many—and still have one bullet left for me?"

What if that were me?

Oh, yes, Angela Brown can just see it.

"If I could just have anything to do with that show I'd never have to have anything else to do with drama," she says.

Angela will tell her mother, maybe her best friend and boyfriend, but otherwise her dream of playing Maria stays locked and hidden. She will not call attention to herself; that's not her style. She is 16, a thin girl with long, straight black hair, brown eyes and a pale complexion. She is poised on the cusp between girlishness and womanhood. Most of her clothes have Mickey Mouse on them, she wears a Mickey Mouse watch, and there is a 5-foot painting of Mickey Mouse on her bedroom wall. She puts potato chips inside her sandwiches to make them crunchy. She goes to church every Sunday. She giggles.

She didn't know she could sing until her freshman year when she tried out for *Oklahoma!* Last year, she sang a solo in *City of Angels.* She loves the way she feels on stage, so special and alive, loves performing so much she can't describe it. It just feels...different.

Angela, you could be Maria, her friends say. It's between you and Angie Guido.

Ever the nice girl, Angela shakes her head.

"You don't want to get your hopes up because there are so many talented people," she says.

She will know soon enough. Vocal auditions are tomorrow night.

One by one, execution-style, the victims enter the classroom. They clutch sheets of music and wads of tissue.

I've got a sinus infection.

I have a sore throat. I can't go any higher.

I think I'm sick.

"We've all got the drama flu," one girl explains.

This is audition week. Student ability will be judged in three areas—acting, dancing and singing. How well they do determines what role they will get. The acting and dancing tryouts are fun, but most would rather find a fresh pimple on prom night than sing alone in public.

Tonight they will stand in an empty classroom and audition in front of Starr, Mr. Shipley, Lisa Rolman, a North County teacher and the show's assistant director, and Neil Ewachiw, the musical director.

Mr. Ewachiw (pronounced e-WALK-q) terrifies them.

He is flamboyant, melodramatic, unpredictable. He speaks as if he is always performing. He will jump from his chair and sprint theatrically to the piano, clapping his hands furiously and shouting, "Sing that again!" During auditions, he will stop students in mid-note and ask them to imitate Elvis, or sing a Christmas carol.

"He's pompous," Eli Senter says, "but he knows his stuff."

Tonight, Mr. Ewachiw wants to hear range. He'll work on quality later.

Unlike the other students, Angela Brown looks forward to her audition. She sings "I Don't Know How to Love Him" from *Jesus Christ Superstar* in a breathy, pretty soprano.

Mr. Ewachiw is intrigued.

"Would you do me a favor, please? I would love to hear the National Anthem, and I'd like to hear it in a C major."

After she finishes, he asks her to sing the phrase, "And the rockets red glare."

She does.

"Now a D major."

She gulps and sings.

Higher and higher, up the scale they go.

"Could I hear it in an E major? I promise not to kill you."

She sings.

"Now an F major."

Angela takes a deep breath. From someplace deep within her, someplace locked and hidden, a sound comes forth, a sound she never has heard before, and her eyes widen in surprise and wonder.

"Thank you," Mr. Ewachiw says.

Her face red, Angela places a hand to her chest. She is breathing hard. She looks stunned, elated and frightened. The girl who walked into the audition is not the same girl who leaves. She has discovered something about herself.

"I didn't know I could do that."

Mr. Ewachiw flips over her audition sheet and scribbles a note:

Has a high C.

Only 10 boys signed up for the vocal audition, too few to perform *West Side Story.* What's more, the ones who try out are tentative and off-key. Mr. Ewachiw listens with the expression of a man forced to drink sour milk.

Eli Senter attempts the theme from *Oklahoma!,* but walks out shaking his head.

"I suck," he says.

Anna Schoenfelder enters, dabbing her red nose with a tissue.

"I feel terrible," she says.

The 17-year-old senior has what Mr. Shipley describes as "the best face for the theater I've ever seen." When the script calls for a femme fatale, Anna gets it— thick blond hair, big blue eyes and dimples you could hide a half dollar in. She also has a full, beautiful voice no cold can diminish.

Mr. Ewachiw turns over Anna's audition sheet.

He draws a star.

It's Angie Guido's turn.

This is it. Her chance to be Maria. Her song, "On My Own," is the heart-wrenching account of a woman's unrequited love.

Angie closes her eyes. She has a rich alto voice, and the words flow effortlessly. When Angie finishes, Mr. Ewachiw asks her to sing it again. Think about the words, Angie. What do they mean?

"There is no music," he says. "There are no notes. Only you."

She closes her eyes.

Without me,
this world will go on turning.
A world that's full of happiness
that I have never known.

"Thank you," Mr. Ewachiw says.

On the back of her audition form, he writes, "Smart. Good instrument. Grown a lot."

One boy is left.

Brian Forte is not like the others. He struts into the music room, wearing a baseball cap turned backward and lugging a guitar over his shoulder. He plops on a desk top, flings a leg over a chair and turns to the piano player.

"You can sit this one out."

Then he plays, "Life by the Drop" by Stevie Ray Vaughan, belting it out in a deep baritone, pounding the guitar. He's confident, relaxed, at home.

The leading man.

Brian is an 18-year-old senior with an FM radio voice, coal black hair and little-boy dimples. He changed the pronunciation of his last name from "Forty" to "For-tay" because, he says, "it sounds more musical." (His parents still use "Forty.") He has played the leading man in North County musicals the past two years and will again this spring.

No one else is even close.

"Thank you," Mr. Ewachiw says after the performance is over. "You don't by any chance know 'Frosty the Snowman,' do you?"

Decision time.

Sixteen drama club members form a circle as light from a sunny Friday afternoon pours through the classroom windows. Mr. Shipley and Ms. Rolman, the teachers, remain in the back. As usual, Starr the Drama Queen is in charge.

"I'm getting the impression that some people are for a certain play because they think they'll get a better part," she says. "They're looking out more for themselves than the group. Be open, guys. Look at it for the club, not just for yourselves."

Once again, they debate *West Side Story* vs. *Anything Goes.* With everything else being equal, there is one enormous difference.

"If we do *Anything Goes,* we might not have a music director," Starr says.

"Why?" a girl asks.

"Because Mr. Ewachiw doesn't like the show, and he doesn't want to spend eight weeks of his life working on it," Ms. Rolman says.

Mr. Ewachiw enters late. Four years ago, he taught music at North County High, but was laid off after a year. Now he's getting a doctorate in vocal performance from Catholic University. He serves as musical director because he admires Mr. Shipley, enjoys the students and, as he puts it, "I'd rather work for the drama club than the Board of Ed."

He will help them do *Anything Goes,* if that's what they want, but first he teaches a history lesson.

"In 1957, there were two big musicals. One of the two took all of the awards and made all the money. *The Music Man.* The one that didn't was *West Side Story.* I never understood that. It says to me that the flavor of the day was fluff. My opinion is, as an artist, I want to do art. When it comes to musicals, it doesn't get any better than *West Side Story.*"

There is silence. He owns the room.

"It was years ahead of its time. It's a story that's timeless. It's a story that's very timely to your lives. It speaks to us all, and it will for an awfully long time."

Sitting under the blackboard, Angela Brown begins to cry.

"There's something else. This is Mr. Shipley's last year, and he's always wanted to do *West Side Story*. It's in your hands."

Eli Senter leaps to his feet.

"Raise your hands," he demands. "*West Side Story*. All in favor."

Each year, some 275 schools and community theaters in the country perform *West Side Story*. This year North County High will join them. The vote is almost unanimous.

Afterward, Michele Miller is in tears. She didn't vote. All of it—Starr's introduction, Mr. Ewachiw's speech, the emotional plea for Mr. Shipley—feels staged.

"I think we were manipulated," she says. "We were manipulated. It's ridiculous for this drama club, with so many girls, to do a play with two girls in it."

She's crying for another reason.

"Somebody is going to be very upset when that cast list comes up. And both of them are my friends."

Angie Guido overhears her. Everyone knows the only person standing between her and the role of Maria is Angela Brown.

"But she has another year," Angie says.

"That's not going to make a difference," Michele says. "This is Mr. Shipley's last year. It's not going to matter if you're a senior."

"It makes a difference to me," Angie says. "A huge difference."

After the students leave, the teachers and Starr cast the four lead roles—Tony, Bernardo, Anita and Maria.

Brian Forte, of course, will be Tony.

"There's no question about that," Mr. Shipley says.

Bernardo, the leader of the Sharks gang, is a problem. Nobody stands out. They'll recruit some more boys.

Anna Schoenfelder will be Anita.

"She will be great," Mr. Ewachiw says.

Casting Maria is just as easy. When the choice is finally made, there is no discussion about who has her heart set on the role, or who will be crushed with disappointment, or who has dreamed of playing Maria since that December night when she saw it on stage.

Only one question matters: Who can do it best?

Mr. Shipley writes the winner's name on a piece of paper.

THE PLAYERS

Angie Guido—She has a vision of herself in the starring role. But wait: Another girl stands in the way.

Brian Forte—Smooth and confident, he's always the leading man. Will he get his comeuppance this time?

Eli Senter—All bony angles and pointed opinions, he fights for his favorite show. The decision will haunt him.

Angela Brown—From this demure girl comes an astonishing sound. Is it enough to make her a star?

Starr Lucas—She loves acting. She's the Drama Queen. So why has she taken herself out of the cast?

Writers' Workshop

Talking Points

1) "A Stage in Their Lives" is a six-part series about a high school musical. How does reporter Ken Fuson introduce the series and explain its purpose? How effectively does this work?

2) Fuson directly addresses the reader: "Find a seat..." "You will meet two girls..." "Come to the practices. Laugh at their goofy jokes." Discuss how effective this device is.

3) The writer weaves lyrics from the musical *West Side Story* throughout the entire series of stories. Do the words retain their effect if a reader isn't familiar with the musical?

4) The subject lends itself to natural drama—what show to perform, which students will get key roles, will the production be ready to open. Note in this installment, and the rest of the series, the devices the writer uses to keep the drama alive from day to day.

Assignment Desk

1) "Nothing ever produced on stage can possibly match the drama of growing up." This series about a high school musical has general appeal because readers will be able to relate this to a similar high school experience of their own. Write a story about another high school experience that would have general appeal to readers.

2) Compare the structure of the series with the elements of a musical—the overture, the acts and scenes, solos and ensemble numbers, the grand finale. Apply this form to a story you write.

3) The writer confronts the stereotype of drama club members in his description of Eli Senter. How could you use this technique in your stories?

4) As the writer did in his introduction, directly address the reader in a story you write.

A stage in their lives, Part 2

JUNE 2, 1997

Dreams hang by a thread as the cast list is posted. 'Who will I be?' they wonder—a timely question about life itself, not just a high school musical.

Angie Guido skips breakfast. She's too nervous. The list will be posted today.

First thing this morning, Angie will walk into North County High School and turn left at the main office, then right at the guidance center. She will come to the intersection of two shiny hallways and pause at a bulletin board reserved for drama club news.

She will look for her name on the cast list for *West Side Story,* the spring musical. Only one role matters: Maria.

"If I don't get it, I'm coming home," she says.

"Call first," her mother replies as Angie heads out. "Break a leg."

Shortly before 7 a.m. on this February school day, Starr Lucas, a senior and the drama club president, begins her trip to the bulletin board, gripping a folder as if it contains state secrets.

The cast list is inside.

Maneuvering through a maze of hallways and classrooms, Starr swivels as she walks—there's a problem with her legs—but she must hurry. When that first bell rings, 40 cast members are going to make a frantic dash to the bulletin board.

Brent McMullen, an apple-cheeked freshman, arrives first.

"I'm a Jet!" he shouts.

Angela Brown, a 16-year-old junior, is in the next wave, bursting with anticipation. She has been excited since the vocal audition when she sang a high C for the first time. This morning, she couldn't wait for school to start, gulping a strawberry Pop Tart and rushing out the door.

She looks.

"Ohmigosh," she whispers to herself. "Ohmigosh. Ohmigosh."

Maria.

Friends hug and congratulate her. She is stunned.

More students arrive, clumping around the list, searching for their part.

"Who the hell's Snowboy?" a freshman asks.

"I'm Action!" sophomore Rob Mackin announces. Then he pauses, perplexed, his voice a mumble. "Whoever that is."

"I'm old," says Lorraine Eakin, a junior who is cast as a teacher. "They always make me old. They say it's because I look mature."

The students look down the hall. Here comes Angie Guido. Everyone knows how much she wants the role of Maria.

One look.

Instantly she collapses into the arms of a girlfriend and begins to sob.

Students turn their heads, unsure how to react. Angela Brown slips down another hallway, out of sight. Friends touch her gently, mouthing "Congratulations." Thanks, she whispers awkwardly.

"I've got to call my Mom," she tells a friend.

Starr, the drama club president, approaches Angie Guido.

You have a great part—Rosalia, Maria's friend—and you will sing in several songs. You're our vice president. We need you.

"I'm not doing this," Angie says.

When Angie's boyfriend, Mark Miller, arrives, she buries her head in his coat. Her face is puffy, her green eyes now red-rimmed and full of tears. A senior, she has worked four years to play a role like Maria. This isn't fair. Mark eventually escorts her down the hall, away from the bulletin board, and out the school doors.

Starr watches, feeling equal measures of empathy, concern and irritation. Wayne Shipley, the drama club sponsor, tells the students repeatedly that every role is crucial, from the stage crew sweeper to the leading lady. They are a team. Angie should know that.

Besides, she's not the only girl who lost her dream.

Four years ago, when she was a freshman, Starr Lucas announced to her family that her destiny was decided:

"You're going to see me on Broadway. I'm going to be a star. I don't even have to change my name."

Starr was a born performer, taking dance lessons since she was 4 and acting in church skits. In high school, she heard Mr. Shipley explain the magic of the theater: The idea is to paint a picture so realistic that the audience experiences a willing suspension of disbelief. Do it well enough, and you can make time stand still.

Starr was hooked. She appeared in 14 consecutive plays, one-acts and musicals. She started calling herself the Drama Queen.

"She seeks the light," Mr. Shipley says.

But Starr rarely landed a starring role. She learned it's not enough to have blond hair and ruby red lips and a movie-star smile.

"Mom," she said, "there's just not many parts for people who walk funny."

She'll talk about it. She doesn't mind.

"I have cerebral palsy," Starr explains.

She smiles, a radiant smile, almost angelic, as if this nervous system disorder is a gift from the heavens. She smiles, almost laughing, as she explains how her leg muscles tighten, causing the hitch in her walk. "I have no ooomph," she says. She smiles again, sanguine, as she says the condition could stay the same or worsen. She could, in fact, need a wheelchair someday. This, too, merits a smile.

"I've always known there was a purpose for me," she says.

So the Drama Queen selected a new kingdom. Instead of seeing her name in lights, Starr now sees herself in the shadows, behind the curtains. She will direct. She plans to major in theater in college next year and has applied to three schools. She's waiting to hear back.

When she tells Mr. Shipley her new dream, he proposes a deal—she can help direct, but that means she will not have an acting role.

How can a young woman who seeks the light willingly put herself in the dark?

"She tossed and she turned," says her mother, Phyllis Lucas. "Then she said, 'If this is the direction my life is going to take, then I have to do this.'"

Starr sees it as logical.

"You can still direct in a wheelchair," she says, beaming.

Wearing a trench coat and his trademark fedora—he owns a half dozen—Eli Senter, a skinny 17-year-old junior, heads toward the cast list. Somebody jokes that he's not on it.

He whirls.

"There's too few guys," he says loudly, as he says most things. "He can't *not* cast me."

Eli figures he will be one of the gang members, a Jet or a Shark, a role in which he can act and not sing.

"I've never sang before," he says. "If I had a choice, I wouldn't. For the audience's sake."

He looks at the cast list. His name is at the top.

"You're Riff," a boy tells Eli.

"Riff's cool," a girl says.

It's not until later that Eli realizes that Riff is the leader of the Jets gang; that Riff sings the first song of the entire show; that Riff sings three songs.

When he learns this, Eli does something entirely out of character.

He becomes very still.

When the phone doesn't ring, Rosemary Guido assumes the news is good. Finally, daughter Angie has gotten a break.

Always, it seems, Angie is the second choice. When she was 3 years old, Angie wanted to be Mary in the Christmas pageant at nursery school. Another girl was selected; Angie wore a donkey suit. Come show time, she squeezed between Joseph and Mary and plopped in front of the manger, stealing the scene.

This is different. Rosemary never has seen her daughter want something so much. It's as if Angie will judge her high school years—maybe her entire life—based on what she finds out this morning.

Sonny, the family dog, barks.

Rosemary looks outside. Angie and Mark approach the house.

Oh, no.

Angie looks shocked, as if somebody died. Her mother hugs her. They cry.

"That's it," Angie says. "I give up."

After she composes herself, Angie is adamant. She is not returning to school today so people can stare at her. She might as well stamp DONKEY on her forehead.

And there is no way she is getting on that stage and watching another girl perform her role. They can do the musical without her. Boyfriend Mark, cast as a Jet, feels the same.

"Angie," her mother says, trying desperately to comfort her, "it just wasn't your time. It wasn't your time to shine."

Then Mrs. Guido calls the school.

Just before first period begins, Brian Forte ambles down the hall, toward the drama club bulletin board, not a care in the world.

A senior, Brian has landed the lead role in the past two North County High musicals. He may, in fact, be the only boy in a school of 1,700 students who can sing the right note on command.

Brian presents the clean-cut good looks of a Boy Scout, the deep-throated voice of a baseball announcer and the devil-may-care soul of a beatnik. Friends say he's one of the most talented students but seldom pushes himself. He would rather sit in the Honey Bee Diner in Glen Burnie, drinking coffee, smoking cigarettes, reading Kurt Vonnegut.

Getting by.

"Hey," he jokes, hands turned up. "I'm a slacker."

Music is his passion. He told his father last year that he might move to New York City after graduation and play his guitar in the subway for spare change. Now he doesn't know. Maybe he'll go to a community college, maybe not. Something will pop up.

As Brian chats, friends notice he hasn't even peeked at the cast list. He laughs, glances over and resumes talking. His expression remains pure nonchalance. So he will be Tony in *West Side Story*. So he will be the leading man for the third straight year. So...ho-hum.

Later, Mr. Shipley pulls Brian aside.

Brian, he says, this will be the hardest show you've ever done. This can't be like the other years. You can't wait until the last week and then let your talent bail you out.

"You're going to have to get your ass in gear," he tells him.

The boyish grin. The what-me-worry slouch. The re-assuring pat on the arm.

"OK, Mr. Shipley," Brian replies.

Whatever.

Mr. Shipley stays away from the bulletin board.

"He hides," Starr says.

He has plenty to do. While the students ponder their roles, Mr. Shipley wonders how they will be ready in time for the April 18-19 shows. He has yet to cast Bernardo and the other Sharks. He will do that tomorrow night, at the first practice.

This isn't the way he prefers to operate, but if Mr. Shipley has learned anything in 30 years of teaching, it's how to adjust.

"High school theater is more about high school than the theater," he says.

This will be Mr. Shipley's last show. At 53, he's retiring at the end of the school year. "I'm tired," he says. He has other hobbies—drag racing stock cars, raising horses, helping run Actors Company Theatre, which produces community shows. But for the next two months he will focus so much on *West Side Story* that his wife rarely will see him.

Mr. Shipley has taught at the school since Andover and Brooklyn Park schools merged seven years ago (he taught in Andover before). He helped design the 900-seat auditorium; he considers it one of the nicest theaters in Anne Arundel County.

He remains oblivious to the daily dramas of high school life. He does not know who just broke up, or who got invited to the junior prom, or who had her heart set on playing Maria. His teaching philosophy is time-tested: This, too, shall pass.

So Mr. Shipley is surprised when he walks into the principal's office and a secretary hands him a pink message slip:

"Call Angie Guido's mother. She says you'll know why."

Angie and Mark skip school all day, watching movies at her house. The phone rings constantly.

Angie, are you all right?

Angie, we want you back.

Angie, we love you.

That night, while Angie works at Blockbuster Video, fellow seniors Michele Miller and Anna Schoenfelder visit.

"You've got to be in it," Michele says.

Angie is confused.

"I don't know. I don't know."

Just the week before, Michele had cried when the drama club selected *West Side Story* as the spring musical over *Anything Goes.* How quickly she has recovered from that disappointment.

"I'm fine," says Michele, who is cast as one of the Jet's girlfriends, a minor role. "I just wanted a part."

It's different for Angie. She has invested everything—her hopes, her pride—in this role. Couldn't they have lowered Maria's high notes to match her alto voice? Now Angie will finish high school without singing a solo. Don't they understand? This shall not pass quickly.

But it must. The word is out: If Angie skips the first practice tomorrow night, she will lose the part.

Mr. Shipley tries three times to return her mother's phone call. He never hears back.

First thing after school, Angela Brown heads to the Marley Station Mall and buys the *West Side Story* CD. All night long, over and over, she listens to it, savoring lyrics that seem written just for her:

Good night, good night,
Sleep well and when you dream,
Dream of me.
Tonight.

She had dreamed of playing Maria. Now she will.

What happens when your dream comes true?

Writers' Workshop

Talking Points

1) In this installment, the writer introduces several students to readers. How does the writer develop these characters?

2) "The idea is to paint a picture so realistic that the audience experiences a willing suspension of disbelief. Do it well enough, and you can make time stand still." The writer summarizes the teacher's explanation of effective drama. Could this description apply to effective news stories? How does this series accomplish that goal?

3) Part Two begins with the resolution of one drama—who will get the role of Maria. It would seem natural to focus on the excitement of the girl who was chosen, rather than on the disappointment of the girl who was not. What is the effect of this focus?

Assignment Desk

1) You could subtitle this installment "Dreams and Disappointments." Write a story about someone dealing with disappointment.

2) The narrative stops in this story to include profiles of several characters. Give characters in your story a chance to be in the spotlight.

3) Rewrite this story without the brief profiles of the characters. What other techniques can you employ to include the biographical information?

A stage in their lives, Part 3

JUNE 3, 1997

Two acts. Fifteen scenes. Thirteen songs.
"Let's try to get through this without hating each other."

They march in place, punching the air like prizefighters, their feet slamming the stage to the pulsating disco beat.

Dressed in gym clothes, the cast of *West Side Story* begins tonight's first practice at North County High School in Anne Arundel County with an aerobic workout. They must get in shape for the dance numbers.

But foreboding has replaced the normal adrenaline rush.

Angie Guido is missing.

When another girl was cast as Maria, the lead role, Angie bolted school for the day and tearfully vowed to skip the spring musical. Friends pleaded with her to reconsider. If she's not here tonight, the director will replace her. Nobody wants that.

Five minutes pass...the music pounds.

Ten minutes...the students march.

Fifteen minutes...and every head turns.

Toward the rear of the stage, slipping through a back door, Angie and her boyfriend walk in and find their places.

Everyone exhales.

Two acts.

Fifteen scenes.

Thirteen songs.

Two months to go.

"You realize when opening night is?" Wayne Shipley, the director, asks the 40 students on stage. "Look at your calendar."

April 18—and they are a week behind.

The days bleed into each other, a melange of practices, voice lessons and dance rehearsals.

"The music comes first, at the expense of everything else," Mr. Shipley says. "They don't realize how hard this is going to be."

The students are sprinting toward a faraway conclusion that tonight looks as gray and undefined as a Polaroid photograph at first snap.

WEEK ONE. THE MUSIC ROOM

Wearing a blue Mickey Mouse T-shirt, Angela Brown, the 16-year-old junior who will play Maria, enters for her voice lesson with Neil Ewachiw, the show's music director.

Push the sound from your abdomen, he tells her. Try singing the word *"tonight"* as if it's pronounced *"tuh-nut."* It will open your throat.

A soaring soprano fills the room, stronger than the high C Angela reached during her vocal audition.

That was the voice of a little girl, pretty and fragile.

Mr. Ewachiw (pronounced e-WALK-q) now hears something different.

"It was huge," he recalls. "Just huge."

Brian Forte, the devil-may-care senior cast as Tony, the leading man, finishes reading the *West Side Story* script. He turns to Anna Schoenfelder, who will play Anita.

"I get to die," he says excitedly.

"Brian, I don't want you to die," she replies.

"I want to. I've never died before."

She laughs, her smile framed by deep dimples. Brian describes Anna as nice, smart, easy to tease. "She makes you feel good about yourself."

They are pals.

"I have always liked Brian," Anna says. "He's different from all the other guys. He's really sweet. He's so open with his feelings."

They make a terrific couple—the leading man and the prettiest girl. They dated for a short time last year, then stopped. Both agreed they didn't want to risk harming their friendship.

Brian leaves for his vocal lesson. He's a baritone singing a tenor's role.

Could it be? Yes, it could.

Something's coming, something good...

The notes are too high. Brian looks frustrated and surprised.

"This isn't going to be easy."

THE CAST IS COMPLETE

Mr. Shipley finally finds enough boys to cast the Sharks, the Puerto Rican gang in *West Side Story*.

Pat Reynolds, a senior, will be Bernardo, the gang leader. Another senior, Eric Schoenbachler, will play Anxious—an appropriate name. This is Eric's first musical; he only tried out after some girls talked him into skipping lacrosse season.

"I used to have something against drama people," he says. "They're kind of obnoxious, frankly. Usually in school, you try not to be around them.

"The more I'm around them, the better friends I get to be, but I'll never be a drama person."

For the mambo dance, Eric is paired with Natalie Colley, a tall sophomore with hypnotically large eyes.

He and Natalie greet each other suspiciously. They complain about each other's dance technique. She calls for detente.

"Let's try to get through this without hating each other."

A few weeks later, sitting in the auditorium, Natalie rests her feet on Eric's shoulders. He ties her shoes together.

A week after that, they begin dating.

A week after that, Natalie confides to a girlfriend: "Eric is so cute. He wants to have four kids—and so do I!"

ANOTHER DAY. THE MUSIC ROOM

"Did it really sound OK?" Angela Brown asks.

"Do I sound like Maria?"

"Trust me, if it sounds bad, I'll tell you," Mr. Ewachiw says. "It'll be very different for you. You can't be afraid of it. Imagine when a snake sheds its skin. It feels weird.

"The singing you've done all your life, it was good when you were young. Now you've got to grow up."

WEEK TWO

The Jets stand to one side, the Sharks to the other. In the middle, Mr. Ewachiw leads them through the quintet. It's a difficult song with five different parts, the musical equivalent of a rumble.

"Are we going to the mall?" Mr. Ewachiw shouts. "Are we going to a retirement home? Are we going to a quilting bee? Ladies and gentleman, I would like to hear the Jets and the Sharks going to a rumble! I want the *AT-TI-TUDE!*"

The music begins. And...

Nothing.

"It sounds like the Sharks are going to sit down with a box of Mallomars and watch *Gilligan's Island*," Mr. Ewachiw says.

He sings the parts as loud as he can, like an opera singer on steroids.

"Can you sing it louder than me? *I DON'T THINK SO!*"

Again, the music begins.

Again, nothing.

It's the musical equivalent of a train wreck. The boys are nervous, timid, self-conscious. This is a test for Mr. Ewachiw's overwhelming confidence.

"I feel like one of my biggest strengths is to take ability that is dreadful and raise it up to mediocrity," he says.

He challenges them:

"Sing it as loud as you can. This time with the right notes."

He goads:

"That was a lovely A. But what we need is a C."

He insults:

"Pitch is a location, it's not an area."

Nothing.

Stomachs have rumbled more menacingly than these guys.

THINK OF AN ASSEMBLY LINE

In the beginning weeks, stage-crew members construct sets after school. On stage, actors rehearse scenes. In a dressing room, two girls practice their lines. In a hallway, dancers stretch.

Mr. Shipley is the foreman. He says his job is to put pictures on the stage. The students do everything else.

But he's worried. The boys are goofing off too much. Actors don't know their lines. The dance sequence is a struggle. Musically—well, they'll need a miracle.

This is the reason the 53-year-old Mr. Shipley has avoided *West Side Story* during a 30-year teaching career that will end with his retirement this spring.

"I may not live through this," he says.

And he has yet to hear Eli Senter.

ANOTHER NIGHT. ON STAGE

The performers will sing every number, one after another, so Mr. Shipley and Mr. Ewachiw can hear how much work needs to be done.

Junior Eli Senter—Riff—has the first song:

When you're a Jet,
You're a Jet all the way...

Sitting in the auditorium, cast members cringe. This is dog-howling bad. Eli throws his fedora off the stage. His long hair, parted in the middle, frames his thin face like parenthetical brackets. He tries again. Horrible. He tosses his script off the stage. Again, he tries. Terrible. He fidgets with his shirt.

Nothing helps. He's so far off-key you would need a search party to find him. He's gulping air like a drowning man.

"I suck," Eli says, his face flush. "I sucked last week and I'll suck two weeks from now."

When he's done, Brian Forte and Angela Brown—Tony and Maria—approach the stage for their duet in "Tonight."

Tonight, tonight
The world is wild and bright...

Angela's voice is captivating. Students doing their homework look up in amazement. Where did this sound come from? The soaring soprano that filled the music room now fills the entire auditorium, up there in the glass-breaking stratosphere.

Everyone applauds when she finishes.

"That was awesome!" Brian says.

For Angie Guido, the senior who lost the part, and with it her dream of playing Maria, this is too much. She still pictures herself in this role, on this stage, basking in this applause.

She runs out of the auditorium in tears.

Two acts.

Fifteen scenes.

Thirteen songs.

Five weeks to go.

Late one night, after another frustrating practice, Mr. Shipley escorts senior Starr Lucas, the student director, to her car. The parking lot is mostly empty; the brown-brick high school mostly dark. Down the hill, traffic is light on Baltimore-Annapolis Boulevard.

"What do you think?" he asks.

"I think it's a mess," she says.

"Yeah, I know," he agrees. "But it's always a mess."

Starr smiles, shimmering in the streetlight. Pile on the jobs—president of the drama club, president of the Thespians, president of her senior class—but you can't crack the Drama Queen.

Nothing gets to her. Not anymore. Not since she was in sixth grade and doctors operated on her legs to relieve pressure on her knees. Starr has cerebral palsy.

She was placed in a cast from her hips to her toes, with a metal bar stretched between her knees to keep her legs spread wide. So wide she couldn't fit through the front door at home; her family had to haul her in sideways, like a sofa. She remained in bed, imprisoned in that cast, for six weeks.

"I don't think she thought life could get much worse," her mother, Phyllis, says.

So what if Mr. Shipley is nervous, and the show is in trouble, and her senior adviser is on her back, and she'll have to stay up until 1 a.m. to finish her homework?

She can handle it.

When she gets home from practice, a letter awaits her.

Dear Starr,

On behalf of Shenandoah University, it is my pleasure to inform you of your acceptance as a candidate for a Bachelor of Arts in Theatre...

She has been waiting for this. The Winchester, Va., school has a conservatory where she can study theater. But the cost is an astronomical $18,000 a year. Her father works for Giant Food Inc.; her mother cares for her sister and baby brother.

She'll need help to afford the tuition.

"I can't do anything about it, so why worry?" she says.

But she does.

Once or twice a week, Lisa Rolman, a North County High teacher and the assistant director, escorts a few cast members to second-hand stores to shop for costumes.

Angie Guido joins one of the trips, but her heart isn't in it. Since losing the role of Maria, Angie has ridden an emotional see-saw—up one day, down the next. This isn't like her. Her friends are concerned.

"I don't like rehearsals," she says. "I don't feel like doing anything anymore. I feel like graduating and not watching other people do wonderful things. I don't even feel like going to school anymore."

She knows Angela Brown has a terrific voice, but it's hard to watch her.

"I guess she's better," Angie says.

Then she sighs, heavy with resignation.

"Yeah, she's better."

ANOTHER NIGHT. ON STAGE

Brian Forte and Angela Brown practice the scene in which Tony and Maria first meet.

They hold hands.

"Uh-oh," a girl says. "Brian just violated the mandatory four-foot no-contact zone."

Angela Brown's boyfriend will arrive soon to give her a ride home. He graduated from North County High last year, and he might not appreciate seeing another boy holding hands with his sweetheart. He is the kind of boyfriend who saves napkins from restaurants he and Angela visit.

One night after practice, Brian pulls the boyfriend aside.

"I'm going to have to be in the play and be romantic and close to her. Is that OK?"

Sure, the boyfriend says, then smiles nervously.

"It's just a play," he says.

He should relax. Brian has his eye on someone else.

Boys. They joke, they gawk, they jump on each other's backs. They flit around like fruit flies.

"It's so difficult to work with guys, because they won't stop talking," says junior Katie Collins, who plays Anybodys, the tomboy who wants to be a Jet. "When they don't understand something, they just keep talking."

Mr. Shipley is fed up.

Usually one or two student leaders emerge to police the ranks. That hasn't happened this year. He'll have to take charge.

"Every time you laugh at somebody or poke fun at somebody, look at the calendar and think about whose butts are on the line here," he says.

"Yours."

Two acts.

Fifteen scenes.

Thirteen songs.

Four weeks to go.

This is the last practice before spring break in March. Tonight Mr. Shipley wants to see all of Act I on stage.

An hour and a half later, Mr. Ewachiw still is working with Eli Senter and the Jets on the opening song.

When you're a Jet...

There is panic in Mr. Ewachiw's voice.

"This is a tune that for the last 40 years people have had in their heads," he says. "It's also the first song of the musical. I cannot share my gripping fear—"

"You don't have to share!" Eli interrupts, shouting. "I've got my own gripping fear!"

The brash facade is gone now. The normally confident Eli looks lost. Before he sings, he braces himself as if he's about to take a cannon ball to the gut. Then he opens his mouth and misses the cue.

"It sounds successively worse," he says. "It's proportional. The closer it gets, the less I can sing. I don't know why they gave me this role."

He got it because the teachers trust him. Nobody tries harder than Eli. Nobody practices more. Nobody else would suffer this much humiliation.

"He won't give up," Mr. Shipley says.

Besides, it's not as if Eli is the only singer struggling. Brian Forte's voice cracks in the upper reaches of his "Tonight" duet with Angela Brown.

"I'm not sure I can do this," he says.

Angela, too, is frustrated. What a roll she has been on—hitting the high C, getting cast as Maria, gaining confidence in her voice—but tonight she hurries off the stage, finds a seat by herself and frowns.

"Mr. Ewachiw kept cueing us too early," she says. "We skipped over tons of dialogue."

She is fearful. What good is it to play Maria—to realize your dream—if the final product is terrible? She has more at stake than she realized.

But on this, the last practice before spring break, there is one reason to hope, one song that looks and sounds exactly as it should.

All night, in the hallway, Ms. Rolman and a half-dozen girls worked on "America," the bouncy song in which one of the characters, a Puerto Rican girl named Rosalia, longs for her homeland and is teased by Anita and the others.

Rosalia: *I like the city of San Juan.*

Anita: *I know a boat you can get on.*

When it's over, Mr. Shipley is smiling.

"Consider that the show stopper, guys," he says.

Mr. Ewachiw also applauds. He compliments Anna Schoenfelder, the senior who plays Anita, then turns his attention to the other girl, the one who sang Rosalia's part.

"Very, very nice," he says, touching her arm.

For the first time in weeks, Angie Guido smiles.

They deserve a weekend night off, a respite from the dreadful musical. They need to see a goofy movie like *Liar, Liar* and act like teen-agers again.

Twenty students head to the theater. Brian Forte and Anna Schoenfelder sit next to each other.

The leading man and the prettiest girl.

Could it be? Yes, it could.

Something's coming, something good...

They don't hold hands, or even share a box of popcorn, but here in the theater Brian and Anna both feel it, an affection that goes beyond friendship. Just sitting here, without saying a word, both sense that their relationship is changing.

Brian: "I've always had extremely strong feelings for Anna. Always."

Anna: "Last year the friendship thing got in the way. This year it's different."

Could it be? Yes, it could.

Something's coming, something good...

If only real life worked like this: Sing a song and fall in love.

But real life is different.

Sometimes you're not the only boy who falls for the prettiest girl.

Sometimes your best friend does, too.

THE PLAYERS

Angie Guido (Rosalia)—She's angry, hurt and bitter. She won't be Maria. Will she boycott the show?

Brian Forte (Tony)—The leading man is distracted: He's falling in love.

Eli Senter (Riff)—He misses cues. He sings off-key. Can he turn it around?

Angela Brown (Maria)—Her voice is changing. Will she change, too?

Starr Lucas (Student Director)—The show is a mess. But she has other concerns: her health and her future.

Writers' Workshop

Talking Points

1) The writer uses numbers in one-sentence paragraphs as a countdown to opening night: "Two acts. Fifteen scenes. Thirteen songs. Two months to go." How effective is this technique?

2) The writer uses dialogue to capture the character of high school students. "I get to die," "Brian, I don't want you to die," "I want to. I've never died before." Look for uses of dialogue that convey more than a narrative voice.

3) The writer engages in wordplay: "Stomachs have rumbled more menacingly than these guys." Find other examples in these stories. What makes them effective?

Assignment Desk

1) Using the structure of this story as a model, write a story using scenes to propel the action.

2) Experiment with different ways to include dialogue in your stories.

A stage in their lives, Part 4

JUNE 4, 1997

Romantic rumblings. Crises of confidence. Teen-age angst. Other dramas unfold behind the curtain—putting a friendship to the test.

On any other night, Brian Forte and his best friend would talk about anything—music, school, girls. Tonight they just stare straight ahead.

There's too much to say, so they say nothing. Only the sound of a car stereo breaks the silence.

Finally, Brian lowers the volume.

"Things are getting pretty complex, aren't they?" he asks.

"Makes life more interesting, don't you think?" his friend replies.

That does it. All the pressure of the past five weeks —struggling through the spring musical, preparing for high school graduation, discovering that he and this friend have fallen for the same girl—finally erupts.

And Brian Forte, the happy-go-lucky leading man, reacts so strongly even he is surprised.

"NO!" he screams.

They're all losing it.

Opening night is one month away—April 18. And everyone involved in the production of *West Side Story* at North County High School knows they need at least three more months.

Several of the songs are shaky. The set remains unfinished. The big dance number is improving, but far from ready. And they still have several scenes to run through.

"Guys, this is in sorry shape right now," Wayne Shipley, the director, tells the Jets as they work the opening scene.

He hurries to the stage. The 53-year-old teacher is getting about four hours of sleep a night. After rehearsals end, he lingers in the auditorium, adjusting the lights, building the set, blocking scenes. The students notice the dark circles under his eyes.

"You guys don't know your lines," he says. "You can't do this show if you don't know the lines. I don't see acting. I don't see anything.

"This show is not going on until this scene is ready.

"Take five."

His disappointment stings.

During the break, the Jets follow Eli Senter to the back of the auditorium to rehearse the scene Mr. Shipley has just criticized.

"Come on, Katie," Eli says.

"I'm not coming," Katie Collins replies. "I know *my* lines."

"That's because you've only got seven lines in the whole thing!" Eli shouts.

"Shaddup!"

Eli can't do it. That's the running joke at the Anne Arundel County school. Last winter, during the one-act plays, the 17-year-old Eli portrayed an impotent character who says, "I'm not physically capable of having sex." Since then, he hears a variation of the Eli-can't-do-it theme at least 10 times a day.

Usually, the wiry Eli laughs. He's comfortable with who he is—a poet, president of his church youth group, a former wrestler and a Boy Scout close to earning his Eagle Scout stripes. You can tease him; his feelings won't be hurt.

When Eli wins a statewide science-fiction writing contest for teen-agers, he appears at a Baltimore hotel to accept the award—two weeks early. He hears about it.

"I was misinformed," he says sheepishly.

This musical has him whipped. Eli's inability to sing Riff's part is affecting his acting. Normally a solid performer, Eli is flubbing lines, missing stage cues and—he believes—disappointing Mr. Shipley. That bothers him most of all.

As the Jets practice, a boy blows a whistle on stage.

"Don't do that unless you have a damn good reason," Eli yells at him.

"I'm practicing my part," the boy says innocently.

"Go home!" Eli shouts.

For the first time in his drama career, Eli doubts his ability. Maybe he really can't do it.

Stand here.

Sing this way.

Move over there.

Smile!

It's too much for Brian Forte, the senior who plays Tony in *West Side Story*. This is the third straight year he has been the leading man in the spring musical, but Tony is by far the most challenging role. He's a deep-voiced baritone singing a tenor's part.

"There's a million things I have to remember," he says. "It's the hardest thing I've ever had to do in my life."

Neil Ewachiw, the music director, teaches him to pronounce words differently. Sing *tonight* as *tuh-nut*. Sing *someday* and *somewhere* as *some-deh* and *some-weh*. The audience won't know the difference, and it's easier to reach the high notes.

When Brian gets on stage, *tonight* still sounds like *tonight*.

"*-NUT!*" Mr. Ewachiw yells.

"*-night,*" Brian sings.

"The only thing I ask of you is to give me everything I ask of you all the time," Mr. Ewachiw says.

"Well, OK," Brian replies sarcastically. "Piece of cake."

Later, Brian approaches him.

"I just can't accept the fact that you know my voice better than I do."

"I'm 10 years older than you and I work with the same instrument," Mr. Ewachiw (pronounced e-WALK-q) says. "I've had years of professional training. Some things you're just going to have to trust me on."

Brian drifts away, frustrated.

As Brian struggles, his best friend flourishes.

Junior Adam Mehok has embraced his role as a Jet since that night when Mr. Shipley explained his character.

"A-rab is just plain crazy."

"All *riiight!*" Adam shouted, slapping hands with a friend.

Tall and lean, with a ponytail that hangs halfway down his back, the 17-year-old Adam is more class wit than class clown. "He's the most right-brained person I've ever met," Brian says. They became friends about a year ago and have been inseparable since.

One night, during a tense rehearsal, the Jets practice the scene in which they physically attack one of the Sharks' girlfriends.

"This is sexual," Mr. Shipley tells them. "It's obscene. It's not playing in a sandbox. Guys, you're looking too much at her face."

"I'm not," Adam says, and Mr. Shipley joins the laughter.

Life is good.

And then it gets better.

Adam invites Anna Schoenfelder, the cute senior who plays Anita, to the junior prom. She says yes.

"I was feeling so high," he says.

The crash will come later.

Two weeks to go.

Starr Lucas, the senior who calls herself the Drama Queen, enters the nightly rehearsal on crutches.

"Every now and then, everything caves in for her," Mr. Shipley says.

Starr has cerebral palsy. She's serving as the student director instead of performing because she hopes to someday work in the theater and believes she will have more career options as a director than as an actress who limps.

Every night, she stays up until 2 a.m., finishing homework and her chores as senior class president. Before tonight's rehearsal, she took a nap, "and when I woke up, it felt like my legs had snapped in two. It was the worst I have ever felt."

She can handle it. Nothing gets to Starr. While everyone else loses their composure, she's the ever-smiling rock.

"I've wanted to be Starr since I was a freshman," says Sarah Huizinga, a junior cast member. "Starr's perfect."

Starr is still waiting to discover if she'll receive enough financial help to study theater next fall at Shenandoah University in Winchester, Va. She has been accepted, but the $18,000-a-year tuition is too steep for her family.

It would be cheaper to go to an in-state school, she says, but "I need a small campus because of my legs."

A breakthrough.

After weeks of Mr. Ewachiw's pleading and pushing, the Jets and the Sharks are beginning to sing their parts in the quintet—the song that leads to the dramatic rumble—as if they mean business.

"Ladies and gentlemen, I think that's the first time I heard the right notes," Mr. Ewachiw announces.

The cast cheers.

She said yes, but what does it mean?

Adam Mehok decides to find out. Late one night after rehearsal, he calls Anna Schoenfelder, the senior who agreed to be his date at the junior prom.

We're just friends, Adam.

"It felt like the ground came out from under me," he says.

Anna doesn't tell him everything. She doesn't tell him that the high-school boy she has romantic stirrings for is Brian Forte, Adam's best friend.

The next night, riding home after musical practice, Brian turns to Adam.

"I think I know how you're going to react to this, but I really like Anna."

Adam sits silently.

"I didn't know how to handle it," he says later. "I didn't handle it very well. I was trying to figure out where I stood and where I should stand and where I will stand tomorrow."

When he gets home, Brian calls Anna. He needs to tell her how he feels; they have danced around the issue long enough. Anna will never forget the conversation.

"We have a problem," Brian says.

"What?"

"Adam."

"I know," Anna says.

"We have a bigger problem."

"What?"

"I really like you, too, Anna."

Like the last lap in a track relay, the pace accelerates as the final week approaches.

Pieces of the set appear on stage as if by magic. The costume rack is getting full. Several of the scenes crackle—good to go, as the students put it. There are moments when Mr. Shipley believes the dance number will actually create a willing suspension of disbelief in the audience.

"We've almost got a show," he says.

Mr. Shipley is all business now. He paces on stage, wearing his trademark cowboy boots, denim shirt and bluejeans, his work gloves waving hello from the back pocket. He always looks like he just finished rustling cattle.

"Characters, guys, characters," he implores, and, slowly but noticeably, the students respond.

Angela Brown is not playing Maria anymore.

She is Maria.

Angela looks so young and innocent on stage in her Mickey Mouse shirt, but she sings with the confidence of someone much older.

"I've seen this show several times," Mr. Shipley says, "and she's the best Maria I've ever seen."

Today they'll work on the scene in which Tony and Maria first meet.

Brian and Angela meet at center stage and hold hands. She gently touches his face. They say their lines.

"There's a kiss in there, isn't there?" Mr. Shipley reminds them.

Angela and Brian gulp.

"Uh, what kind of kiss?" Brian asks, stalling.

A boy in the back: "The kind of kiss where you shove your tongue halfway down her throat."

Mr. Shipley laughs so hard his face turns red.

Angela does not laugh. After rehearsal, she says, to no one in particular but loud enough to be heard, "That whole kissing thing—yuck!"

"Was it *that* bad?" Brian says, sounding hurt.

"I didn't like that," she says in her best little girl voice. She's rehearsing. Undoubtedly Angela will use the same voice later, when she tells her jealous boyfriend what happened.

On a Sunday afternoon in April, Angie Guido pulls into the parking lot at Holy Trinity Catholic Church in Glen Burnie.

She thinks her band is playing here. Angie, Brian Forte and some other friends formed a band they called Ground Zero. After growing tired of the name, they changed it to The Artists Formerly Known as Ground Zero.

But this is no gig.

"SURPRISE!"

Angie jumps. About 30 family members and high school friends are here to celebrate her 18th birthday.

The surprise is on Brian, too. His 18th birthday is fast approaching; the party is for both of them.

Angie is Angie again. She cried when the cast list was posted and she lost the role of Maria. Now it's as if she has moved through the stages of grief—including shock and anger—to grudging acceptance.

"It was really hard for me," she says. "I didn't realize —whoa—how good Angela is. I was just so disappointed. I don't want people thinking I was looking for a pity party."

She was so close. When the cast list was compiled, Mr. Shipley first wrote down a different name for Maria:

Angela Guido.

Realizing his mistake, Mr. Shipley slowly traced over the capital "G," transforming it into a capital "B," and he did this with each letter until the name "Guido" became the name "Brown" and Angela Brown had the part instead.

So you can understand the pain in Angie Guido's voice when she sings a sultry rendition of "Who Will Save Your Soul?" at her birthday party.

And you can understand why, when her friends and family reward her with applause, she smiles and says, "I feel really good right now."

The spotlight is hers.

Adam Mehok sits by himself at Angie's birthday party, saying little.

"What's wrong with him?" a boy asks.

"It's me," Anna Schoenfelder says.

"Go talk to him."

Since that night when Anna uttered the two words that have scarred many a teen-age soul—*just friends*—Adam quit talking to her.

Anna approaches him in the church parking lot. Adam says something funny, and Anna cries because she realizes how much she misses him. She holds out her hand—come back to the church with me. Maybe later, he says.

It's confusing to Adam. One day Anna agrees to go with him to the junior prom. The next day he finds out that his best friend, Brian Forte, likes her, too. The day after that, he discovers that Anna likes Brian.

"I was basically destroyed by the whole thing," he says.

After the birthday party, Brian gives Adam a ride home. It is then, during the awkward silence, that Brian reaches over and lowers the volume on the car stereo. It is then that Brian loses it.

"*NO!*" he screams.

He hates what's going on. He pounds the steering wheel. He doesn't want to lose Anna or Adam. He begins to cry.

Adam: "He just erupted. I was taken by the emotion. I really envy him for that."

Brian: "I've always held my feelings back. For some reason, this time, I couldn't. My feelings were just too strong."

Instead of taking Adam home, Brian drives to Anna's house. They need to talk about this. The three of them sit on her front porch.

"Brian was scaring me," she says. "He was really upset. I didn't know what he was going to say."

The next night at practice, Brian sits in the second row of the theater, his legs dangling over a chair. He watches Anna as she sings on stage.

"Isn't she wonderful?" he says. "I get goose bumps."

He describes yesterday's meeting with Anna and Adam as "the purest thing in the world" and says the experience "will go down in history as the weirdest day of my life."

He and Anna are together. He and Adam still are friends.

"It's amazing."

In his nightmare, he falls off the stage.

A piece of the set collapses and smacks him in the head.

Instead of pretending, another cast member actually stabs him during the rumble.

And when he opens his mouth, nothing comes out.

Eli can't do it?

Less than a week before opening night, he can't even sleep.

Writers' Workshop

Talking Points

1) This installment opens with an episode taken out of chronology. Discuss the effectiveness of the opening paragraphs. Would the story be stronger or weaker with a different, more chronological opening? Does the opening anecdote have more power or less power because of its placement?

2) What is the mood of this installment? What tools does the writer use to depict the confusion, chaos, and desperation of getting the show ready?

3) The writer uses brief sentences of stage direction: "Stand here. Sing this way. Move over there. *Smile!*" Study how this style creates a sense of urgency.

4) The writer opens with Brian and Adam talking to each other. Later in the story, the writer quotes their reflections of that moment. Do their later insights add to the story or interrupt the narrative flow?

Assignment Desk

1) This story includes powerful moments of brief dialogue using colons. "Adam: 'He just erupted. I was taken by the emotion. I really envy him for that.' Brian: 'I've always held my feelings back. For some reason, this time, I couldn't. My feelings were just too strong.'" Experiment in a story with different ways to include dialogue.

2) Report and write about people involved in another last-minute crunch—a football team preparing for the big game, accountants facing the April 15 tax deadline.

A stage in their lives, Part 5

JUNE 5, 1997

*On the eve of opening night, their nerves are shot.
Their voices are cracking. And the trumpet section is
under orders: No snickering.*

Attention Cast of *West Side Story*

*This is it, guys. The week we've all been waiting for.
There's no more time. Know your lines, know your
cues, know the MAMBO. We are on in less than five
days.*
—Sign posted on drama club bulletin board.

MONDAY

After school ends, senior Starr Lucas, the drama
club president, stands near the North County High
School entrance and talks to Keith Jeffcoat, who plays
one of the Jets in *West Side Story,* the spring musical.

Keith is on crutches. His left ankle is in a brace.

"You've got to be ready," Starr says.

"Mr. Shipley told me that if I'm not walking by
Friday he'll break both my kneecaps," Keith replies.

Early Sunday, while he was delivering newspapers,
Keith plucked a red tulip for his girlfriend. Jumping
back into the truck, he tore ligaments in his ankle.

This is a problem. Keith plays Diesel, the biggest
member of the Jets gang. He and one of the Sharks begin the fistfight that leads to the gang rumble. Wayne
Shipley, the show's director, choreographed the scene
blow-by-blow. If Keith can't walk, how can he fight?

"I'll be there," he vows.

Maybe they're jinxed. Last week, Jason Morgan,
who plays Chino, one of the Sharks, suffered a collapsed lung. He's still recuperating at home.

"I may have to be Chino," Starr jokes.

"You're a goofball," Keith tells her.

"I didn't mess up *my* ankle," she counters.

"You're just jealous because that flower wasn't for
you," he says.

"Ha!"

Starr heads outdoors, where ballplayers practice on the fields that surround the Anne Arundel County high school. She transforms her blue Volkswagen Beetle into a mobile billboard for the show, taping *West Side Story* posters on the hood. She's going to drive the car in the local Little League parade this weekend.

"I don't know how I'm going to make it this week," she says. "A lot of people aren't cooperating. They don't understand."

They will tonight.

The taped music plays. Pat Reynolds and Eli Senter circle each other, knives brandished. Eli plunges forward, Pat counters and—

"You haven't gotten that right once," Mr. Shipley says, interrupting them. "Listen to the music. You're 12 bars early."

This is the rumble, the final scene in Act I, the dramatic high point of the entire musical. It's the scene in which the leaders of the Jets and the Sharks are killed.

Pat and Eli—the gang leaders—have rehearsed their fight for weeks, practicing fake kicks, an over-the-shoulder flip and an ankle trip. The problem is, they must coordinate their moves precisely so that the fatal blow is delivered at the exact moment the music roars to a crescendo.

"Guys, you should be listening to this music," Mr. Shipley pleads. "There is no other agenda. What we're seeing just doesn't work. You don't realize the seriousness of your situation."

Tonight, for the first time, the cast members will sing each of *West Side Story*'s 11 songs with the orchestra playing. Neil Ewachiw, the 27-year-old music director, has hired two dozen professional musicians; the drama club foots the bill.

"Ladies and gentlemen, you're on my clock now," Mr. Ewachiw (pronounced e-WALK-q) announces, tapping his baton on the metal stand.

Up first: Eli Senter, who plays Riff.

Eli snaps his fingers. The music begins. He looks at Mr. Ewachiw, gulps a deep breath and, as usual, misses the cue by a half-beat.

Ah—When you're a Jet
you're a Jet all the way...

But Eli trudges onward. By his vocal standards, this isn't horrible. He actually hits a few notes, and he almost nails the ending.

Orchestra members peek at the stage as Eli finishes. Mr. Ewachiw has reminded them not to laugh. Last year you could hear the trumpet players snicker.

Next comes Brian Forte, the senior who plays Tony, the leading man. In past musicals, this is the week when the normally nonchalant Brian gets serious.

Tonight, though, something is wrong. Brian's voice cracks, he forgets lyrics, the high notes are impossible. He seems—this is a first—nervous.

"I don't know how to sing this part, Mr. Ewachiw," he says after one song.

"Don't yell at me for doing it wrong when you were doing it right."

"Mr. Ewach—"

"You were doing it right!"

When he slumps off stage, Brian no longer exudes the panache of the leading man. He's no longer the happy-go-lucky teen.

"I'm just feeling miserable," he says. "I'm feeling really horrible about the musical aspect of this musical. The mikes, the orchestra, the mood, myself not excluded. Everything is just very malingering."

Mr. Shipley corners him.

"What I saw was a little scary," he says.

Mr. Shipley sits by himself in the theater, jotting notes on a yellow legal pad.

After 30 years of teaching, this will be his last musical. At 53, he's retiring at the end of the school year.

"You know," he says, smiling wanly as the students struggle, "I think the thing I dislike most about musicals is the music."

Friends arrive to help. In addition to Mr. Ewachiw, a former North County teacher who returns each spring to work on the musical, Mr. Shipley relies on other adults. There's David Richardson—the kids call him Dave the Piano Guy—who plays at rehearsals. There's David Garman—Dave the Light Guy—a former student who helps with the theater lighting. And there's Mike Strehlen, who handles all the guns, knives and cigarettes used as props, enough weaponry to intimidate the boys from calling him Mike the Gun Guy.

"I couldn't do it without them," Mr. Shipley says.

Next on stage are Anna Schoenfelder and Angela Brown, whose characters—Anita and Maria—sing the last songs in the musical: "A Boy Like That" and "I Have a Love."

Shortly after they begin, a scream punctures their sweet duet:

"NOOOOOOOO!"

Something has irritated Garman as he works on the lights. His voice is so loud and surprising that Mr. Ewachiw stops the orchestra and turns around angrily.

"Please don't do that," he snaps. "This is my rehearsal."

"It's my rehearsal, too," Garman says.

"I'm on the orchestra's time clock," Mr. Ewachiw says. "You're wasting my time."

The students watch, mesmerized. This is better than the rumble. Maybe the adults will duke it out.

Calm prevails. Typical last-week jitters, Mr. Shipley says later.

Flustered, Mr. Ewachiw tries to remember where the song was interrupted.

"Let's just do it over," he finally says.

It's worth hearing again. This is the best song in the show. The harmonies—Anna's alto and Angela's soprano—mesh perfectly.

As the two girls finish, Mr. Ewachiw calls Brian Forte to the conductor's stand.

"Look," he says, pointing to his arm.

Goose bumps.

TUESDAY

Some cast members are spending so much time at school that their parents bring supper to them.

When Phyllis Lucas arrives, Starr unloads.

"Mom, I'm sick," she says. "I'm running a fever. Shipley's yelling at me because people aren't here. The senior adviser is mad at me. I tried to take a nap on that mat over there, but I was interrupted seven times."

Her face is flush, her forehead hot to the touch.

"I'm not responsible for people not being here," she says.

"I know," her mother says.

This is what Starr needs; somebody to listen. Here, at school, Starr is the mommy, even for the teachers. *There's a problem in the costume room.* Talk to Starr. *I need more tickets.* Talk to Starr. *I need to add something to the program.* Talk to Starr.

Starr can handle it.

But not always.

Every night, she goes home and anxiously checks the mail. She's waiting to learn if she will get enough financial help to go to Shenandoah University, a Virginia college where she can major in theater. The school is perfect: Because Starr has cerebral palsy, she needs a small campus to avoid weakening her legs. If she can't afford to attend the college, she's not sure what she will do.

"I have my moments," she says, "but I keep them to myself."

The other students don't realize how difficult this show has been for her. For the first time, she's directing instead of acting.

"She would love to be on that stage, dressed up and in makeup," her mother says.

But she won't even get a curtain call.

An hour later, her face still red, Starr addresses the cast in a classroom.

"Tonight what we're doing is running the show from beginning to end, without the music," she says.

"We will run this at speed," Mr. Shipley adds. "If there are any train wrecks, figure out how to get out of them."

There are no prompters in a Wayne Shipley production. If cues are missed, the students are expected to improvise their way around them. There is no curtain on his stage; he believes it detracts from the audience's willingness to suspend its disbelief. If the script calls for a nightstick, then he wants a real nightstick, a wooden one, with a real leather handle, not some cheap-looking piece of plastic.

"All right, guys," Starr says. "Let's go. We're doing this in two minutes."

Afterward, back in the classroom, Mr. Shipley is upbeat.

"We were almost good," he says. "But Riff got killed 12 bars before he was supposed to. I want the

Jets and the Sharks here tomorrow at 5:30 to go over that fight scene."

He looks around. The students are tired and apprehensive. Their expressions say, *This* is going on in three nights?

"We have a show," Mr. Shipley reassures them. "But we have a lot that needs to be done."

Starr climbs into her car and heads home. The *West Side Story* posters on the hood flap in the spring breeze.

She needs sleep.

They all do.

WEDNESDAY

Time is running out. During a free period in school, Mr. Shipley grabs Brian Forte and Angela Brown to work on their love scenes.

Maria's balcony is finished. It is covered with spray-painted Styrofoam, but it looks like a brick facade. Mr. Shipley waited to finish the set until now; he knows it will send an excited buzz through the cast.

With Brian and Angela perched in the balcony, Mr. Shipley directs Brian. Wrap your arms around her as you sing. Sway with the music. Look happy, for crying out loud, you're in love.

Tonight, tonight,
The world is wild and bright,
Going mad, shooting sparks into space.

Mr. Shipley likes the way it looks. It will present a nice picture for the audience.

Brian, though, has a secret.

"When I'm singing to Maria, I'm thinking about Anna," he says. "When I'm cradling and kissing her, it's Anna."

Just last week, Brian and Anna Schoenfelder, who plays Anita, realized they liked each other as more than friends.

"The stuff that I tell Anna sounds like song lyrics," Brian says. "I know it's hokey, but that's how I feel."

During a class, a friend notices Anna's face. She is pale.

Anna has hardly eaten since lunch the day before; she says there wasn't enough time.

"Are you OK?" the friend asks.

"I feel like I'm going to fall over," she says.

The friend escorts her to the health room. They find an orange and some soup.

After school, several cast members head to their refuge, the Honey Bee Diner in Glen Burnie.

"Hey, look," Brian Forte says.

He turns his eyelids inside out.

Angie Guido groans, then laughs.

She has mostly recovered from her disappointment over not getting the role of Maria. She has a key part in two songs—"America" and "I Feel Pretty." She sings them well, but without much joy. Like everyone else, the drudgery of rehearsing is wearing her out.

"I'm ready to graduate."

Tonight is dress rehearsal with the orchestra, the last scheduled practice before opening night on Friday. Mr. Shipley wants to give the cast Thursday off.

Jason Morgan is back. A collapsed lung kept him out of school nearly a week. He says he should get through the show, even if it happens again.

"I'll ignore it," he says. "I won't die from it right away."

In a classroom, Mr. Shipley addresses his troops.

"Listen, guys, there is no—"

"Other agenda!" a half-dozen students shout in unison.

"Let's do it," he tells them.

Mr. Ewachiw pulls Brian Forte aside.

"High notes can smell fear," he says. "Don't be afraid of them. It doesn't have to be loud, just comfortable."

The opening act is rugged.

During the song "Cool," sung by the Jets, two members of the Sharks gang mistakenly strut on the set while Eli is singing. They look around, then walk out.

In the back of the theater, Mr. Shipley nearly tosses his legal pad.

"If I ever do another high school play, I hope somebody castrates me and dumps the body in the Atlantic Ocean."

Intermission. It's already past 9 p.m., the time they usually stop.

"We're not going anywhere yet," Starr tells them. "Call home if you have to. We're having an early night tomorrow so I don't want to hear any complaints."

The students are exhausted, their faces drawn, their bodies slumped.

Mr. Shipley reviews his Act I notes.

"The Jets song, frankly, sucks raw eggs," he says. "We're going to work on it tomorrow so it's credible. Plan to be here until we nail it."

He turns to the Jets' girlfriends.

"I'm not getting any characters from you," he says. "Eli has this great line—*got a rocket in my pocket*— and you just sit there. Ladies, what would you do if you heard that?"

"I'd laugh if Eli said it," one girl says, and the room erupts.

Mr. Shipley holds a hand in the air.

"Guys, this show has a real chance of being fantastic, it really does, but it's going to take every ounce of concentration that you have."

He wants to go over the opening number again tomorrow. And the fight scene. And a couple of other things.

So much for having Thursday off.

THURSDAY

The normal after-school energy is sapped.

"I'm just so rushed," says Rob Mackin, a sophomore who plays one of the Jets. "I have school to worry about. I don't see my parents enough. I have track practice. I've gotten four hours of sleep every night for the past three weeks."

Anna Schoenfelder still looks tired.

"I came to school late today," she says. "My dad told me I had to stay home and sleep."

First Jason's lung collapsed.

Then Keith hurt his ankle.

Then Anna nearly passed out.

Now this.

"I'm in pain today," says Angela Brown, who plays Maria. "My throat hurts."

Mr. Shipley works on the opening scene. He has put in several sight gags—the Jets play keep-away with an apple; one of the Sharks swings on a rope from the balcony; there are some tumbles—and he wants to make sure they click.

He stalks the stage, urging the students to stay in character. He's getting less sleep than anyone but looks the most energized.

"It's crunch time," he says. "That's half the fun."

They finish the scene.

"That's good enough," one boy says.

Mr. Shipley corrects him.

"It's *never* good enough."

In the music room, Mr. Ewachiw works with Brian and Angela one final time on their wedding duet, "One Hand, One Heart."

Don't sing so loud, he tells Brian. Just be soft and gentle. Think about the words.

"You're doing a very good job for us as far as the technical stuff is concerned," Mr. Ewachiw says. "You're not singing it the way I want to hear it, or the way I would sing it. You know why? I don't think you've ever been in love like this before.

"The first time I heard this song after I got engaged, I nearly wept. I think that's what's missing. That absolute conviction. It's just a matter of feeling what you're saying."

This is a setup. Mr. Ewachiw knows about the romance between Brian and Anna. Without saying it specifically, Mr. Ewachiw is asking Brian to sing to Anna.

Brian nods.

Then Mr. Ewachiw turns to Angela. She wears a shirt with Mickey Mouse on it. He has heard about her sore throat.

"Rest your voice tonight," he says. "Don't talk, whisper. Wear a patch that says: I'm on voice rest. You've got a big job tomorrow."

Angela nods. Her throat still hurts.

Eli Senter is the last to leave.

"You look fabulous up there," Mr. Ewachiw tells him.

"Why?" Eli says, disbelieving.

Mr. Shipley answers. "You're just"—he pauses— "Riff."

Another pause.

"Even without a rocket in your pocket. Go get some sleep, ace."

Eli falls asleep reading his *West Side Story* script. It's the first thing he sees when he awakens on Friday morning. And with it comes the heart-pounding and frightening and magnificent realization:

This is opening night.

Writers' Workshop

Talking Points

1) The structure of this story is clear: A day-by-day account of the last week. What's the pace of the story? Does time seem compressed? Does it seem to drag out?

2) This story opens by quoting the words of a sign on the bulletin board. How does this note set the tone for the story?

3) The writer repeats the use of the word "tonight," building on the lyrics from one of the songs in the musical. What's the effect?

4) Rather than relying on the mainstay verb "says," the writer uses a variety of words in depicting dialogue: "he vows.... Starr jokes.... Keith tells her.... she counters." How do these words affect the pacing? Would the use of "says" be more effective or less effective?

Assignment Desk

1) A burst of short sentences can convey a sense of expectation. "First Jason's lung collapsed. Then Keith hurt his ankle. Then Anna nearly passed out. Now this." Use this technique in one of your stories.

2) Rewrite this story without the strict chronology, using a summary lead or a different theme as your structure.

3) Use the lyrics from a song as a thematic device in a story.

A stage in their lives, Part 6

JUNE 6, 1997

Opening night! The curtain rises, and our high-school actors step boldly into the spotlight, into a pure moment they will have forever.

Wayne Shipley looks at the clock.

1:55 p.m.

The school bell rings. Most of the students flood the halls of North County High School and scamper outdoors to begin this April weekend, but a few race to the auditorium.

This is opening night.

At 7:30 p.m., the orchestra will begin playing the overture to *West Side Story,* and 40 cast members who have been working at an exhausting clip for the past two months will finally have their moment on stage.

But not yet.

There's too much to do.

Mr. Shipley, the director, surveys the auditorium. Some of the sets still need final touches. He must review scene changes with the stage crew. He wants to practice the opening scene and the rumble one more time. He needs to make sure the key actors know where to stand so the spotlight hits them.

"This is the thrash," he says. "Everybody loves the thrash."

"What time is it?" Eli Senter asks.

2:45 p.m.

The 17-year-old Eli has reached some metaphysical state where testosterone and adrenaline converge.

He's wired, bounding across the stage, singing lines from the musical.

And there's nothing for me but Maria...

Eli plays Riff, the leader of the Jets. He will sing the first song in the entire show, a prospect that has given him nightmares. But he's too jumpy to worry.

Every sight that I see is Maria...

Lisa Rolman, a North County High teacher and the assistant director, grabs him. They head to a grocery store to buy produce for a fruit and vegetable stand that's used in the opening scene.

Ms. Rolman knows Eli needs to get out of the auditorium for an hour or so. She does, too. She's almost as hyper as he is.

Last year, on the afternoon before opening night, Ms. Rolman and Eli worked off their pre-show jitters by reupholstering a couch.

"I want to get you something for dinner," she tells Mr. Shipley.

"Just grilled cheese," he replies. "That won't kill me."

As Ms. Rolman and Eli depart, Angela Brown arrives.

This is the night her dream comes true. Last December, Angela watched a touring company performance of *West Side Story* at the Lyric Opera House in Baltimore and fell in love with the part of Maria.

"It's not just like I'm acting like another person," she says. "You *feel* like another person."

She carries a dress, humming to herself. Her throat hurt so much the previous day that she was told to quit talking.

"It's better," she says. "I didn't talk all night."

In fact, the healing power of opening night is astonishing. Students who looked ready to faint the day before now bounce into the theater.

Angela skips down a hall.

"What time it is?" she asks.

3:17 p.m.

Starr Lucas, the student director, the 18-year-old senior who calls herself the Drama Queen, arrives, lugging a chair. She has taken all the chairs and several old Coca-Cola signs from her parents' kitchen to use as props.

"My Dad's asleep," she tells Mr. Shipley. "Boy, is he going to be surprised when he wakes up."

Starr wears a silver jacket and black slacks. She's almost fluorescent.

"I got the money," she whispers.

No wonder she's so happy. Last night, when she returned home from the final musical rehearsal, Starr learned that she had qualified for almost $10,000 in financial aid to attend Shenandoah University, a Virginia college where she will study theater. This is what she has been waiting for: The campus is small enough that Starr, who has cerebral palsy, can walk around without weakening her legs.

"That's fantastic," Mr. Shipley says, patting her back.

Four hours to go.

Fill your head with hair,
Long beautiful hair...

The dressing room rocks with taped music.

Josh Gembicki, who plays Doc, is first on the hair schedule. He wears a bald cap. A girl flattens his hair by soaking it in laundry soap.

A freshman boy brings in a bucket of fried chicken and a cooler of soda pop.

"My Dad couldn't be here tonight, but he wanted to do something, so he bought this," he says.

In another corner, Anna Schoenfelder brushes her formerly blond hair. She has dyed it black to play Anita in the musical.

She shivers.

"I just thought about it," she says. "We're going on!"

Ms. Rolman and Eli return from the grocery store, carrying sacks loaded with fruit and vegetables.

"Don't eat the props!" Eli yells.

He jumps in the air. He snaps his fingers. He practices the mambo dance.

Mr. Shipley watches him. This is why he loves the theater. This is why it will be so hard to retire after these shows are over.

"You can't walk away from this without experiencing something you're not going to experience anywhere else," he says. "There's no other experience like this in education. Everything else is about competition.

"You take a kid like Eli. He has all this energy, all this aggression, and he channels it into something creative.

"Eli's heroic, really."

He looks at his watch.

4:20 p.m.

"Come with me," Neil Ewachiw, the music director, tells Brian Forte. "I want you to hear something."

They head outdoors, to Mr. Ewachiw's car, where he has a tape of *West Side Story* songs. He wants Brian—who plays Tony, the leading man—to hear the song, "Tonight."

"Right here," he says. "Listen."

Tuh-nut...

"Hear that?" Mr. Ewachiw says.

Brian grins. For weeks Mr. Ewachiw (pronounced e-WALK-q) has pleaded with him to sing the word *tonight* as if it sounds like *tuh-nut*. Doing so will make it easier to sing the high notes. Now here's the proof.

"It's still not natural," Brian says.

"All you have to do is just do it."

Angela Brown is still humming Maria's songs.

"I feel like bouncing off the walls," she says, adjusting a white headband. "I'm getting so excited I can't stand it."

4:55 p.m.

The makeup room is full. Angie Guido puts lipstick on Mark Miller, one of the Jets.

They have been dating for more than a year. Two months ago, Angie and Mark left school for the day after Angie lost the role of Maria. They were going to skip the musical, then reconsidered. That feels like a million years ago.

"I can't work with people like this!" Angie jokes. "These actors' egos!"

In the hallway, Keith Jeffcoat limps. His left ankle is purple—he tore ligaments last weekend—but he's ready. Maybe too ready.

"I'll tell you the truth," he says conspiratorially. "I pick up more girls in make-up."

Two boys sprint the length of the hallway, leap and slam into each other's chests.

"Guys are really scary," Angie Guido says.

On stage, Eli Senter jumps on another boy's back.

Starr enters the makeup room at 5:45 p.m. There are two huge lipstick kiss marks on her cheek. She leaves them there all night.

"Anybody seen Pat?" she asks.

Pat Reynolds is late. He plays Bernardo, the leader of the Sharks gang.

Starr sighs. "If I laid down to take a nap, I'd never wake up."

Cast members roam the hall between the stage and the hair and makeup rooms. Brian Forte rummages through the costume rack.

"Anybody seen my tennis shoes?"

In the auditorium, Mr. Shipley vacuums the stage.

6:30 p.m.

An hour to go. Orchestra members arrive.

Pat Reynolds is still missing.

"Where could he be?" Starr asks. "He knows he's supposed to be here."

A few minutes later, to everyone's relief, Pat storms into the makeup room. Apparently his ride never showed.

"Where have you been?" somebody asks.

"Obviously, I wasn't here," he snaps.

Angie Guido quickly applies his make-up.

"You look very good," she says. "Very Spanish."

"Yeah, a Spanish transvestite."

At 7:15 p.m., a crowd mingles in the school. A line forms at the ticket table and stretches down the hall.

"Usually, right now, I feel so nervous," Anna Schoenfelder says. "I don't even feel nervous."

A beat.

"I don't think that's a good thing."

Another beat.

"I'm nervous now."

Starr's voice fills the hallway.

"To the green room!"

This is what the cast calls the classroom where they gather before and after the show.

They squirm in their chairs.

Eli taps his foot.

Angela hums another of Maria's songs.

In my eyes, in my world...

"Quiet, guys!" Starr says. "We have a full lobby out there."

A roar.

The teachers enter at 7:24 p.m.

"We have one of the best opening nights I have ever seen," Mr. Shipley says.

Another roar.

"It's been a semi-hoot," he says. "I've never been so tired and so energized at the same time. Let's get in a circle."

The cast members form a giant circle and hold hands.

"Thirty seconds," Mr. Shipley says.

They close their eyes. The room is silent. Somebody's lucky charm—a Beanie Baby—tumbles to the floor.

"Go have some fun," Mr. Shipley says.

Off they go.

"I need the Jets!" Eli shouts. *"WHERE ARE ALL THE JETS?"*

The overture begins.

The stage lights come on.

Forty years after it opened on Broadway, *West Side Story* comes to North County High School in Anne Arundel County.

Alone, on stage, stands Eli Senter.

He snaps his fingers. He looks at Mr. Ewachiw for his cue, takes an enormous gulp of air, opens his mouth wide and—

When you're a Jet,
you're a Jet all the way...

Let the record show that at 7:49 p.m. on April 18, 1997, Eli Senter does it.

He hits the note that has eluded him for two months.

He actually sings.

Like an expectant father in a hospital waiting room, Mr. Shipley paces the back of the theater, his arms folded, grinning.

It is not a perfect opening night.

Angela Brown's microphone goes on the fritz during one of Maria's scenes. The buzzing makes it sound like she's surrounded by locusts; her soaring soprano is mostly lost during the quintet.

The lights come on too late during the big dance number.

A police siren sounds too soon.

During the dramatic rumble, one of the Sharks can't open a gate; the audience laughs as he and the gang members crawl through a hole in the fence instead.

The lights come on too soon before Act II. Angela Brown, Angie Guido and several of the Shark girls improvise on stage for several awkward minutes while the orchestra plays the second-act overture.

As Brian Forte—Tony—sneaks out of Maria's window after their love scene, he accidentally kicks down the curtain. The audience laughs.

When Tony is shot in the dramatic final scene, the gun is so loud everyone in the audience jumps, then laughs again.

And none of it matters.

They are the best they have ever been.

"Great job, guys," Mr. Shipley says in the green room. "We have some technical things to take care of for tomorrow night, but it was lovely. The audience said it all. Go see your folks."

"Wait!" Mr. Ewachiw says. "I have an announcement."

Slowly, he puts his hands together and begins to applaud.

"Where's Anna?" Brian Forte says in the hall. "Have you seen Anna?"

He looks frantic. The carefree Brian has been replaced by an urgent young man. Suddenly he realizes that it's almost over. He's a senior. He has less than a month before this safe harbor called high school is gone. He has fallen for Anna Schoenfelder, and she with him, and now Brian understands that some things in life deserve to be taken seriously.

"I've got to get revved up for tomorrow night," he says. "Then I've got to get revved up for the rest of my life. I need to find Anna."

The hallway is a mob scene—parents, friends, roses, balloons.

When Brian finds Anna Schoenfelder, he hugs her tightly.

Holding on.

Angela Brown needs to find someone as well.

During the song, "I Feel Pretty," Angela's eyes gave away her panic. It's the look singers get when they suddenly realize they can't remember the lyrics.

Angie Guido, one of the girls in the chorus, sensed the problem. So Angie—the girl who desperately wanted to play Maria, who sobbed when the cast list was posted, who nearly quit the show in anger—helped the girl who won the role instead of her.

Her back turned to the audience, Angie looked at Angela and mouthed the words, "I feel charming."

That's all Angela needed.

I feel charming,
Oh, so charming—
It's alarming how charming I feel...

She didn't miss a beat.

Now, in the hallway, the girls find each other.

"Thank you so much," Angela says.

The next morning, a Saturday, Angela Brown sings the National Anthem at the opening of the Brooklyn Park Little League. Starr Lucas drives her blue Volkswagen Beetle, the one covered with *West Side Story* posters, in the parade.

"That was good," Starr says of opening night. "But we can do even better."

And so they do.

It begins, again, in the green room.

"I want to thank you for giving me the opportunity to do this show," the 53-year-old Mr. Shipley says on his last night as the director of a high school musical. He's retiring this year. "It is a perfect cast. I find very little in life that is perfect, but this comes close."

Mr. Ewachiw is next.

"Last night never happened," he says. "Tony and Maria have never met. Riff and Bernardo are still alive. You have to do it again and you have to be at the top of your game."

The orchestra begins.

The stage lights come on.

Magic.

Eli Senter hits his cue. Brian Forte sings *tonight* as *tuh-nut*. The dance number sparkles. The rumble works; Riff gets killed just as the music reaches a crescendo. Angela Brown has a new microphone—and the voice of Maria leaps from the stage, so strong and powerful the audience gasps. Brian wraps his arms around her in "Tonight," and they sway to the words.

Tonight, tonight,
The world is wild and bright...

Cast members are improvising, performing stunts they never have tried before. The audience feeds on their energy. When Brian and Angela finish singing, the audience is not just applauding. It's cheering like a football crowd.

One of the Jets—Adam Mehok—steals the "Gee, Officer Krupke!" number when he wraps a handkerchief around his head and sings like an old woman. The audience interrupts the song with applause.

Not long ago, Adam and his best friend, Brian Forte, fell for the same girl. Brian won, and Adam was crushed. He needs this victorious moment.

"I nearly stopped singing—'Wait, we're not through yet,'" he says later.

Look at Angie Guido. The girl who longed to play Maria commands the stage in the "America" song. She sings the same line twice, but the audience is too enchanted with her scene and her voice to notice.

And listen as Angela Brown and Anna Schoenfelder harmonize during the final duet.

When loves comes so strong,
There is no right or wrong,
Your love is your life!

Goose bumps galore. The audience cheers before the two girls finish.

During the show's final scene, after the gun is fired and Maria cradles Tony's lifeless body, a small child in the rear of the auditorium turns to her mother.

"Was that real?"

The audience stands and cheers as the curtain call begins.

Last night, Starr Lucas remained backstage. Directors, even student directors, don't make curtain calls. But this is different. This is her last high school musical.

Beaming, shining, Starr walks on stage, heading straight for the spotlight. Then she and the cast members point to Maria's balcony, where a boy unfurls a banner with this message:

A Bow For Shipley.

The tears begin on stage and escalate in the green room. The cast members can't stop crying. They hug and cry and hug some more. The boys who aren't crying are spitting out one-liners as fast as they can to keep from crying.

Eli stands in the middle, his face a puddle.

All the girls—Angie, Angela and Anna—are bawling.

"You have just experienced a pure moment," Ms. Rolman tells them. "It's infrequently in life that you can say, 'On this day, I did my very best,' but you can say that tonight."

Each of the seniors receives a red rose, a North County High tradition.

"We have one more senior tonight," Starr says.

She hands Mr. Shipley his rose.

Mr. Shipley—the old cowboy—maintains his composure. His moment comes later, when the room is mostly empty. The piano player, David Richardson—Dave the Piano Guy—comes to say goodbye.

"I was sitting there, listening to that last duet, thinking how I will never have an experience quite like this again in my life," he says. "I just sat back and enjoyed it."

A willing suspension of disbelief...

Mr. Shipley blinks back the tears.

After the show, Angela Brown hands Mr. Ewachiw a thank-you card.

I don't know how you did it, but you're right—my voice has completely changed. Today at a Little League opening day ceremony I sang the National Anthem and people actually cried!

Mr. Ewachiw cradles her face in both hands and kisses the top of her head.

A junior, Angela will have another year to see where this voice can take her. But tonight is for basking.

She races to the auditorium.

"Wait for me!"

You can't take a cast photograph of *West Side Story* without Maria.

As Angela hurries to the stage, her arms overflowing with roses, balloons and congratulatory notes, a Mickey Mouse balloon floats gently to the theater floor.

She doesn't even notice.

Later that night, after tearing apart the set, the cast celebrates at an ice-cream shop that remains open just for them.

Let's leave them here, giddy and triumphant—the fedora-topped Eli Senter nuzzling his girlfriend; Brian Forte and Anna Schoenfelder flirting with each other; Angie Guido laughing as her boyfriend clutches a rose in his teeth; the shimmering Starr Lucas digging into a mountainous ice-cream sundae; and Angela Brown wearing the exultant expression of a young woman who has discovered this wonderful gift—a voice so pretty people cry when they hear it.

Years from now, Angela will happen upon a copy of the *West Side Story* program from the 1997 spring musical, and the memories will wash over her...the first time she hit the high C...seeing her name next to Maria's on the cast list...watching Eli persevere...

Angie's help...the duet with Anna...Starr's curtain call...Mr. Shipley's final show.

The program will have faded, but if Angela closes her eyes—if she's willing to suspend her disbelief for just a moment—she will feel it again, all of it, every instant of that stage when the girl she was became the woman she is, two glorious nights when the world was wild and bright and time stood forever still.

Writers' Workshop

Talking Points

1) Study and compare the opening scenes for each of the installments. For example, one opens with an anecdote that foreshadows the day's theme. Another uses a note pinned to a bulletin board. Which techniques work best?

2) At the end of this story, the writer directly addresses the reader as he did at the beginning of the series. "Let's leave them there." Then in the final two paragraphs he uses an authoritative voice to project the future emotions of the characters. Is it necessary? Is this appropriate? Is it effective?

3) This series focused on high school students. How would it differ if it focused on college students? Professional actors and musicians? What changes in tone would be necessary?

4) The cast of characters in the series is almost as big as the musical itself. How effectively did the writer protray the characters and keep them identified clearly to readers from day to day?

Assignment Desk

1) Using the different opening scenes as models, try different ways to open one of your stories.

2) "Years from now, Angela will happen upon a copy of the *West Side Story* program from the 1997 spring musical." Write a different ending to this story without using this reflective tone. What are some other ways you could conclude the series.

3) In addition to the headline every day, "A Stage in Their Lives," each of these stories includes a one- or two-sentence secondary summary. These draw the reader into the story. Try writing these for several of your stories. Do they help you focus the story? Do they change the way you structure the story?

A conversation with

Ken Fuson

ROY PETER CLARK: How did you come to do this story?

KEN FUSON: It was on my list of ideas for a while, those that you never get to. I was having a conversation with Steve Proctor, he's our feature editor, before Christmas, and we were just chatting about his two children being in the *Nutcracker.* They're both child actors. And he was talking about going back and forth to the practices and how much fun that was.

I was telling him, "Yeah, you know, when I was in high school I was Charlie Brown, in *You're A Good Man, Charlie Brown,*" and how much fun that was. I don't remember who said it first, but at some point we both came up with the idea that it'd be a lot of fun to go watch kids put on a musical and write about it. And he said, "Why don't you go to North County High School. Give them a call."

So I called the director, Wayne Shipley, and from the very first instant, he knew exactly what I wanted to do. He loves the creative process.

Did your memory of being in a school play make a difference for you?

A little bit. But you have to understand, there were 55 people in my high school class, and probably there are several hundred in each class at this high school. Their level of drama, what they do, is so much more advanced than mine was.

Yeah, but that's not really what the story is about, right? It's about a rite of passage.

Exactly. And the thing is, I have very vivid memories of being in high school and what it was like to stand on the stage, and that did influence me. I knew there were going to be three things that would happen. One, somebody always doesn't get the part. You could do that story every single year a spring musical is done. Somebody will not get the part that they've always wanted. Number two, somebody will fall in love. Usually it's the leading actor and the leading actress who fall in love, just because they're doing all these love scenes and high school kids get carried away. And number three, I've never visited a show that didn't look like a complete disaster the week before.

Now, those are three things I was looking for right from the start. But then some other things happened that I wasn't ready for.

Angela Brown really blossomed from a little giggly girl to a young woman during the course of this. That was a surprise for me. I wasn't expecting that. I didn't remember how hard it was to get up in public and sing until I met Eli, so that was another surprise that came to me. And finally, Starr is a girl with a physical disability. I never would have expected that. And see, you have all those things at one high school.

Talk about the process of "casting" stories—choosing who will be the perfect characters, and who will not.

My colleague, Lisa Pollak, had a big part in this. When I started off, I sat in the back of the theater and took notes on everything. I figured there were probably 15 or 20 kids that I thought might be interesting. Then I got down to like, OK, I've got 10 characters here. There's no way I can tell really long stories about 10 people; nobody will care. How do I narrow it down? And it was really, really tough.

There was a girl named Amy Balonis, who is a sophomore, who did all the choreography for the show. And she's an amazing kid, great grades, a great kid— she would come to practices in her softball uniform, because she pitched that day in the softball game. Her name is not in the series, which is horrible. I can't look that kid in the eye. When I was struggling on who to use, Lisa Pollak told me, "Pick the kids who have the most at stake. Who has the most at stake?" And each one of those kids I used represents something.

Angela Brown represents a girl becoming a woman. Angie Guido represents what happens when you don't get what you want. Brian Forte represents the kid who's always had things go his own way and now, all of a sudden—number one, it doesn't go the way he wants it to and, number two, he's got to grow up. He's graduating. Eli Senter is a boy who is guts personified. How can you have enough guts to stand in front of everybody and sing when you can't sing a note? Guts above talent. And he also provided a sense of humor to the whole thing. He's a very funny kid. And I used him for that.

What about Starr?

Starr Lucas decided, "I can't be a star, so I'm going to become a director." And by the end of the show, Angie Guido grows up, too, but Starr made a very adult decision right before this thing. So each one of those kids had big things at stake and represented themes that I could carry through each story.

The other thing is, different things happen to them during the course of this, which you need in a serial. Part 3 has to be different from Part 1. Brian Forte starts off, "Everything's great. I got the part. Of course I did, I'm the only one who can sing." The second story, "Gee, I'm not sure if I can really do this. This music's tough." Third part of the story, "I've fallen in love, and so has my best friend." So each day things changed with them.

Have you seen the movie, *The Full Monty?*

I haven't.

Go see it. You'll enjoy it. But one of the interesting things about it is that the narrative structure, as it follows these five or six steelworkers from Northern England in the middle of this deep economic recession, is that each one of them has something different at stake.

Brings something different to the stage.

In one case, it's a sexual identity crisis. In another case, it's a marriage that's falling apart. In another

case, it has to do with custody of a son. In another case, it has to do with a wife who doesn't realize her husband is unemployed. So they all become Chippendale dancers as a common way to overcome their individual problems. The narrative is generated in terms of these individual streams that eventually flow into this great stream.

I'll give you an example of this. There was a girl I finally decided I *wasn't* going to focus on. I would have bet any amount of money early on that Anna Schoenfelder, who played Anita, would have been a huge part of this, one of the main characters. She's bright, she's funny, she was falling in love with Brian. There was a lot going on with her. The thing with her, though, is she was like a female Brian Forte. She was good at what she did, she always got the good role, and she was graduating from high school. She didn't bring anything distinctive that Brian didn't. So while she's in there, and she's a big part of this, she wasn't one of the five kids. You do have to pick people who will bring something different if you're going to do a serial like this.

I want to ask you one other thing about characters. Did you like the characters that you chose?

Oh, yeah. Angie was your typical spoiled little kid. And people who read it felt that way about her, early on. "I didn't get the part, I'm not going to play, and I'm not going to be part of it. I'm going to go home, I'm going to pout." In the beginning, she got on my nerves a little bit. Through the course of this I grew to really care about her, like her, seeing what she went through. But I have to tell you, there weren't any kids in this that I wouldn't have liked. There wasn't some really jerky kid.

When Tom French of the *St. Petersburg Times* wrote about high school students in his series, "South of Heaven," he was quite surprised when some readers didn't like the characters that he really liked. Did you have that experience?

A friend of mine, whom I had read this to early, didn't like the Brian Forte character at all. He just thought, "Typical goof-off kid," and I said, "Brian's a terrific kid." And so you do run that risk.

I made it a point to sit down with each one of these kids and really go over the story—not read it to them, but really go over it. "Brian, I'm writing about you and Anna and breaking up," or "Angie, I'm talking about when you ran out of the auditorium."

So there are no surprises for these kids?

Exactly. Because I have a theory about newspapers, that when you write about somebody, that when they first read it, they don't read it logically. They don't read really what you mean to write sometimes. They're totally over-sensitized to it.

Do you have any personal inhibitions against showing drafts of your stories to sources?

None. See, when I went to school at the University of Missouri, you used to have to call up sources and read the story back. They called it "fact checking." And I've always thought it was a great idea, but I know other reporters, investigative reporters, hate it.

This is different than investigative reporting. You're almost collaborating with the source.

In fact, Gary Smith of *Sports Illustrated* talks about having to convince the person that this is their story as much as it is your story. They have to work with you on it, and that's so true.

Now, there's an article in *Columbia Journalism Review* that highlighted your series. The author uses a term I've not used or hadn't heard before. He talks about "immersion journalism." Do you like that term? Does it describe what you're trying to do in a series like this?

What else would you call it? It's not your typical feature story. You're really living with somebody.

Just to give a sense of the level of your immersion, were you attending every practice?

I went to every single practice except one, and to all the auditions. I went to Angie Guido's birthday party. I went with Brian after school to his basement where all these kids hung out. I went to the Honey Bee Diner. I really tried to be there when things were happening. And in the beginning—I'm a 40-year-old, middle-aged guy, who needed to connect with 18-year-old kids—I knew that if I just showed up once a week they weren't going to trust me. But if I was there day after day, I'd become a part of the scenery.

In the beginning, they wouldn't say much; but eventually they'd come by and sit down and talk, and I was kind of like their mascot after a while. I mean, they really wanted me to be there. "We're going to have a Saturday practice. You going to be there?"

"Sure, I'll be there." And I knew I connected with these kids when, the day after spring break and we'd been apart for a week, I walked into the first practice and Anna Schoenfelder and Michele Miller and another girl who were kind of my spies during all this, came running up the aisle of the theater saying, "Ken, Ken, you won't believe...Anna's going out with Brian! Anna and Brian are dating!" That was the sort of thing you're looking for.

I know you're a student of writing and writers and of journalism. Give me some sense of the kinds of reading experiences that may have influenced the shape or direction of this particular piece, since a lot of people are trying to figure out how to use reading to help reporters write.

"South of Heaven" by Tom French would have been an influence for this, definitely. I loved how close he obviously got to these kids. And that was one of the goals I had—is to feel like you knew these kids on the stage.

Other stories—there's not one I can really point to. I admire Gary Smith. He talks about how you've got to find those moments that really change people. That really have an impact.

So in your series, give me an example of a moment that changes a person.

Angela Brown hitting a high C at the audition. When she hit that high C—if you remember, they're singing "The Star-Spangled Banner"—you could see it in her face that something had clicked with her. And she was just so excited. That was a big moment. That was a huge moment for her. That's what I'm talking about, one of those really life-changing moments.

With Starr, there were more things that had happened to her in the past. Being carried by her dad, like a piece of furniture, into her house because of her cerebral palsy. When she told that story I almost cried listening to her tell it; you could tell how much it hurt her to go through that.

You're not an eyewitness to that.

Right.

Any difference in the way that you reported this?

I describe it more. The one I do with Angela singing the high C is a scene that I witnessed. With Starr, it's more me telling you something that happened. It's more—exposition, is that the word? More exposition. I tried very hard not to have to re-create a whole lot that I wasn't there to see. And I have different feelings about that. I sometimes think that it weakens my writing.

There's a quote here when Brian and Adam are in the car. They're rivals and best friends. Brian lowers the volume and says, "Things are getting pretty complex, aren't they? Makes life more interesting, don't you think?" "That does it," Brian screams, "No."

I wasn't there in the car. They told me about that. But I'm writing it as if I'm there. I tried not to do that very much. I do it a little bit. Then I throw in these quotes. Adam: "He just erupted. I was taken by the emotion. I really envy that." Brian: "I'd always held my feelings back. For some reason, this time I couldn't. My feelings were just too strong."

Now, I think most people who do narratives would think that's a really weak thing to do right there.

Tom French calls that, "stepping on the narrative."

And I do that occasionally. And if I went back and rewrote it, I'd get rid of all the things like that. Or I'd tell it from a point of view that's different.

So you want the train to be moving on the track the whole time—no whistle stops where you stand back and look retrospectively at what happened?

Yes. But it's very difficult for me to write really involved, specific re-creations. I don't think readers trust them that much. I think you've got to be really careful. And I was probably too careful there. Where I stopped the train right there for, "Now here's a word from Adam." You know?

But if you can't do re-creations, then you can't use the scene where Starr is carried by her father.

Right. So my next level of evolution in this is to figure out a way not to stop the train. There aren't many moments like this, because Jan Winburn, my boss, would get rid of them, or she'd point them out to me.

I read these re-creations—I did a judging of magazine work, and this one guy had this really gripping story about a murder that happened five years ago. There's a scene in a bar. Now he wasn't in that bar, you know he's not, and he's talking about, "He took a drink on a Budweiser and then cleared his throat." Well, how does he know that? I don't believe it. I don't believe he'd know that. I don't even think a person would remember someone clearing their throat. When I read "Angels and Demons," Tom French is very careful about just how specific he gets when he re-creates something. It's the one thing that I work on, that I struggle with the most in writing, is how much can I really re-create a scene.

What I did do here—this is going back to an earlier question—I basically feel like a narrative apprentice. I always have. I've wanted to do these kinds of stories ever since I read Frances Craig in the *Des Moines Register.* She wrote a story about a baby getting open-heart surgery where you felt like you were in the room. I mean, you could hear the doctors playing music, and there was tension, and you didn't know if the baby was going to live. I've always wanted to write stories where you felt like you were there.

And you called her up or wrote her a letter?

I called her up at work and said, "You're going to win an award." She won the Penney-Missouri Award.

How old were you then?

I think I was a senior in high school.

So since then you've thought of yourself as an apprentice?

Yeah, but I wanted to do stories like that where you have a feeling that you're there, and it means something to you to be there.

My other thing was I used to go to Drake University basketball games when I was in high school, and it'd be exciting and people would be screaming, and the next day you'd pick up the paper and it would say, "Willie Wise scored 20 points and..." I never thought that captured the event at all, and so I always, in the back of my mind, have thought, "I want to try to capture the event." So anyway, I'd play around with stories and features, and then I read Jon Franklin's book, *Writing for Story,* and that made me realize what structure of story is, and so I tried to play around with that. Franklin talks about how you've got to do the apprenticeship, you've got to do the "day in the life" of the garbage man and all that.

So I did this story on a small town in Iowa, which was a finalist for this award. And if you go back and read it, it's not very good. The thing was, I did not narrow it down to people who had something at stake. I wrote about this town and it just seems like 500 characters. They're all interesting characters, but I was just writing it as if the town was the main character, and all these people just come and go. That was a mistake. By Parts 3 and 4, where I narrowed it down to a certain number of folks—the town drunk, the town mayor—then it had some narrative momentum. But the first part is not very good. It just doesn't grab you.

So then I did this story on a small-town baseball team. And that story was better. I had this great story: They're losing their team, their school, but they beat the big school, they beat the big school for the state championship.

But again, I was thinking about this as a story about a town. And you never got to know the kids. You never got to care about who the players were on the team. You care about the coach a little bit. I didn't hit the home run with it. I remember thinking, "Gosh, if Tom Wolfe had this material, what could he do with it? I know I've got great material here," but it just didn't connect the way I wanted it to.

So then, several years ago, I had a similar sports story about a girls' softball team. One of the girls had been killed and her dad continued to coach the team. I focused on the kids there, and it's a much better story because you care about these kids. So that leads me in, that's the evolution of what I brought to this series. I said to myself, "OK, I've got to find kids that I care about, I've got to get to know these kids. I can't sit back and just talk to the musical director because we're about the same age. I've got to go hang out with the kids, I've gotta be there."

And now, from this point, the next story I do, I will get rid of these whistle stops. That's the next thing. I'll concentrate more on the point of view of Adam or Brian right there, and tell this story right there through their eyes. I could have gotten all this in without interfering. And that's the one thing I give myself credit for in this business: I do try to get better. I think about it. How can I, by the time I'm 65, write a really good one?

You'll be ready to write. Talk about the value of serialization and the momentum from one chapter to another.

At the end of each chapter, there has to be that, "I want to go on." You have to have the big cymbal crash, the big door slamming, the "Oh my God" event.

Let's talk about that. Some people call that a cliffhanger.

The best cliffhanger here is the first one. Mr. Shipley writes the winner's name on a piece of paper. Who gets the part of Maria? I've led this whole thing up to somebody's going to have their dream come true. Is it Angie or is it Angela? And you don't find out. Now, I didn't write it that way the first time.

How did you do it?

I was so proud of myself. I had this great vignette, this thing I'd seen. When they were casting everybody, and they came to Maria, Mr. Shipley wrote down her name, "Angela Guido." You have Angie Guido, you have Angela Brown. He wrote down "Angela Guido."

A merger of their two names.

And he looked at it, and I'm watching. He's got a pencil. And he looked at it and he realized that was wrong, and over the name "Guido," over the big capital "G" he wrote a capital "B." And he kept doing that, over and over again, until the name "Guido" had been transferred into the name "Brown." And it was so poignant when you think about Angie Guido and how she was that close. He went right over her name, he just steamrolled right over it. And I thought, "I've got this great moment." I was so proud of myself for seeing it, you know. It's one of those, "Boy, this is a nice little reporter's moment. I actually saw him do this."

And I ended it with, "And Angie Guido will forever know the meaning behind the words she sang in her audition," which was from *Les Miz,* and I used earlier— "Without me, this world will go on turning. A world that's full of happiness that I have never known." And that was going to be the end of Part 1.

Now, if I had left it like that, it would have been perfectly fine, but there would have been no reason for anybody to read Part 2. Really. I didn't have any sort of suspense built in. My colleague Laura Lippman read it and she said, "You can't tell us who gets the role at the end of Part 1. We have to find out when that girl sees it on the cast list." She was very adamant about this. And I thought, "She's right, she's absolutely right." That was a great piece of advice. That's the cymbal crashing.

The more I thought about this, the more I thought each one of these sections had to have a little bit of mystery to it. Or I tried to. They're little scenes. But I have this image of Tarzan on the vine. In a story, you want the reader to go from one vine to the next vine to the next vine, you know, just something that keeps them moving. I don't know if that's a good image, but that's how I've got it. And I think the best ones are when there are little-bitty dramas going on within the actual story. In other words, don't just save your one big problem or climax for the very end. Try to have a few interspersed within the story.

Tell me some of the ways that readers responded to the serialization of this story.

Early on, the people I work with were like, "Six parts on a high school musical?" In the beginning I was going to do five, and I told them, "No, it's going to be six." They almost laughed right in my face. And I don't think they really understood what it was we were going to do.

I think readers liked it. I think it's frustrating, to some extent, when you leave a question hanging. Readers are not used to that; they're used to having answers in newspapers, not questions. I think women readers really liked it. I don't want to sound like a sexist here, but I heard more from women than I did from men on this. And I don't know if it's something about soap opera serialization or just a sense of story, you know, like with the Olympics coverage—they try to do more stories that have a heart to them. I don't know if that's what appeals to them.

What kind of evidence did you get that people were following the story?

I heard from people I didn't know at work who said their kids were reading it every day and they were enjoying it. That was great.

The best compliment I got from the whole thing was a woman who sent me a postcard saying how much she liked it and that she went to the local Sam Goody's, or whatever it's called, to buy a CD of *West Side Story*.

And the teen-ager at the counter said, "You must be reading the series, because we've been selling it. We've been selling that all week." And I thought, well, you know, that's the best.

You had them humming the score.

Right from the start, I wanted those songs in people's heads. I don't think I overdid it, I tried not to. I wanted the sense of music in this thing, and the way you do that is with these little moments where I use italics. The last story was the easiest one to write because I just wanted to go zip, zip, zip, zip, right to the performance. Everything's really quick and fast.

And there's a little moment in here where—let's see. Eli plays Riff. "He's wired, bounding across the stage, singing lines from the musical, 'And there's nothing for me but Maria.'" You get that established, and people hear that in their heads I think, subconsciously, and they get that sense of the show going on.

So really, it's almost as if this were a movie we were watching.

Exactly. Background.

It'd be a musical score, the score on the story.

That's right.

I didn't want to overdo it. One thing I did in this series that I've never done before was plant seeds early on that I'd come back to later. And I don't even know if readers caught it or not. But I definitely tried to plant some seeds.

There's one in the beginning about Starr—you don't learn about Starr's cerebral palsy until Part 2. During Part 1 I say, "A senior walks to the front. She has a radiant smile and a faint limp." In Part 2 I say, "Maneuvering through a maze of hallways and classrooms, Starr stumbles as she walks—there's a problem with her legs." And I don't think anybody really is going to remember from Part 1 that I mentioned she has a limp. I don't know. I'm playing around with that.

The other funny thing. The ending—a lot of people told me they really liked the ending. People would say, "Let's leave them here," that line. And I totally had the sense when I was writing that of a camera panning back. Or an audience walking out of the theater. And it's almost like an epilogue there. But the funny thing is, I wrote this the night of the last show. I was as wired as the kids. I was really excited for them. The photographer, Nanine Hartzenbusch, and I went to the ice cream store. We left because we really didn't feel like we belonged there.

And then we went and had coffee with the teachers. And we sat there till 6 in the morning, talking—just coming down. Decompressing. And I went back and wrote the ending for the whole thing on a legal pad, before I ever wrote anything else.

So the ending came first.

My advice to young people is to know what your ending is before you start writing.

As people venture into narrative for the first time, they wonder just how to take all the basic raw material they've got and what do they do with it then? So you need to walk me through it, let me see it. You've got notebooks, you've got printouts. What's the raw material?

I took a notebook every night to the practice, and the next morning I'd come back and type up all my notes, the very next day because you can't wait till the very end and then go back to your notes. You can't. I think on any kind of project, the great challenge is to control your material. Because you're going to get 10 times more than you need. So I type up everything that happened on that day, April 4, and then here's all the material.

And after a week or two: Here's all my notes about Mr. Shipley. I had a daily log of notes, and then by person. So by the end, I had this big list of Angie Guido notes that I could go back to.

All right, so you have printouts. Are you making copies of the printouts?

Yeah. I typed up my notes and then I had them all printed out. I've got a sheet of paper that's got this by day. And then I go through all these notes in the computer, and anything that happened that day that has to do with Angie Guido, I'll pull out and make a separate printout of that.

So you're moving stuff from Computer File 1 to Computer File 2, looking for all the stuff on individual characters.

So I have my daily list of notes plus my character notes. And what I'm really trying to do is pick out, like you said, the ebbs and flows. I mean, these kids had to have a certain kind of conflict for each day, really. Something had to happen to them for each day of the story.

You're mining the raw material, not only in terms of breaking stuff out for each character, but you're also taking out material that could be used in the creation of scenes ?

Right, right, exactly. And I knew the audition was a scene. I knew I had a great scene there. I knew posting the cast list was a scene. And so, at the beginning of the story, to organize it, my first two days were really elementary, as far as organizing it.

Let me interrupt, because there's one other thing I want to try to figure out. When it's time to write a particular scene, how do you find it in your notes or materials?

Oh, I'm very anal retentive—what's the word, "compulsive." I go through all my notes and look for scenes. I've got this sheet of paper, a legal pad that's got "Posting cast list, Angie runs out of auditorium."

But do you have a page number where you can find it in your notes?

By then I've read it in the notes so often, I know where it is. You practically memorize it

You're saying you just internalized it by then?

Yeah. Usually I have. I tend to organize like this. I actually draw it out in blocks. What's first, what's second. And then, for each story, I'll even do this for scenes. This is going to be the Eli scene, this is going to be this scene. And for some reason, that helps me see it. It's not sitting down with an outline, but it's a way of outlining.

So basically you start off with the big blocks, which are the global structure for the story. Is this going to be five days, going to be six days, going to be seven days? You start to figure that out. And then, within each of those blocks you have subsections, which are mostly scenes.

Exactly. Then you figure out how to tie them in.

You do have chronological order, right?

I do some flashbacks. It's not a real strength of mine. I tend to think chronologically still. That's something else I'm working on.

You told me a funny story about how the alternative newspaper in Baltimore dissed your story.

They had their "Best of Baltimore" section, and they called the series the "Most Overblown Feature Story of the Year." I won the award. They called it a "Technicolor Fluff Fest."

It was really well written. That was one of the hard parts about it. It said, "We can't wait for what Fuson takes his florid pen to next, 'A Splice in Their Lives: The Story of the Audiovisual Club.' Or, 'Page in Their Lives: The Story of the Yearbook Club.'" I totally understand that. This is not going to be anybody's sense of hard-hitting journalism. But this isn't written for the hipsters at the alternative paper. I wanted to get a slice of what it's like to be in high school, and this is a part of high school that's never written about. We write about sports teams, we write about kids in trouble. These are good kids, doing something creative, and having it change them. Now, what's wrong with that?

The New York Times

N.R. Kleinfield

Finalist, Non-Deadline Writing

N.R. (Sonny) Kleinfield is a senior writer on the Metropolitan staff of *The New York Times,* largely engaged in feature stories and long-range projects about the ordinary and the unsung. He was born in Fair Lawn, N.J., and began his career as a general interest feature writer at *The Wall Street Journal,* where he spent five years. He joined the *Times* in 1977.

Kleinfield was part of the team that covered the bombing of the World Trade Center that won a Pulitzer Prize for local reporting, as well as the team that wrote about the downsizing phenomenon that won a George Polk Award. He has also received the Gerald Loeb Award and the Meyer Berger Award, among other honors.

In addition to his newspaper work, Kleinfield has contributed articles to many national magazines, including *The Atlantic Monthly, Harper's, Esquire, New Times,* and *The New York Times Magazine.* He is the author of seven books, including a book about the development of the MRI scanner, an ordinary race car team and its driver trying to win the Indianapolis 500, floor traders, the life of hotel workers, and the civil rights movement for those with physical disabilities.

Kleinfield demonstrates the value of immersion reporting and the power of narrative writing in the last installment of his moving series about James Velez, a profoundly disabled man who seeks a normal life after spending two-thirds of his life in institutions.

With round-the clock help, young man joins the world

JUNE 24, 1997

In the dappled morning light, a small young man walked out of the back entrance of Building 2 of the Brooklyn Developmental Center, a loose-muscled swing to his shoulders. The act itself was unremarkable, and he was attended by only a handful of familiar faces. For him, though, it was like the Earth shifting. His shoes rasping on the macadam, he scuffed toward his mother's van.

"I got there," he said emphatically. "Now let's get out of here."

With these few steps, his long confinement was over. Fifteen years after entering an institution as a scared and profoundly disabled 7-year-old, James Velez crossed the threshold of a proximate world that had always seemed unreachable.

He had feared he would never witness this moment. For so long, as thousands of others were being ushered out of institutions and into the community, he had found himself burrowing ever deeper into the institutionalized world.

Relatively speaking, those who had moved out were the easy cases; Mr. Velez was a hard one, and a medical riddle: He feels imaginary bugs swarming over his skin and scratches himself to the point of self-mutilation. He has to be constantly watched. And yet, his intelligence is within the range of what is considered normal. And so he yearned for a "normal" life, in a place of his own.

Now, on this Tuesday morning, last Nov. 12, after two and a half years running a gantlet of obstacles, Job Path, a small Manhattan social-service agency that is part of the Vera Institute of Justice, was placing him with a roommate in an apartment in Queens, one of the boldest attempts ever to grant so acutely disabled an individual his independence.

Nobody was likely to take his old room. "They're closing institutions, you know," a supervisor at the center said with a shrug.

Peter Uschakow, the deputy director, watched him go. "He should do very well," he said. "Having his own place is the best thing for him."

But would it be? Would this daring and expensive experiment turn out as everybody hoped? Could he be kept safe from himself and still have some version of an independent life? Waves of disabled individuals had entered the community, but few had truly become "of" the community. They had not found jobs or made friends beyond those paid to be with them.

Because of Mr. Velez's intelligence, his advocates had higher aspirations for him still; a good job, maybe college. If all went well, his case could be a beacon for others left in institutions. But deep was the well of his past. People in institutions become practiced in not making decisions. Though he could read at a 12th-grade level and do ninth-grade math, he did not have a high school diploma and was indifferent about further schooling. He read little beyond *TV Guide.* He was 22, but quite immature. He had never mopped a floor or cooked a chicken. Could he shrug off his institutional indoctrination, and at what price to those laboring on his behalf? And, ultimately, would living better make him better?

Nobody expected quick answers. This was about a young man and an apartment, but it was no simple undertaking. With an annual budget of around $200,000 in state and federal money, a considerable apparatus had been erected around him and his much less needy roommate. Seven aides had been trained. Work internships had been arranged. A behavioral consultant would chart his progress. Administrators and state auditors would look in.

Now, Mr. Velez slid into his mother's van, bound for the ground-floor apartment in Ozone Park.

"I'm going to cry," said Lisa Pitz, Job Path's housing coordinator. No one had worked more indefatigably on his behalf. Her body canted backward, she was snapping pictures as keepsakes.

"I've never seen my son this happy in years," beamed his mother, Daisy Velez, over the clatter of voices. Roselia Suarez, his grandmother, exulted, "Finally! James deserves his chance."

He had not had breakfast and so they stopped at Dunkin' Donuts, where he ordered an egg sandwich, coffee with seven sugars and a box of doughnuts for later.

"Did you get the 'Keep Out' sign on the door?" he asked.

"No, I forgot it," his mother said.

"But I colored it," he said.

"Do you want to go back for it?"

"No," he said. "I don't ever want to go back, not for anything."

RITUALS OF COMING HOME

His mother stuck a family portrait on the refrigerator. Everyone cast aside their diets and dug into the doughnuts. His grandmother boogied around the kitchen. She did a headstand. She was having the time of her life. Mr. Velez rooted her on. Contagious laughter rattled through the apartment.

Soon Mr. Velez, whose long social isolation had left him a TV junkie, went into his bedroom and switched on *Godzilla vs. Megalon.* He climbed into his rocking chair; he is only comfortable while in motion.

Ms. Pitz busied herself putting away kitchen items. She arranged a black loose-leaf binder on the kitchen table. Each day, the aides were to record the highlights of their shifts; over time, the notebook would become the record of Mr. Velez's new life. It was a way to judge progress, and it was necessary for state audits. She also inserted a stack of data sheets. The aides were to mark down when he scratched and what else was going on at the time, to see if certain factors influenced his behavior.

Around 4, his roommate, Manny Sanchez, 25, got home from day treatment. Mr. Sanchez is taciturn, with a reedy voice and an informal smile. He is severely retarded, but also fairly self-sufficient. He heated up some chicken and rice. Supper smells drifted through the apartment. He sat down at the table to eat. Mr. Velez walked in and settled across from him. After dinner, they would make their first grocery list and go shopping. Ms. Pitz would urge them to clip coupons to stretch their dollars.

And so, in this sequence of everyday events, the next symphonic movement of the effort was under way. The years and the tireless work, the meshing of all the strands, seemed to come down to this: two young men seated across a dinette table.

"How you doing, man?" Mr. Velez said.

"OK."

"So we're finally here."

"Yeah. Finally here."

"We're in our place."

"Yeah. Our place. Welcome to our place."

* * *

In successive days, celebration seemed less in order. Mr. Velez drew within himself, and his demons spoke up with fury.

Some days, he did not want to leave the apartment. He was supposed to spend three days a week helping out at the Brooklyn College radio station (he aspired to become a disk jockey), but when it was time to go to work, he said he felt sick. He was snappish, constantly ill at ease.

The aides looked at him with furrowed perplexity. After so much anguish, he had what he ached for. Why wasn't he happy?

"It must all seem like such a nonreality to him," Ms. Pitz hypothesized. "He's waited so long. He has a lot of institutional behavior he has got to unlearn."

He liked his independence. "I love it all," he said. "I've never had something like this." And yet he behaved like a recluse.

He would sleep record long hours, refusing to be wakened. Only asleep, he said, did he escape the bugs. For days, his legs itched relentlessly. Then it was his head. The bugs seemed to redirect their focus by the day or the week. The aides were trying to teach him to massage himself rather than scratch, but they found themselves doing virtually all the massaging. If an aide told him to stop scratching, he was supposed to comply. But he would argue.

Dan Moulthrop, an aide: "Stop scratching."

Mr. Velez: "I was not scratching. My hand was flat. I was rubbing."

He was not cleaning his room. He was not even taking showers. He had to be badgered just to wash himself.

Ralph Sanchez was sternest of the aides. He took no sassing. Mr. Velez, in turn, would give a look that could propel a person across a room, and tell him, "Stop pushing me."

Hearing about his sloth, Ms. Pitz called and read him the riot act: "You finally have your own house and your room is dirty and you have dirty laundry lying around. What are we going to do about this, James?"

He said, "It would help me if I had a schedule so I won't forget."

A schedule was stuck on the refrigerator.

For years, he had been bothered by an ulcerated sore on his right heel, and it was flaring up, so Job Path got him a wheelchair to use while it healed. This only made it harder for him to pitch in around the house.

One morning, snoring like a band saw, he was finally roused by the blare of the "Space Jam" CD that Mr. Moulthrop had put on: "Good morning, Earthling." Mr. Velez tends to sleep with his legs stretched out in front of him and his upper body fully bent over, so his head rests on his knees.

"I'm very uncomfortable," he said. He was given a massage. His legs were driving him to distraction.

He tried to dress himself and had to clamber into his rocking chair. He began to rock furiously, trying to quiet the bugs. He got up and tumbled onto the floor, writhing in discomfort, calling, "Mommy, Mommy."

Mr. Moulthrop talked to him about trying deep breathing, but he said, "I can't think about anything but the itch when I itch. Everything is the itch."

* * *

Lisa Pitz spoke with the others and they agreed. The staff needed to get together. Three weeks into freedom, while Mr. Velez ate with his parents, everyone assembled at the apartment to evaluate where they were.

When Mr. Velez heard of the meeting, he said to Ms. Pitz, "Why, so everyone can sit around and say how much they hate me?"

She said, "No, that's for the second meeting."

One curious matter had come up. Some nights, Mr. Velez asked to be alone in his room, and the aide on duty had complied. But how long could they leave him in solitude and be sure he was safe?

It was a delicate issue. Ms. Pitz had phoned Fredda Brown, the behavioral consultant, who told her: "As long as James needs people to take care of him, he is never going to have privacy as we know it." She suggested small doses—15 or 20 minutes.

He had begun his new life with a small savings account, but was spending it with abandon, ceaselessly buying pay-per-view shows and music tapes. He wanted a sports car. ("Yeah, I'd like a car, too," Ms. Pitz told him.) As it was, Shelley Azumbrado, Job Path's fiscal officer, was finding that her budget had overlooked innumerable minor expenses. She had forgotten haircuts. She had forgotten cable TV. Nor had she assumed that Mr. Velez would make two calls to a psychic help line: $145. She called the psychic and said her powers should have revealed that they wouldn't be paying.

"This is the first freedom he's had," Ms. Pitz said. "He's milking it. He goes grocery shopping and he puts everything in the cart he can get his hands on. The only way he's going to learn is through his wallet when he gets the bills."

Everyone complained of his torpor.

Larry Seldon, an aide: "I told him one night, I'm only here so you don't hurt yourself. I'm not here to be your maid. He has this attitude, 'Get me this, get me that.'"

Ms. Pitz: "I think we have to find a delicate balance. James is so smart. The survival technique for him his whole life has been to read you and to take that information and use it to his advantage. He has had so little power and control over his destiny that I was blown away that I had to tell him to shower. He has lived his entire life with people doing everything for him."

The aides said he was requesting massages almost constantly and wouldn't massage himself. Ms. Pitz offered some thoughts from Ms. Brown: "Continue to offer massage as a proactive thing, but say, I'll rub you for 20 minutes if you'll rub your own legs for one."

Another suggestion was that a massage be contingent on participating in one activity, like setting the table.

This did not sit well. Given that he had spent his institutional life rigidly controlled, Ms. Brown had told the group he should be free of contingencies, at least for a while.

Now, Ms. Pitz said, "She said that if he can't make a commitment, then we have to ask for some small contingencies."

Ms. Pitz sipped some coffee from a mug Mr. Velez had just given her for her 30th birthday.

"James is requiring more of everyone's attention than I ever thought," she sighed. "He's a handful."

* * *

Three pins went down, clacking on the hardwood. Not great, but better than the last ball, which hugged the gutter the entire way.

"Ugh," Mr. Velez shrugged. "Guess I'm a little rusty."

Inexorably, as the weeks passed, he began to find the rhythms of freedom. He began to taste: styles, commerce, travel. Not only did he go bowling, he saw a lot of movies. He ate out. And he steadily took on more responsibility. He would pick up the vacuum and go at his carpet with zeal. He would always take a shower. He spoke about finding a job at a record store.

Though Mr. Sanchez sometimes felt Mr. Velez teased him unremittingly, the roommates were getting along. One weekend, they went to the nearby Green Acres mall and Mr. Velez bought a watch that could store 150 phone numbers. He acquired a bird; he found it a soothing presence. Sometimes, he would look at the bird and beseech it: "Stop scratching. Stop scratching."

There were days when he would itch a lot and his mood would sour, but also days when he would not scratch even once. If his metamorphosis was going to be slow, the clock of his life had a lot of time left on it.

From the log book, hopeful moments:

"James doing well with cooking. Seems to know what he needs to do in general, but some difficulty with specifics: how much oil to put in frying pan, how hot the stove should be."

"Made deal with James so he can do more stuff on own."

"James did not scratch at all."

In small ways, he began assimilating into the community. He shot baskets with the two young boys next door and came to know some local shopkeepers. But he had not found any contemporaries to be his buddies. Most of his contact was with the staff.

His right heel was improving. And while he did open a couple of other sores, it had been more than a year since he was in the hospital, once a routine destination.

Ms. Brown began to see a pattern in the scratching data. The milder sieges came throughout the day, while the more severe ones tended to erupt either early or late, when he had nothing to do. Distraction obviously made a difference. Yet how could the staff occupy him every instant?

Ms. Brown suggested he practice a relaxation sequence: tighten one fist, relax it, tighten the other fist, relax it, tighten the neck, relax it. Then, at times of extreme discomfort, he could resort to it.

On a chilly Saturday afternoon, the roommates threw a housewarming party. Most of the guests were Mr. Velez's relatives. Mr. Sanchez's girlfriend from his day treatment program also came. All the key people in the quest were there. The mood was decidedly upbeat. Even Julio Velez, whose emotional turmoil through the early years of caring for his son had left him leery of the new living arrangement, now spoke hopefully.

"It was harder for me to see the truth," he said. "Now I'm happy for all of us, and for him especially."

His son uncorked a bottle of champagne and a toast was proposed by Fredda Rosen, the project director of Job Path. Looking fondly at him with her glass raised, she said, "I don't know if you remember that Saturday two years ago when we first met you at Job Path, but I was wondering back then if you thought you'd be sitting here now?"

"I don't know," he said, "but I want to drink the champagne."

* * *

One night in April, something truly wonderful happened out of something awful.

Mr. Velez was eating with his parents. His aide understood he would return home at 9. His father dropped him off at 8. As was his custom, his father waited in the car until Mr. Velez got inside and waved through the window. After he had driven off, Mr. Velez noticed that the apartment was quiet. "Anyone here?" he called. No one answered. He was terrified. He had never been alone.

Quickly, he phoned Lisa Pitz. She was frightened, but kept her wits and said, "Listen, someone will be there shortly. Do something to occupy yourself. Keep your hands busy. I'll call you every 15 minutes."

"I'm scared," he said. "I've never been alone."

"I'm scared, too, James," Ms. Pitz said. "But this is a golden opportunity. See what you can do."

He kept his boots on to make sure he wouldn't scratch his feet. He folded some clothes. He played video games.

Ms. Pitz called: "How's it going?"

"Good. Good. I'm folding clothes."

Ms. Pitz called: "How're you doing?"

"I've still got my boots on," he chirped. "I'm doing the dishes. I can't believe I'm here alone. I'm doing OK."

At 9, his aide showed up. Mr. Velez was beaming. He was 23 years old, and for the first time in his life he had spent an hour by himself, and the bugs had not come.

* * *

Every good spell seemed to be followed by a bad one. He got better, got worse, got better, got worse. But was he going forward two steps and then back one, or was it forward one and back two?

As he passed the six-month mark of his release, his scratching remained in check. Over Memorial Day weekend, he went to a movie alone and did not scratch. Yet he was again retreating into laziness. He began losing interest in going to Brooklyn College, his sole work experience. He didn't know why. Strapped for money to pay his cable bill, he agreed to do clerical work once a week at Job Path's office. Mostly, though, his routine mimicked that of an indulged teen-ager on summer break. He slept, saw movies, played video games, watched TV—hardly the life either Job Path or the state ultimately envisioned for him.

Part of it, Job Path realized, was he was almost always in physical discomfort. Ms. Brown managed to interest Dr. Judith Willner, a geneticist affiliated with Mount Sinai Medical Center, in his case, and Mount Sinai agreed, over a period of time, to subject him again to intensive testing. "We can stop him from hurting himself," Ms. Brown said. "But we can't take away the torture."

Dr. Willner's early suspicion was that some rare neurological condition, perhaps something no one else in the world suffered from, was the source of his problems.

Still, it was hard to sympathize when you were his servant. And the more the aides pestered him, the more defiant he became. Finally, Ms. Pitz told them, "OK, just let it go. I don't care if he has dirty laundry piled up to the ceiling." The bathroom and kitchen had to be cleaned—after all, another person lived there—but his room would be an experiment. It was up to him to clean it. A chart was posted to record how he did.

The strain on the staff was intensifying. One aide likened caring for Mr. Velez to working in a radioactive plant. After so much exposure, it begins to do something to you. Ralph Sanchez had a recurrent dream in which he kept encountering Mr. Velez's head. Mr. Moulthrop dreamed that a friend bore on her neck an enlarged version of a scar Mr. Velez had on his foot.

Job Path had expected that it would be a struggle to retain a salutary staff. For all the stress, the work paid only $10.75 to $12 an hour. Now, one of the seven aides was injured in a car accident and had to quit. An overnight aide was dismissed after falling asleep several times. Mr. Moulthrop, who was pretty frazzled, was promoted to a job as a training consultant with Job Path.

Lisa Pitz rounded up replacements, though it got dicey at times. Then, a few weeks ago, it was her turn. After two and a half years, she asked to move on to new projects. She was burned out to the ashes.

"I need to do some other things for me," she said one day. "For the last two years, this has been the last thing I thought about before I've gone to bed and the first thing I thought about when I woke up. I believe a lot of good things will happen for James. Overall, I think he'll do better and better. But I feel I've traveled the part of the journey with him that I should have. I need to stop for me."

Ms. Pitz expects it will take a few months to find a successor.

This turnover spoke to a greater issue as more and more demanding cases left institutions. The constancy of aides, studies suggest, benefits the person under care. Yet where were the people able to cope for any length of time with the enervating nature of the work? No one had a good answer.

One evening, Job Path had a psychotherapist named Cheryl Dolinger Brown meet with the staff. She passed out literature about secondary traumatization, something that afflicts people who witness someone else's pain, and then she listened to them. They articulated their abiding affection for Mr. Velez, but also said they felt hopeless, sad, devoid of control. One person confessed he felt guilty, because he was always feeling grateful that no one in his family had whatever Mr. Velez had.

Ms. Brown advised them to find outlets for the stress. One person said he worked out with a punching bag. Several said they took long walks or escaped in books. Another confided that he prayed.

When the aides vented the frustration that their diligence could not arrest this metronomic cycle of good days followed by bad, she told them that given his torment, this was how it went: evolution at a snail's pace.

"You can only see glimmers," she said. "And even those glimmers won't tell whether he will ever achieve the ambitions for him. He may not. But there's a soul. And there's been contact with that soul."

* * *

And so a young man who scratches himself had moved into his own apartment and was trying to act in the world. Was this, then, a story of transcendence? Perhaps, though no one was prepared to pronounce its coda. But, then, how could they? A fog of uncertainty may always surround James Velez. So far, all that had happened was his first big step toward leaving behind the wreckage of his past.

Eleven o'clock. Friday morning. Mr. Velez had a rare good shift at the radio station. He was tapping his feet to the salsa and bantering with the disk jockeys. He hung around a half-hour after his time was up.

When he got home, he was in a carefree mood. He settled into his rocking chair. Joanne Lauro, an aide, stopped by to deliver a prescription, and he started horsing around with her, playfully shoving her down on the sofa. "James, what has gotten into you?" she said.

He watched *Saved by the Bell,* a comedy about high school. One scene showed a student who had a problem with itchiness. He scratched his back and scratched his neck. Mr. Velez watched and said nothing.

His roommate came in, slid briskly into the kitchen and made a pot of coffee. He poured himself a cup and fixed one for Mr. Velez, spooning in the excess sugar. Mr. Velez arranged himself at the kitchen table. "C'mon, sit down, man," he told Mr. Sanchez. "Join me."

He sat down. "So what's up?"

"Nothing," Mr. Velez said. "You have a good day?"

"Yeah," he said. "Tired."

"You're working too hard, Manny. Take a vacation."

"Yeah, right."

Mr. Velez suggested going out later to buy a cake.

"Sounds good," Mr. Sanchez said. "Get a big one."

They had some time. They caught a couple of sit-coms on TV. Both were in musing good spirits on this desultory day. They couldn't stop laughing. They teased each other. Outside, the light fell dyingly on the street. Cars sank into the dusk.

Good company, amusing entertainment, the prospect of cake soon, his own apartment—yes, James Velez was feeling chipper tonight. There were many currents in this room—a commingling of hope and doubt—but presiding above them all was joy—pure, unadulterated joy.

He tilted his head back. He laughed and laughed.

Lessons Learned

BY N.R. (SONNY) KLEINFIELD

Few categories of people are more ignored than the disabled, especially the severely disabled. And I have always felt that most of the journalism about the disabled has fallen into two camps: impersonal coverage of the politics of disability that is chilly and distant from the human element; and pumped-up, saccharine portraits of the valor of a disabled person. Look, he can sort mail at the post office! Look, he can tie his shoelace!

Both of these camps miss something essential, which is that living with disability is always a decidedly mixed bag, full of complex subtexts.

When a small social services agency approached *The Times* about possibly following an ambitious effort to move a severely developmentally disabled young man out of an institution and into his own apartment, I was automatically interested. I saw this as a chance to write about meaningful social policy through the lens of a particular life. And I saw this as a chance to write about the multi-faceted nature of disability.

At first, I imagined this project might consume a few months. As it turned out, getting someone this disabled out of an institution was more difficult than staging a successful prison break. Days became weeks became months became years. I was lucky that I had patient editors. I was even luckier that, after a while, they forgot that this story even existed. Between other projects, I would say, "I'm going out today on the Velez story," and they would sort of nod in a puzzled way, but it never pays to offer editors more information than they need.

James Velez had all the time in the world, but getting to know him proved to be next to impossible. When I first met him, he was still pretty miserable about his lot, and institutional life had left him shell-shocked. On top of all this, he didn't entirely understand me. He had been put under all sorts of microscopes by doctors and psychiatrists, and he was understandably wary of fresh investigators probing his soul. Why, he wondered, would some reporter want to write about him? Who would read a word of it? On several occasions, he said to me, "I don't think my life is very interesting." I told him right back that I could hardly imagine a more interesting life, but my own enthusiasm did little to dissuade him of his doubts.

During my initial encounters with James, he barely spoke to me. He answered questions with nods and grunts and one- or two-word responses. So I settled for spending hours and days, often idly, simply doing whatever he did, which was often not much more than sleeping or watching less than mesmerizing television shows. After some months, when James's chances of getting funding approval seemed truly bleak, he withdrew even more. He would be belligerent. He would refuse to see me at all. He regressed to an ornery isolate.

Fortunately, he and his parents permitted me to receive all his medical records, and they freed all the doctors and psychiatrists who had seen him to speak freely about him.

The trajectory of James Velez's life, even now when he has gotten what he so dearly wished for, has the same sort of wild gyrations as the stock market. At times, he is the most endearing person. At times, he is the most irascible and annoying. At times, it seems as if he can accomplish almost anything. At times, he seems capable of nothing. I wanted all that expressed in what I wrote about him. I spent much of the time in the writing of this story fumbling to try to show a reality.

What one does, I suppose, is look again and again at notes and recollections and weigh them on some sort of imaginary scale as one might weigh spices. And without being insidious or deliberately mean-spirited, you try to cool your own emotions and in your selection of material do your best to portray faithfully what you have seen rather than what you hoped to see. We're not after distilled water here, but we are after a reality.

The most rewarding aspect of all the time I spent with James was getting to know someone most people cower from and to share that experience with others. Over the years, I've increasingly become convinced that the greatest moments are contained in the lives of the unknown and the ordinary. If someone tells me they have never spoken to a reporter before, that's when I pull up a chair and listen.

Newsday

Irene Virag

Finalist, Non-Deadline Writing

Irene Virag is a Pulitzer-Prize winning reporter for *Newsday* who is now the paper's garden columnist. Virag joined *Newsday* in 1982 as a town beat reporter on the Long Island desk and eventually became a special writer on general assignment. She wrote a feature column called the Long Island Diary about the people and places of suburbia. From 1992 to 1995, as part of *Newsday*'s on-going breast cancer project, she wrote a series of articles on the human side of the disease. The articles form the basis of her book, *We're All in This Together: Families Facing Breast Cancer.*

In addition to her garden column, for the past two years she has also written a general interest column on nature and the environment.

Virag won the 1984 Pulitzer Prize for local reporting as a member of a team that covered the Baby Jane Doe case. She has also won the Newswomen's Club of New York Front Page Award for column writing and the 1995 New York State Associated Press Association award for feature writing for one of her breast cancer stories.

In 1997, she won two Quill and Trowel Awards for column writing by the Garden Writers Association of America.

Virag studied literature at the University of London, and holds a bachelor's degree from Boston University and a master's from the Medill School of Journalism at Northwestern University. She was a Nieman fellow at Harvard University in 1988.

In this installment of her detailed and painfully honest account of her battle with breast cancer, Virag brings the reader face-to-face with cancer, the murderous medicine of chemotherapy, and the patient's see-saw ride with despair and hope.

Chemo: The slayer and the savior

JULY 3, 1997

Snow flurries twirl in the sky and cold grips my soul. I sit in my car on a gray afternoon in January and look my chemo in the eye.

We're all alone in a parked 4-Runner outside my oncologist's office. Just me and my chemo—two shopping bags filled with boxes and bottles and vials. Chemotherapy is a slayer and savior all in one. The drugs kill cancer cells, but they destroy other rapidly dividing cells, too. They're not very smart—they can't locate, identify and destroy the enemy. They have to kill the whole village.

The drugs wipe out white blood cells. They threaten menstruation and endanger your bladder. They sap your energy, shove you out of the driver's seat of your own life. In order to do battle with the cancer, I have to surrender to the chemo. But ultimately it can give me back my life—my cancer-free life.

Forever? For a while? I'll find out.

My friend Paula Leahy, who stabbed her mammogram and wore jewelry to her lumpectomy, called her chemo Rambo. Maybe I'll call mine Xena after television's warrior princess. I could use a warrior princess. I know I'm not one.

It's not that I can't leave home without my chemo drugs. It speaks to the arrogance of our managed care system that I have them with me. My insurance carrier, Oxford, was so behind in reimbursing my oncologist's practice for drugs that the doctors couldn't afford to wait any longer. And so they're requiring patients like me with drug plans to buy them instead.

I'm glad I have an oncologist with a sense of humor. "Here," she said when she wrote out the prescriptions. "Give your pharmacist a stroke."

Actually, my pharmacist was pretty cool when I handed him the 15 prescriptions. "I'll have to order these from the warehouse in New Jersey," he said.

Now I open the first box, marked Cytoxan 500 mg. My regimen of chemo is known as CMF—C for

Cytoxan, M for Methotrexate, F for 5 Fluorouracil. The vials of Cytoxan are so tiny. Clear glass vials with bright yellow lids—not even a quarter filled with white powder. The folder inside explains that it is used in treatment of certain malignancies. "The following malignancies are often susceptible to CYTOXAN treatment. 1. Malignant lymphomas. 2. Multiple myeloma. 3. Leukemias. 4. Mycosis fungoides. 5. Neumblastoma. 6. Adenocarcinoma of the ovary. 7. Retinoblastoma. 8. Carcinoma of the breast." Bingo—that's me.

I want to open the vial and hold that white powder in my hand but I'm afraid. Afraid I'll spill it accidentally or on purpose. Mix it with the snow. Afraid I'll swallow it—get chemo over in one great gulp.

The second box is marked Methotrexate. Brown bottles the size of Mercurochrome bottles. The stickers on the bottles of bright yellow liquid have pictures of an X-ed out sun and warnings to avoid exposure to sunlight. And the labels inside the bottles are terrifying. "Deaths have been reported with the use of Methotrexate...Patients should be closely monitored for bone marrow, liver, lung and kidney toxicities." The labels cite side effects such as extreme fatigue, dizziness, gingivitis, rashes, renal failure, infertility, loss of libido, diabetes and reversible lymphomas.

I don't have a choice with chemo—not really. There are people who tell me they'd never take chemo. Eat broccoli, they tell me. Take antioxidants. Try shark cartilage. Trust nature. Well, nature did its thing. It gave me breast cancer on the eve of my 41st birthday. I've chronicled the struggles of 20 women whose lives were irrevocably changed by breast cancer. I've seen what this disease can do. Until the experts find a cure, I'll up my odds by taking this thing called chemo. As barbaric as it seems, it's the best we have. Go, Xena.

The third drug is Fluorouracil, aka 5-FU. What a fitting acronym. I say it out loud—five times. The bottles are three-quarters filled with a clear liquid. It looks like water—but the list of precautions from the pharmacist advises "contraceptive measures are recommended for use in men and women while taking this medication. Do not become pregnant while taking this drug." The drug manufacturer's label is even more explicit—telling of tests on mice and rats where the Fluorouracil "crossed the placenta and entered into fetal circulation causing cleft palates, skeletal defects and deformed appendages, paws and tail." Of course the dosages used on the mice and rats were one to three times the maximum recommended for humans.

I remember my oncologist warning me not to get pregnant. "There should never ever be a pregnancy," she said. "Breast cancer flourishes under a pregnancy state because there's estrogen flying all over the place. These cells are just looking to be stimulated by hormonal states like pregnancy. You can't take the risk. Don't even think about it."

I already have three grown stepchildren—the oldest is a year older than me. But my husband and I did think about it. David Isadore for a boy, Rachel Anna for a girl. Maybe one day I'll have a grandchild to hold.

And so I've gotten to know my chemo drugs, just me and them alone in a parked car outside the office of a doctor I'm entrusting my life to. I've shaken them, read about them, cursed them. I look at my watch and I'm surprised to see I've been sitting in the cold car for an hour and a half. Snow still twirls in the sky as I carry my shopping bag into the building.

There are four chairs in the treatment room—two gray and two blue ones in each corner. Prints of tulips and luminous lakes and snow-capped mountains remind me of a world beyond chemotherapy. Three chairs are occupied. A nurse hovers over one of the patients, who has a pale face and is holding a paper towel to her mouth. I'm new here—I think that she must have vomited. Later, I learn that she was sucking an ice cube. I look away quickly but I catch the woman's eye anyway. Her eyes are dark and hollow and frightened.

I feel too robust, too healthy, too alive to be here. My smile is inappropriate. But I can't make it go away. This smile that has always been my shield. Or my mask. I have a love-hate thing with my smile. If I had a knife in my hand as I stand in that doorway I'd slice it off. I don't want it here in this room. I smile at a tired looking woman in another corner and she smiles back. Then she retreats into her own thoughts. The third woman has her eyes closed. Thank God. I stand in the doorway feeling like I'm trapped in a place I don't belong. Waiting.

I stare at the empty chair in the corner—the gray one with a high back and a foot rest and a pillow invitingly placed on it. My chair. Soon, I'll be one of these women hooked up to an IV in a room with tulips on the wall. I'm just beginning to understand what my friend Cathy Langan once told me. "I've looked at life down the barrel of a chemo tube, I'll never be the same again."

I'm just beginning to accept what my oncologist told me at our first meeting. "You have a potentially fatal disease that could recur."

I've thought about my mortality in the past. I used to worry that my stepfather would kill us in our sleep when he was drunk, or that I'd be stabbed by some intruder, or mangled in a car wreck. I always thought about death, my death as a thing that would come suddenly, violently. I never thought about disease or suffering. Now I do. I hope that whatever my future holds in terms of cancer that I travel through it with grace and courage and honesty. I stand in the doorway and say a silent prayer that I'm able to.

I offer my bags to the nurse. "I'm a little busy right now," she says. She is busy, too busy. I think about dropping the bags on the floor, letting the white powder and the clear and yellow liquids spill out. I wish I could run away.

But I can't. This is my journey. And essentially I must make it alone. My husband can hold my hand and wipe away my tears. He tells me my lumpectomy scar is exotic. He says I'm beautiful. I've never seen myself that way and I see it even less these days. It occurred to me recently that I still haven't touched my scar with my bare hand—just with a wash cloth in the shower. I don't really like to look at my breast even though it looks better than it did after the surgery. My nipple is no longer inverted. The swelling and redness are gone. One night before going into the shower I raised my hand just to see how high I could reach. Suddenly, my breast hardened, the aureole puckered and turned a pale yellowish color. My husband was frightened. I was frightened. In a few minutes my breast returned to normal. I wonder if I ever will. Just as there is a new definition of normal for my breast, there will have to be one for me.

For now, chemo will be part of the definition. The nurse takes my bag. I glance back at the treatment room where the empty chair still waits for me. I leave the office and make it to the elevator. I push the UP button and lean on the elevator door and cry.

* * *

My hard winter melts into spring and blossoms into summer. Six months have passed and Xena is wielding her sword. I sit in the gray chair with an IV in my arm for two hours once every three weeks. I sit there when my white blood count is high enough. There is a Catch-22 here. Chemotherapy makes your blood count drop. But if it's too low you can't have chemotherapy.

I can usually tell when my white blood counts are low. I get tired—so bone-aching tired that it hurts. I can sit in a chair all day and do nothing—literally. Not even turn on TV or read catalogs or pay bills. Those are the times when my smile leaves. When the world overwhelms me. When getting out of bed and facing the day seems like an accomplishment. But there are columns to write, office stress to overcome, weeds to pull, annuals to plant. There's a part of me that thinks if I can do this or that or whatever I feel like, then I'm still who I was. Well, I'm learning that I'm not who I was.

I focus on the things I'm not getting done and beat myself up. My husband reminds me of the things I am doing.

"What's wrong with me?" I cry.

My husband gets frustrated. "You have stage two breast cancer. You're on chemotherapy."

My oncologist reminds me that doing less doesn't mean I'm giving in to the cancer. "It's a time to be kind to yourself," she says.

My oncologist, Paula Schwartz, is a little tornado. She makes the office whirl. She has her own style—she looks good in everything from slim-cut slacks to ankle-length dresses to above-the-knee skirts. She has bright eyes and looks like Margot Kidder when she played Lois Lane. She doesn't believe in spouting statistics and we talk about more than cancer. "Foxglove is my favorite perennial on Earth," she told me at our first meeting, after observing that so many plants have medicinal purposes. That day, she and my husband talked about growing tomatoes and learning Yiddish and her daughter who likes to write. My oncologist is studying to be a Torah reader at her temple. She's married to a gastroenterologist. "We're blood and guts," she says, laughing. In the book I wrote about breast cancer, I talked about "real women who were not just breast cancer patients but who also were mothers and daughters and wives and sisters." Paula understands that. I'd like to have her as a friend.

She lectures me about the chemicals in diet soda and warns me about the evils of the sun. "I don't like this— your hands are getting tan," she says as I remove my watch before standing on the scale. "Don't forget your hands when you're putting on sunblock. And don't worry about your weight. On CMF, you can gain 10 to 15 pounds. Your metabolism, your whole body, is affected by these poisons I'm pumping into you. I don't want you dieting while you're on chemo."

I've put on a few extra pounds and I was overweight to begin with. I hate it. And there are other effects besides the fatigue. Nausea. Constipation. Mood swings. Insomnia. Dizziness. Agitation. After my first chemo session my husband and I walked on the boardwalk at Sunken Meadow State Park. I was like Beavis and Butt-Head on a junk food high. I walked 20 paces ahead of my husband, who has a much longer stride. Then I turned around and walked back to join him. I shot ahead of him again. I broke into a jog.

Oh, yes. My period stopped after my fifth treatment. I don't know if it will come back. My husband and I both had dreams about babies that week. I didn't need my therapist to explain why.

And there was the day I didn't want to go to chemo. It was my third treatment. "You can drive me there," I told my husband. "But that doesn't mean I'm getting chemo." Suddenly I was afraid of the needles, I was afraid of the drugs. What if I go through all this, I thought, and the cancer comes back anyway? When we got to the oncologist's office in Plainview, my husband parked the car and I jumped out and said I was walking home. I didn't care that it was snowing. "It's 25 miles," my husband said. I made a face and stomped ahead. My husband followed me, pleading. We walked about a mile in the snow when suddenly he grabbed me and kissed me. "Please," he said. "I love you. Please get the chemo. I don't want you to die."

Our shoes were drenched, our ears were red from the cold. We walked back to the doctor's office holding hands but separated by our thoughts. I was still upset. All Paula had to do was look at our faces. We talked. "It's OK," she said tenderly. "I know this isn't fun."

But it's not as bad as I thought. I don't look any different. Most of the time, at least in public, I don't look sick. I'm not losing my hair. I'm not taking Adriamycin, the chemo drug that claims every strand of hair on your body. That's because the 25 lymph nodes that were removed during my lumpectomy were negative for cancer. If I'd had as few as three positive lymph nodes or if my tumor had been larger than five centimeters, it would have been a different ballgame.

My tumor was negative for estrogen and progesterone receptors, which is common among pre-menopausal women. This means the cancer cells didn't have the tiny antennae that search for hormones to feed on and grow. It's why I won't be on Tamoxifen—an anti-cancer drug designed to block the signals on those receptors.

I've made peace with the gray chair. More than that. I take a certain comfort in it. Smiles have their place in the oncology office. "Come on in back, sweetie," Jackie Mott, the office secretary, calls when it's my turn. I met her once on the boardwalk at Sunken Meadow, and we embraced like old pals.

Music plays softly in the treatment room—everything from "Yesterday" to "I Fall to Pieces" to "Tomorrow." The cast of characters changes. Men with lung, colon or prostate cancer. Women with lung, colon or breast cancer. Paula says lung cancer kills more women than breast cancer. She is vehement about the deadliness of smoking. "And now cigars are the thing," she says angrily and I'm frightened for my stepson.

I listen to the other patients. A man says Percoset isn't helping his pain, a woman asks when her port will be removed. But they also talk about jobs and vacations and families. A wife chides her husband for not eating breakfast—"at least you could've had a piece of fruit." A man smiles proudly when his little grandson does a Michael Jackson dance imitation in the hallway. An elfin man in a navy blue cardigan charms my husband

and me with descriptions of his native Italy. "You should go to Lake Como," he says, and I think that I'd need a strong sunblock in the bright light.

I chat with Sharyn Parness, the RN who administers my chemo. First come the trio of anti-nausea drugs. Compazine, which is given by injection. Decadron, a steroid that is pushed though an intravenous tube and causes intense burning and itching. Sharyn calls it "the ants-in-your-pants drug." Kytril, which takes about 30 minutes to drip through the IV in my left hand. Where would I be without my anti-nausea drugs? In the bathroom throwing up, I guess. And I have Compazine in pill form and another, more powerful anti-nausea drug called Zofran that I take at home when I feel like I'm on a tiny boat in a heaving sea.

These drugs set the stage for Xena to come in fighting. Methotrexate that looks like liquid lemon Jell-O coursing into my hand as Sharyn pushes it through the IV. Cytoxan, a clear fluid dripping down the narrow tube from a plastic bag. And Flouroucil, with the acronym I love to repeat.

Sharyn has a talent for finding a perfect vein in my left hand—on the first try and painlessly—and an equal talent for making the time pass. She tells my husband and me stories about her vacation in Monte Carlo and her younger son's bar mitzvah and her older son's 3.87 grade average at New York University. Or I take a nap or read a mystery or work on a garden column or jot notes in the journal of my cancer. The journal of my life.

I am both reporter and subject now. I think it's easier to be a reporter. I've made a career out of asking strangers questions that I often think I have no right to know the answers to. I'm always surprised and grateful when they open up to me. I was never more aware of this than when I was writing about breast cancer. Now it's my turn. I can write things I would never tell you in person. Maybe I'm paying back all the people who let me into their lives. Maybe I'm simply acknowledging the truth in the title of my book. *We're All in This Together.*

I have one more chemo session left. Paula says everything is going as it should. The chemo I feared so has given me courage. Thank you, Paula Schwartz. Thank you, Xena.

Next come six weeks of daily radiation treatments. As always, my husband will be with me. I'll wear the sapphire and diamond ring he bought me after my lumpectomy. The ring I've worn to every chemo appointment. It reminds me of dark night skies and twinkling stars to wish upon. When I was a child, I'd wish for grand things like happiness. Or things that seemed impossible—like my stepfather leaving. Or my getting away.

Now, I wish for life.

Lessons Learned

BY IRENE VIRAG

I learned about life as well as journalism in writing about my own breast cancer. The lessons about life were especially meaningful. Breast cancer is a crap shoot and we don't have much choice about how the dice fall.

I thought I knew a lot about breast cancer. For three years, I'd written about a disease that is every woman's fear. I'd written a newspaper series and a book about the tragedies and triumphs of women who could be me. But there are degrees of separation. As much as I felt for the women I wrote about, I knew that I could never really know their tears. And I surely didn't want to.

I guess that somewhere in the inner recesses of the soul where we cling to omens, I thought that writing about breast cancer would keep the darkness from my own door. But it didn't. Breast cancer has no rules; it knows no boundaries.

A little more than a year ago, I was diagnosed with stage two breast cancer and underwent a lumpectomy. I found out what it's like when time blinks and your whole universe shifts. What it's like to go from just living your life to wondering how long it will last. I found out what it's like when the tears are your own. When you wake up and stare at the darkness that is deeper than night, and you know that for as long as you live the fear of recurrence will hover on the outskirts of your universe.

And I learned about the Catch-22 of chemotherapy. Will your blood count be high enough for you to undergo the very treatment that made it drop? I learned that chemo is no picnic. That's what I wrote about in "Chemo: The Slayer and The Savior."

The piece gave me new insights into our craft. A wise writing coach I'm now married to once told me that if you're going to be a writer, you have to be willing to take on your own terrors and turmoil, and that writing begins with reporting—with scenes and details and dialogue. I tried to do that. My reporter's notebook was the daily journal I kept of what was happening to me and how I felt about it. I started this piece with the moment that I'm sitting in my car outside my oncologist's office with bags of drugs I have just picked up from the pharmacy "and look my chemo in the eye." I guess the piece is about staring chemotherapy down. I wrote in the present tense because that offered the most immediacy.

I gained a new appreciation and respect for the people I've written about in the past. It's not easy to expose your life in the pages of a newspaper—to expose your fears and your hopes and your dreams. In the series I had written previously, I had asked women with breast cancer to let me into their lives during the most traumatic times of triumph and tragedy they would ever experience. So when I agreed to write a series about my own breast cancer, I wanted to be as brave and honest as they were.

I learned that it's harder to write about yourself than about other people. As a reporter chronicling the lives of other people, you can take refuge in what we call objectivity. I'm not sure that true objectivity exists, but you can pull back and put a little distance between you and your subjects. It's much different when you're the subject.

If you're not honest when you use the "I" key, it shows—in the tone, in the writing. That's why I wrote about the dark side of my childhood and about the moment when I tried to run away from treatment and my husband held me in the snow. Sometimes honesty hurts.

I tried so hard to explain the way it was—to go behind the statistics and give a human face to breast cancer, to chemotherapy. To tell the story through the warnings on the drug bottles and the emotions as well as the side effects they elicit. Through the sights and sounds of a treatment room where I stared at the empty chair that waited for me.

As I said, this story was part of an occasional series about one of the most difficult chapters in my life. I believe that good stories have protagonists and narrative drive. I was the protagonist in this story. The narrative drive came out of my treatment for a disease that could kill me. And from where I sat in the treatment room, there was nothing pleasant about chemotherapy.

Clearly, the story was colored by my own perceptions—my own feelings, my own point of view. Sometimes, journalistic objectivity is a myth. It's not that simple. A writer's ultimate responsibility is to her perception of the truth.

This story is my truth.

John J. Keller
Deadline Reporting

John J. Keller is a *Wall Street Journal* news editor responsible for telecommunications coverage. He also serves as deputy editor of the Science, Health, and Technology group.

The 44-year-old Keller made business reporting a career when he landed a job at *Communications Week* in the early 1980s. He covered the global communications and high technology beat created in the wake of the AT&T breakup. Keller built the international telecommunications beat there and then left to become telecommunications editor at *Business Week* in 1986. Three and a half years later he moved to *The Wall Street Journal* to cover the same beat.

Keller finds the beat compelling because he learns about the impact telecommunications and high technology can have on him, his family, his friends, and his readers. He believes "business is the glue that holds everything together." The development of products and services and the technologies behind them fascinate him.

The telecommunications beat also enables him to track companies with billion-dollar budgets and global impact. And it keeps changing. "The telecommunications beat is the most dynamic in the world," Keller says.

His long tenure as a telecommunications reporter, his ability to develop knowledgeable sources, and his tenacity enabled Keller to capture the leadership change at AT&T in a way that showed the personalities and technological change driving the upheaval.

Although Keller had little more than an hour between the unexpected announcement that AT&T's president would resign and his deadline, he managed to craft a 50-inch story that captured the drama and the significance of the sudden shift in power. He drew upon his in-depth knowledge of the company to explain what had happened and how it had affected the company. Subsequent page one stories took readers inside AT&T as it made the decision to change its CEO.

Keller also wanted people "to see the story...to see the action when they're reading about it" because he knows businesses are run by personalities. His deadline stories on the AT&T power struggle offer readers an inside view often only allowed to a privileged few.

—Aly Colón

AT&T's Walter quits after boardroom rebuff

JULY 17, 1997

AT&T Corp. President John R. Walter, whose relations with Chairman Robert E. Allen had grown increasingly strained, resigned abruptly after the company's board said it wouldn't name him chief executive as planned by Jan. 1.

The stunning decision by AT&T's board, which hired the former printing-industry executive only last November after a high-profile search, capped an unusually public drama played out in the executive suites of a telecommunications giant struggling with seismic changes. AT&T's board took the extraordinary step of airing its low opinion of Mr. Walter in a conference call with reporters yesterday, during which outside director Walter Elisha declared Mr. Walter lacked "the intellectual leadership" to run AT&T.

Mr. Walter, 50 years old, was told of the board's decision yesterday morning after an evening of intense talks among outside directors and Chairman Allen. These directors, including Mr. Elisha, will launch yet another search for a successor to the 62-year-old Mr. Allen, an indication that Mr. Allen will have a lesser role in this search than in Mr. Walter's hiring. Mr. Elisha made it clear last night that AT&T is looking for a new CEO.

Mr. Walter's exit seems to leave AT&T adrift at a time when it can least afford to be distracted. The company's core long-distance business continues to erode. AT&T is under intense attack in virtually every one of its markets, including wireless services. And its international strategy is in disarray as competitors such as the team of British Telecommunications PLC and MCI Communications Corp., as well as Sprint Corp. and the Baby Bells, lock up key alliances.

AT&T's shares closed yesterday at $36.3125, up $1.3125 in New York Stock Exchange composite trading.

Mr. Walter defended his tenure as president yesterday, in a statement in the very AT&T news release that announced his resignation. "I believe I am perfectly qualified to be CEO of AT&T right now," he stated. "I have worked tirelessly on behalf of the shareholders of AT&T."

Mr. Walter, who declined to comment, will leave the job much richer than he began it. He received a $5 million bonus in October when he left his job as chairman of R.R. Donnelley & Sons to join AT&T. And now he will get $3.8 million in severance, plus $22.8 million to cover what he would have potentially earned at Donnelley had he stayed.

"Mr. Walter's services will be in great demand," said Mr. Walter's attorney Robert Barnett, of the Washington law firm Williams & Connolly. "He is one of the world's experts on information services and communications. John Walter will be just fine."

Now with Mr. Walter gone, scrutiny of Mr. Allen's troubled tenure is certain to intensify. Mr. Elisha acknowledged last night that Mr. Allen has become "a lightning rod" of blame for AT&T's current malaise, but he defended the chairman as "doing a terrific job under very trying circumstances."

Many analysts and AT&T watchers had been skeptical of Mr. Walter's abilities to run AT&T since he had never worked in the telecom industry. "He wasn't even close to the best person that could have been tapped to run this company," said David Beirne, a corporate headhunter who has lured several top AT&T executives to other companies.

However, while some questioned Mr. Walter's capacity to run far-flung AT&T, people close to the company said a bigger reason the telecom novice was dumped might have been Mr. Allen's inability to get along with his No. 2. It is a problem that has plagued AT&T's chairman during his nine years in the top job. Mr. Allen had gradually taken away much of Mr. Walter's responsibilities, including merger talks AT&T had been conducting, while offering only lukewarm public support for his colleague. Mr. Allen wouldn't comment.

People close to AT&T weren't surprised by Mr. Allen's actions. For eight of his years as CEO, he refused to name a president with his board's full compliance. Mr. Walter, brought in under an agreement in which Mr. Allen agreed to retire two years early, is now the second president to quit AT&T in a year. Alex Mandl resigned last summer after Mr. Allen wouldn't designate Mr. Mandl as his heir apparent.

Mr. Walter was tapped in October after a three-month search by AT&T's directors and the recruiting firms Spencer Stuart and Korn Ferry. Among those considered for the job were current Eastman Kodak CEO George Fisher, who turned AT&T down at the time. Mr. Fisher has since been elected to AT&T's board, igniting speculation once again that AT&T will try to offer him the job. Mr. Elisha will only say he admires Mr. Fisher and that he would be an obvious candidate, but he wouldn't say whether AT&T would make him a new offer. Mr. Fisher hasn't commented on such speculation. He has a couple of years left on his contract with Kodak.

Only a few weeks ago, Mr. Allen said he had "full confidence" in Mr. Walter. But AT&T insiders knew differently. "Bob very reluctantly agreed to accelerate his own retirement by two years to get John, but when the day for that to happen got closer he didn't want to give up the reins," said one executive.

The tension at the top of AT&T rose during the recent failed merger talks with Bell giant SBC Communications Inc., when Mr. Walter was cut out of the negotiations by Mr. Allen and AT&T's chief counsel, Vice Chairman John Zeglis. It turned out that it was Mr. Walter who first got the call from SBC Chairman Edward Whitacre to do a deal, angering Mr. Allen. "After that, Bob took the SBC deal over for himself and Zeglis," cutting Mr. Walter out of the loop, said one executive.

And all the time Mr. Allen was critiquing Mr. Walter's performance to Mr. Elisha and other noncompany directors. The increasingly critical reviews came during private sessions between Mr. Allen and the board's outside directors, dating back to mid-April, said Mr. Elisha, who is Chairman of Springs Industries Inc. "Bob talked to us for awhile [at the April meeting] and expressed concerns to us," the director said, but he wouldn't elaborate on what Mr. Allen told the directors. Later in May at another session, "the caution light was on," Mr. Elisha added.

The AT&T board met in a special executive session late into Tuesday night over the Walter succession issue.

The final showdown came yesterday morning in a 90-minute session between Mr. Walter and directors in a small conference room in AT&T's lower Manhattan headquarters where he outlined what he felt were his accomplishments at AT&T. The directors left the room and caucused among themselves. Mr. Elisha later met with Mr. Walter again and told him of the board's decision to refrain from naming him CEO in January. Mr. Walter decided at that point to leave, and later working out a suitable news release with the company.

"John was very able" as an executive, Mr. Elisha said yesterday. But he noted the CEO's job at AT&T requires more than just good management acumen. As Mark Twain used to say, Mr. Elisha recalled, the "difference between president and vice president is like the difference between lightning and a lightning bug."

But it remains to be seen whether the telecom experts who remain at AT&T will be able to dust the company off from the latest brouhaha. AT&T said the company's counsel, Mr. Zeglis, now would assume all of Mr. Walter's responsibilities for operations, while AT&T moved Mr. Zeglis's responsibilities for legal, human resources and public relations under Mr. Allen's direct control.

Mr. Allen's closest confidant, Mr. Zeglis was recently elevated to vice chairman, undercutting Mr. Walter's position significantly. Mr. Zeglis gets high marks for his intelligence, particularly in navigating the current regulatory issues surrounding the competitive telecom market, but his new assignment is bound to cause controversy, since he has never run a business.

Mr. Elisha defended the choice of Mr. Zeglis as operating chief, calling him a "very able, knowledgeable and insightful executive...who's also a lawyer." But he would only endorse him as one of a "final 10" list of executives that might be qualified to someday run AT&T. AT&T will look inside and externally for its next CEO, a search that might necessitate Mr. Allen having to stay on longer than expected, he said.

Mr. Walter had grown popular with the troops and senior managers at AT&T, some of whom called analysts incessantly in recent weeks to see if speculation was true that the new president might soon quit. "There are going to be a lot of executives looking to jump ship after this," said one executive recruiter last night. "People here loved John and hated Allen."

The two executives made for an extremely odd couple. The laconic Mr. Allen rarely meets informally with his top executives and is slow to give praise. Executives close to AT&T said that in the past year he has grown increasingly remote after having endured several years of blistering news coverage over his multibillion-dollar failures in the computer business and other investment misfires.

Mr. Walter, on the other hand, "is a born salesman," noted one AT&T executive. "He's energetic, he has charisma; he takes charge."

Mr. Walter adopted an aggressive tone at AT&T almost from the moment he arrived, telling *The Wall Street Journal* in a front-page story that he hadn't taken the job at AT&T "to be No. 2."

In only a few months, he took command of AT&T's disparate operations, ordering a wide-scale cost review; survived a showdown with the company's hard-charging former consumer-services president, Joseph Nacchio, who resigned; promoted several senior executives to command AT&T's core businesses; and traveled extensively to meet with corporate customers and AT&T employees.

Those workers must be thinking "what now," said Brian Adamik, a senior analyst at Boston research firm Yankee Group and a former AT&T executive. "Nothing amazes me about AT&T anymore," he added. "The company appears to be out of control with a lot of senior defections, a very publicly failed merger attempt with a Bell and its core long-distance business continues to erode."

A committee of independent directors of AT&T will conduct the new CEO search. The group includes Mr. Elisha; Kenneth Derr, chairman and CEO of Chevron Corp.; Donald McHenry, president of IRC Group; Ralph Larsen, chairman and CEO of Johnson & Johnson; and Thomas Wyman, senior adviser of SBC Warburg Inc.

Writers' Workshop

Talking Points

1) This article is really a story inside the story. What's the news angle? What's the behind-the-scenes story?

2) How many key players are in this story? How does the writer keep them clear to readers?

3) What impression do readers get of Mr. Walter from the story? What tools does the writer use to develop this picture?

4) Note the number of named and unnamed sources in the story. How does that affect the tone of the story?

Assignment Desk

1) Who are the readers of *The Wall Street Journal?* Rewrite this story for a general news publication.

2) Compare *The Wall Street Journal* coverage with the coverage in your local newspaper. What is different? What is similar?

AT&T's Walter failed to court the man who counted: Allen

JULY 18, 1997

In the end, AT&T Corp.'s new president, a former star salesman, failed to woo and win over his most important customer: Chairman Robert E. Allen.

Plucked by Mr. Allen from the obscurity of a printing company and made heir apparent at one of the world's most powerful corporations, John R. Walter faced a tough situation from the start. He had to share the executive suite with a chief executive who had agreed to give up the reins early in order to land Mr. Walter, but who didn't really want to do so.

Rather than cultivate Mr. Allen, Mr. Walter managed to alienate him—with a hardball style, concern with image and what the board depicts as an inability to grasp the complex competitive and regulatory issues roiling the telecommunications industry and AT&T.

It was a major miscalculation. Mr. Walter underestimated the sway that Mr. Allen still had with directors. During the past four months, Mr. Allen delivered tough critiques of his new No. 2 in private discussions with outside directors, even as he gave little critical feedback to Mr. Walter himself. By Wednesday, Mr. Allen had convinced the directors that Mr. Walter lacked the "intellectual leadership" to run AT&T, in the language of outside director Walter Elisha, who delivered the news to Mr. Walter that he wouldn't become CEO next year as planned.

In undermining his designated successor, Mr. Allen may, in fact, have inadvertently hastened his own departure. Mr. Elisha made clear Wednesday that to recruit a strong Walter successor, the board will have little choice but to offer the candidate the CEO title from the start. "We are now searching for a CEO," he said.

Mr. Allen has always found it hard to work with a No. 2. The reason the job Mr. Walter got was open was that its well-regarded previous occupant, Alex Mandl, had quit when denied the heir-apparent designation.

Mr. Walter, who is 50 years old, thus came into AT&T under extraordinary circumstances. The company, lacking enough bench strength, had searched extensively last fall for a president who would eventually move up. But marquee names in American business, such as George M.C. Fisher of Eastman Kodak Co. and James Barksdale of Netscape Communications Corp., wouldn't consider the job unless they could get the CEO reins immediately. Mr. Walter agreed to wait a little over a year for them.

To accommodate such an arrangement, Mr. Allen, now 62, reluctantly agreed to retire two years sooner than he had intended. Even so, Mr. Walter exacted a lucrative price for coming: a $5 million signing bonus and at least $25 million in severance and potential pay if he didn't ascend to CEO by the agreed-to date of Jan. 1, 1998.

As Mr. Walter's power grew in the company and he garnered increasingly favorable press coverage, Mr. Allen, whose own reputation had been damaged by years of bad investments and competitive misfires, is said to have grown resentful and mistrustful. In private, he would accuse Mr. Walter of missteps ranging from not backing the chairman's deal strategies to talking with newspaper reporters. Several executives say Mr. Allen had phone records checked at the company, looking for any calls that might have been made on the sly to reporters. AT&T denies this. Neither Mr. Allen nor Mr. Walter will comment.

The former chairman of R.R. Donnelley & Sons blew into AT&T like a cool autumn wind last November. Knowing well Mr. Allen's reputation for being aloof with AT&T employees, middle managers and Wall Street, the new president played to all three constituencies. He urged the rank and file to e-mail him about their concerns. He could warmly greet the lowliest subordinate with an arm around the shoulder. He called the executive suite in AT&T's plush Basking Ridge, N.J., offices "Carpet Land" and ordered the executive dining room closed, forcing senior managers to use the company cafeteria as everyone else did.

He showed little deference to his boss. Although Mr. Allen appeared to welcome a mentoring role, sometimes commenting that he hoped "my 40 years in the phone industry would be a valuable resource to anyone new that we bring in," Mr. Walter didn't build many bridges to the old-style, conservative manager. The two men met infrequently at work and almost never outside the office.

Mr. Walter didn't help matters when he told *The Wall Street Journal* he hadn't joined AT&T "to be No. 2." Privately, he groused about being called a telecommunications novice and about how the negative reaction to his inexperience had hurt the stock price. "He'd say, 'The problem's not me, it's Bob,'" one executive says.

Mr. Allen, though, soon began to wonder if the problem wasn't Mr. Walter. The new president had a stormy showdown in early December with AT&T's aggressive consumer-services president, Joseph Nacchio, who had been passed over for the presidency. Mr. Walter said he would transfer Mr. Nacchio to a new assignment, but Mr. Nacchio had already lined up a new job running a start-up company, and he quit.

That weekend, however, Mr. Walter told the *Journal* he had taken Mr. Nacchio "out of his job." Says one AT&T executive: "Bob felt that was too harsh. Things just aren't done that way at AT&T."

Later, when AT&T transferred Ron Ponder, the executive in charge of its beleaguered efforts to build a new national billing system, it was reported that Mr. Walter had ousted Mr. Ponder. Mr. Allen and other senior executives "suspected Walter of giving the story to the press," a person close to AT&T says. Mr. Walter heard of the suspicions and strenuously denied to associates that he had leaked anything.

Mr. Allen's suspicions aside, it became clear by spring that Mr. Walter was having an impact on AT&T, its managers and workers. He had named two senior executives to powerful new positions, including rising star Gail McGovern, who became head of the $26 billion consumer unit. Mr. Walter held meetings with middle managers in which he would push them to act like owners of AT&T. He rewarded those who found ways to cut costs on everything from real estate to paper clips.

"Senior managers were loving the guy," says Ken McGee, an analyst at Gartner Group Inc. "I'd never seen AT&T's groups acting so coherently and singing from the same song sheet as they were this year."

MEETING THE ANALYSTS

Burnishing his image with investors, Mr. Walter held AT&T's first meeting in two years with securities analysts, who had all but written off Mr. Allen for years of management misfires such as the botched takeover of computer company NCR Corp.

Mr. Allen had won applause for breaking up AT&T last year and spinning off its equipment businesses, including NCR and the now-highflying Lucent Technologies Inc. "Bob Allen had done a terrific job," Mr. Elisha said. But AT&T still faced billions of dollars in spending in numerous sectors, and morale was still poor after years of downsizing.

With Mr. Allen's credibility at an all-time low with analysts, the job of delivering tough news to the Street about the spending and earnings outlook fell to Mr. Walter. Over two days, he and other executives described in detail the financial hit likely in the next two years as AT&T expanded into the local-phone market and upgraded its long-distance and wireless networks. AT&T would spend $9 billion, nearly a third more than last year, on capital improvements; but it would cut more than $2.5 billion in costs over that time and strive to deliver annual earnings of $5 to $6 a share within a few years. Analysts were skeptical that Mr. Walter could deliver but thankful for the meeting just the same.

Little did they know that Mr. Allen had already begun to write Mr. Walter off. AT&T had held merger talks with SBC Communications Corp., the aggressive Bell company in San Antonio, in early 1996, only to have SBC pull away in disgust over the lack of progress in the talks, according to executives close to the two companies. Then last winter, AT&T's new president got a call from SBC Chairman Edward Whitacre, who knew him well from Mr. Walter's days at Donnelley printing SBC directories. Mr. Whitacre asked for a meeting to revive merger discussions, and Mr. Walter agreed.

Although Mr. Walter told Mr. Allen of SBC's renewed interest, Mr. Allen is said to have been incensed. "Allen was angry that his subordinate got the first call," says an executive close to AT&T.

The call only seemed to reinforce the chairman's suspicions that Mr. Walter couldn't be trusted. It also helped to promote the only real competitor Mr. Walter now had within AT&T for Mr. Allen's seat: John Zeglis, the 50-year-old general counsel and Mr. Allen's closest confidant.

Mr. Zeglis, a quiet lawyer whose involvement at AT&T goes back to the 1984 Bell System breakup, is as cerebral as Mr. Walter is a salesman. Mr. Allen came to rely on his acute legal mind. "Zeglis is bright enough to project forward where the industry is headed and how the complex regulation will affect AT&T's ability to expand," says an investment banker. "His brainpower is pure wattage, and he's also affable. Allen loves him."

Mr. Allen took over the SBC talks, pulling in Mr. Zeglis to run the complex negotiations and figure out how to win over regulators to such a controversial deal.

Mr. Walter was kept on the periphery. And it was agreed SBC's Mr. Whitacre would take command of the combined company, leaving Mr. Walter without a job and allowing Mr. Allen to stay on for the possibly two years it would take to complete the complex merger.

Mr. Allen, who never publicly acknowledged the talks even though he lobbied for the right to do such a merger, hoped to put together a deal with the large Bell company to jump-start his own flagging efforts in local phone service. He also saw a merger as a way to neutralize a Bell threat to AT&T's long-distance business.

Bell companies and GTE Corp., which control eight U.S. local-phone regions, aim to beat AT&T in the long-distance market. While GTE is already in the game, the Bells are awaiting a regulatory green light. By combining with SBC, which has a lock on the two Bell territories in the Southwest and California-Nevada, Mr. Allen could effectively take AT&T out of two fronts in the eight-front war and use SBC to help fund AT&T's push into local territories elsewhere.

But Messrs. Allen and Zeglis never got a chance to sell regulators on their deal. News of the talks surfaced in *The Wall Street Journal* in late May, fouling Mr. Allen's plan. He suspected Mr. Walter of leaking news of the merger to the *Journal.* Mr. Walter denied the accusation, but Mr. Allen remained unconvinced.

BOARD GETS AN EARFUL

Mr. Allen had already begun to critique Mr. Walter's performance to directors, Mr. Elisha confirmed in an interview Wednesday. Between April and this week, Mr. Allen held numerous private sessions with Mr. Elisha and other outside directors, saying he was concerned that Mr. Walter wasn't focusing enough on the details of regulation, an important factor in AT&T's business.

Other senior managers had approached Mr. Allen privately about some concerns they had with the president, say people close to AT&T. They said he had angered executives in AT&T's wireless unit in Seattle by acting uninterested in its technology and taking a hard line on its spending. "People questioned whether he really understood the technology and how important it was for us to use it to fight the Bells, since it was so hard to use the Bells' own local phone lines," one executive close to AT&T says.

Several of the wireless business's senior managers have since quit, including Wayne Perry, the well-regarded vice chairman, who directed AT&T's bidding recently for $2 billion in wireless licenses.

Outside directors also did their own homework. Mr. Elisha said they began interviewing senior managers regarding Mr. Walter. The managers' input, Mr. Elisha said without elaborating, helped the board decide finally not to make Mr. Walter AT&T's next CEO. Mr. Elisha told Mr. Walter of the decision Wednesday morning in a 90-minute session during which Mr. Walter ticked off what he felt were his numerous accomplishments at AT&T. Mr. Walter then resigned and worked with AT&T to put out a news release.

It quoted him as saying, "I believe I am perfectly qualified to be CEO of AT&T right now." But Mr. Elisha and the other directors had concluded otherwise. "He underestimated the complexity of AT&T and the difficulty of making an impact on the organization," Mr. Elisha said.

A NEW LEADER

With AT&T now needing more than ever to recruit a dynamic CEO, Mr. Allen may have written the last chapter of his own tenure. But one way AT&T could find his successor would be through a Bell merger such as the failed SBC deal. There are rumors that AT&T has been drawing up studies of possible mergers with several other companies; how far along any such deal might be is unknown.

In the meantime, outside directors have taken command of the new search. While Mr. Allen will have input, Mr. Elisha said, the board will find the new CEO. Kodak's Mr. Fisher, who is an AT&T director, is a strong candidate, although lately he has been having his own problems at Kodak, whose earnings are dropping as it comes under increasing fire from aggressive Fuji of Japan and Hewlett-Packard Co. in digital photography.

There is also Mr. Zeglis, who for the past couple of years has told AT&T executives that he has no interest in running a company, even as he has strived to make himself indispensable to the chairman. Mr. Zeglis, who recently added the title of vice chairman, has never run a business, but on Wednesday he was put in command of AT&T's operations world-wide.

It will take some time before he or any candidate can restore the power that was once AT&T. "Walter was supposed to save AT&T," says Scott Cleland, director at Legg Mason Precursor Group, an adviser to big institutional investors. "Every time AT&T takes one step forward, it takes two steps back. This is a major oops."

Writers' Workshop

Talking Points

1) The first three paragraphs of this story use an authoritative, analytical voice. Does this carry through the rest of the story? How is the tone supported with opinions from other sources?

2) The story offers a glimpse into the world of corporate management. How does the writer depict that world?

3) Note the balance of narrative voice and quotes from other sources in this story. When are quotes most effective? When does a narrative voice work best?

Assignment Desk

1) Similes compare two things that are essentially unalike, often using the words "like" or "as." Metaphors make an implied comparison. In this story, the writer says Mr. Walter "blew into AT&T like a cool autumn wind last November." Look for other similes and metaphors in these stories.

2) Rewrite this story without the authoritative voice of the writer. How does it change the story?

3) What is the theme of this story? Express it in a word, a sentence, and a paragraph.

Board faces twists and turns in search for new CEO

OCTOBER 13, 1997

NEW YORK—Picking a new pope may be easier than this.

As AT&T Corp.'s hunt for a new chief executive drags on into its third month, company directors face an especially difficult choice. If they pick Mr. Inside, the untested Vice Chairman John D. Zeglis, they risk inciting the wrath of some big shareholders who see the brainy lawyer as merely an extension of AT&T's embattled chairman, Robert E. Allen. But if they go outside and tap a superstar, they could lose Mr. Zeglis and possibly a cadre of AT&T senior executives who support him.

Mr. Zeglis, a veteran AT&T lawyer who helped devise the breakup of the old American Telephone & Telegraph Co. nearly 14 years ago, has let it be known he might walk if he gets passed over for the top job. He has never run a business before, but many AT&T senior executives would rather work for him than take their chances with a stranger; directors fret some of those executives would quit with him.

The AT&T directors could reach a Solomonic solution as early as this week that could keep Mr. Zeglis and yet bring in an outsider. In one particularly startling scenario, a few directors recently discussed tapping C. Michael Armstrong and, if necessary to land him, making a multibillion-dollar bid for the company he runs—satellite giant Hughes Electronics Corp., a unit of General Motors Corp. In the process AT&T would get not only great technology but a thriving satellite-TV business in which AT&T already owns a stake. Some AT&T directors believe the Hughes CEO, who turns 59 this week, could lead AT&T as its new chairman and CEO with the hope that Mr. Zeglis, 50, would stick around as heir apparent.

A potential Hughes purchase has gotten some support from AT&T Director Thomas Wyman, who is also a director of GM and its Hughes unit, according to one person close to the search. Mr. Wyman won't comment. But

Mr. Allen opposes the plan. He rejected Mr. Armstrong for the job once before and doesn't want to be overruled by his board. Moreover, handing the company to Mr. Allen's longtime lieutenant, Mr. Zeglis, would mark a more graceful exit for the AT&T chairman.

In another scenario, which could actually be the easier path, Mr. Allen is advocating that AT&T's directors recruit an elder statesman CEO who could act as a caretaker while Mr. Zeglis would serve an apprenticeship in the No. 2 role. Mr. Allen wouldn't comment for this article.

Directors were still wrestling with the conundrum over the weekend. Clearly they must act soon. AT&T has seemed paralyzed in the meantime, unable to wage a bold counterstrike just when there is turmoil in the telecommunications industry. The company's No. 1 share of the long-distance market, slipping for a decade, could slide even more sharply if the Baby Bells gain entry into the business in the next year or two. Two weeks ago, WorldCom Inc. launched an unsolicited $30 billion bid to acquire AT&T's biggest rival, MCI Communications Corp.

News reports immediately had AT&T talking to GTE Corp. about a merger. But executives close to AT&T and GTE say the reports simply aren't true. While the two telecom giants briefly discussed joining forces a few months ago, the WorldCom surprise didn't prompt AT&T to reignite the talks—in part because the board collectively has been reluctant to dictate any major new course before deciding who will be in charge of pursuing it.

"They are afraid to approve a new strategy for AT&T, whether it be a merger or a new marketing alliance, because they don't know yet who the leader is," says one person close to the search. "If the directors choose an outsider, they don't want to stick the new guy with a plan he didn't devise."

Their caution may be understandable; AT&T's board has been burned twice in trying to select a leader to guide this $52 billion-a-year behemoth into the 21st century. Among the twists in this prime-time telecom soap, "Search for Tomorrow's CEO":

Oct. 12, 1995: AT&T's board anoints insider Alex J. Mandl as president and heir apparent to succeed Mr.

Allen—eventually. Ten months later (Aug. 19, 1996), Mr. Mandl tires of waiting and unexpectedly quits to join a telecom start-up. Two months later (Oct. 23, 1996), John R. Walter, the little-known chief of printing company R.R. Donnelley & Sons Co., is the surprise pick as president, with the promise of rising to chief executive in a little over a year. But things sour in eight months as Mr. Zeglis is promoted to vice chairman (June 19, 1997). Four weeks pass—and on July 16, Mr. Walter quits after the AT&T board balks at keeping its promise to make him CEO.

That last untimely exit was an embarrassing blow to AT&T, and even more so for Mr. Allen, who is 62 years old. He had personally led the search, interviewing candidates and selecting just one—Mr. Walter—to present to the AT&T board. Chastened, Mr. Allen has been reduced to a role of advising from the sidelines as two AT&T directors, textiles executive Walter Elisha and former CBS Inc. Chairman Mr. Wyman, control the quest for a successor he had hoped to pick.

On the morning Mr. Walter resigned, AT&T's board bypassed Mr. Allen to ask Messrs. Wyman and Elisha to form a search committee to find a new CEO. Later that afternoon Mr. Elisha, chief executive of Springs Industries Inc., talked by phone with headhunter Thomas Neff of Spencer Stuart. The firm had worked on the search that produced Mr. Walter a year earlier. Soon Mr. Neff presented the committee with the shortlist of other candidates from that first go-round.

The directors were impressed with the top-notch prospects on the list, which included Mr. Armstrong, head of GM's Hughes Electronics unit, and Richard Brown, a former Bell executive who is CEO of Britain's Cable & Wireless PLC. Some directors were miffed that Mr. Allen hadn't bothered to recommend them, according to people close to the matter.

So began another episode of this search saga. Messrs. Elisha and Wyman ordered Mr. Neff, the headhunter, and rival recruiter Gerry Roche of Heidrick & Struggles to find out whether any of the prospects were still available. They started background checks, and by late last month they narrowed the list to a few executives, including Messrs. Armstrong and Brown. The two headhunters also began preparing separate assessments of Mr. Zeglis, AT&T's only internal candidate, after interviewing him in late August.

Along the way, AT&T's board has kept one eye on the finalists and the other on the company's stock price, wary that a wrong move will add to the stock's woes. The directors were high on Mr. Zeglis, confident he has the talent to guide AT&T through the arcane rules that govern the newly deregulated telecom market. But they also worried about picking a man viewed by many on Wall Street as Mr. Allen's aide-de-camp.

"Directors feared that the investment community would throw stones if they picked Zeglis," says one executive involved in the matter. Mr. Zeglis's prospects improved a bit after *The Wall Street Journal* reported on Aug. 29 that the Allen confidante had emerged as a front-runner for the top job; AT&T stock held its own.

Mr. Zeglis helped himself a few weeks later, when directors took his measure as he presented a new strategic initiative at a gathering of the board and senior executives at the plush Greenbriar resort in West Virginia on Sept. 19.

Mr. Zeglis's Greenbriar pitch included a bold plan to franchise the AT&T name to other carriers. He also briefed the directors on the strengths and weaknesses of possibly merging with any one of several potential candidates, including GTE, Cable & Wireless and BellSouth. He declined to comment for this article, but the lawyer-turned-operator has other plans in store: a global Internet play with Microsoft Corp. or another major partner, and the possible sale of financial stakes in AT&T's network to the Baby Bells and other players, risking easing their way into AT&T's long-distance market in exchange for their capital and their help in letting AT&T offer rival local services.

But the board reserved judgment on whether to approve Mr. Zeglis's ambitious blueprint for the same reason many big decisions are on ice at AT&T these days: They hadn't yet decided on a new CEO.

Still, AT&T's stock price rose more than $2 a share in three days after Mr. Zeglis's franchising strategy drew headlines, and his own stock with the board rose accordingly. As the Greenbriar confab ended that weekend, directors agreed privately that they must find a way to retain Mr. Zeglis. Yet they still worried about his lack of operating experience, a critical point given the vastness of AT&T and the impressive combat records logged by a few outsiders under consideration for the top job.

The searchers took a hard look at those outsiders last month. A small contingent of headhunters and directors flew to London to meet with Mr. Brown of Cable & Wireless. They came away believing that he would be a strong prospect to run AT&T, based on his years as a top executive at the Chicago-based Bell, Ameritech Corp., and his CEO credentials since then in turning around C&W.

The drawback: Mr. Brown is 50, about the same age as Mr. Zeglis, which would leave little room for the AT&T insider to ascend to the starring role as long as Mr. Brown is running the show. But two weeks ago, AT&T's directors learned they won't have to worry about it after all: Mr. Brown took himself out of the running and signed a new employment contract to run Cable & Wireless for another three years, according to people close to Mr. Brown. C&W's CEO declined to comment.

The search focused more intensely on Hughes's highly regarded chief, Mike Armstrong. Mr. Armstrong had been down this path before, in the summer of 1996, when AT&T's Mr. Allen had interviewed him for the job of president. But the personal chemistry between the two men was bad. And it wasn't helped when the Hughes chief bluntly told his AT&T counterpart that he wouldn't take the job unless Mr. Allen agreed to step down as CEO a few months after Mr. Armstrong arrived. Mr. Allen never passed that exchange on to his board, and some directors are hopeful a better result might emerge this time around.

Mr. Armstrong's older age might let AT&T's directors hold out the promise that Mr. Zeglis could eventually succeed the new hire after spending a few years in an apprenticeship. But by late last month, Mr. Armstrong's candidacy was clouded by other factors. Lately he has been busy restructuring Hughes and spinning off its multibillion-dollar defense business to Raytheon Co. Next month he is scheduled to begin a road show to pitch the newly restructured Hughes, now in the satellite and telecommunications businesses, to institutional investors. This would make it difficult for Mr. Armstrong to just up and leave, and it is why some AT&T directors have talked about making a bid for Hughes.

"It's much more complicated this time," Mr. Armstrong told an associate in describing the latest AT&T approach. The Hughes head declined to be interviewed for this article.

Even some of the people who are intimately familiar with the search are unsure of which course AT&T's board will take. The directors may yet arrive at a "power sharing" solution aimed at pleasing as many sides as possible. They could hold off on making Mr. Zeglis chief executive for now, in favor of an "elder statesman" who would serve in a caretaker role for two years or less while Mr. Zeglis cuts his teeth running operations.

That approach worked especially well at AT&T's equipment spinoff, Lucent Technologies Inc. Mr. Allen tapped AT&T board member Henry Schacht, former chairman of Cummins Engine Co., to run Lucent as chairman and CEO and named the unit's chief, Richard A. McGinn, as president and heir apparent. Lucent has since done very well as a public company, and last week Mr. McGinn ascended to CEO as planned.

Mr. Schacht now would be free to serve in a similar role at AT&T, but he has made it clear he isn't interested in doing so. Another possibility is to name a nonexecutive chairman: Donald Perkins, a former AT&T director and the retired chairman of Jewel Foods Inc. Mr. Perkins played such a role at Kmart Corp. after leading an ouster of the company's chief, Joseph Antonini, a few years ago. But Mr. Perkins has let associates know he wouldn't want the AT&T assignment.

The former CBS chief, Mr. Wyman, has lobbied to have himself appointed nonexecutive chairman, but his fellow AT&T directors haven't shown much enthusiasm for the proposition. Unknown to Mr. Allen, Mr. Wyman tried much the same maneuver a year ago when he interviewed Mr. Walter for the job. But Mr. Walter brushed off the suggestion, knowledgeable observers say. He won't give interviews.

Until the board decides, the intrigue continues—as does the uncertainty for AT&T's future course. For now, says one person privy to the matter, AT&T "is like an unguided missile with no one to direct where to strike. Or when."

Joann S. Lublin contributed to this article.

Writers' Workshop

Talking Points

1) The writer begins this complex story with a short statement: "Picking a new pope may be easier than this." How does this set the tone for the story?

2) Note how many of the primary players in this story decline official comment. Study how the story is constructed without their contributions.

3) In one paragraph, the writer prefaces the background of the story citing "twists in this prime-time telecom soap." How does the tone of this paragraph balance the following paragraph of names and dates?

Assignment Desk

1) Stock performance is a factor in making a decision at AT&T. *The Wall Street Journal* articles covering AT&T affect the price of the stock. Its news coverage becomes a factor in the news-making process. Discuss whether this should influence the paper's news coverage.

2) This is a complicated story with many elements, themes, and players. Write an outline of this story to see how all the material was organized for readers.

How directors decided it was time for change at the top

OCTOBER 20, 1997

NEW YORK—Ma Bell, in distress and facing the fight of her life, finally has a new leader: C. Michael Armstrong.

AT&T Corp.'s directors may announce their choice of Mr. Armstrong, the chairman and chief executive of Hughes Electronics Corp., as early as today. That would wrap up an intensive three-month search that has ended as it began, with a big jolt of surprise: The board has decided that Robert E. Allen, 62 years old, will resign within weeks as chairman, CEO and a director after a 40-year career at AT&T.

It is a dramatic denouement to Mr. Allen's stormy nine-year reign atop AT&T, a period of unprecedented tumult in the telecommunications industry and, even more so, at AT&T itself. Its directors were long criticized as one of the most passive boards in corporate America. They had unstintingly supported Mr. Allen for years as he eliminated more than 100,000 jobs, incurred billions of dollars in losses in a disastrous misadventure into computers, and ultimately split the company into three, stripping AT&T of deep management talent and some of its greatest assets, including Bell Laboratories.

That isn't to say Mr. Allen didn't produce some wins. The 1995 three-way breakup freed AT&T's equipment business, Lucent Technologies Inc., which since has been a stellar performer and a hot stock. AT&T also expanded aggressively in wireless services on his watch. And the job cuts, though painful, were necessary: AT&T simply was too fat.

The board forgave myriad miscues but lost patience in the end, prodded by some newer members less loyal to Mr. Allen and by one final humiliation: Mr. Allen's engineering the ouster of his own chosen successor, John R. Walter, whose surprise resignation as AT&T president in July kicked off this extraordinary search.

Mr. Allen had opposed the selection of Mr. Armstrong, 59, whom he could have hired a year ago but refused to because of the Hughes chief's insistence that Mr. Allen step aside within a few months. The AT&T chief had hoped to salvage his legacy and hand the CEO job to his confidante and general counsel, Vice Chairman John D. Zeglis. The board will meet him only halfway on the score. Trying to keep Mr. Zeglis, 50, on board, they are promoting him to president and chief operating officer and tacitly assuring him he will succeed Mr. Armstrong as chairman and CEO in three years. Messrs. Allen, Armstrong and Zeglis wouldn't comment for this article.

The board thus has paired a new chief from outside AT&T with his main rival for the top job. How the two men get along—and whether AT&T can quell the past year of soap-opera dramatics and return to the orderly transition of power that had long been its history—will be worth watching.

Mr. Armstrong would be the first outsider to lead AT&T, one of the nation's oldest and most revered corporations, since financier J.P. Morgan installed visionary Theodore N. Vail in the top job at the turn of the century. By now, Mr. Armstrong is accustomed to the outsider role. He joined Hughes as CEO in 1992 over the heads of many inside candidates, and he confronted resentment in the executive suite by stroking the egos of those who played along—and throwing out those who didn't.

At AT&T, Mr. Armstrong must quickly decide whether to wade into the $30 billion takeover battle raging for the company's biggest rival, MCI Communications Corp. Should he try to buy one of the bidders—WorldCom Inc. or GTE Corp.—or perhaps counter by coupling up with a Baby Bell such as SBC Communications Inc., the Texas suitor AT&T had courted a few months ago? Less pressing is whether to make a bid for Hughes in the future as a few AT&T directors had discussed, now that they have hired Mr. Armstrong without having to do so.

Mr. Armstrong also must chart a strategy for staving off declines in long distance, reviving flagging fortunes in local service and on the Internet and shoring up senior-management talent.

Some of these problems must seem eerily familiar to Mr. Armstrong, who once harbored CEO ambitions at a once-fading giant: IBM. He had spent 31 years at International Business Machines Corp. but left to lead Hughes, a unit of General Motors Corp. IBM went on to regain a solid financial footing under the helm of another outside superstar, Louis V. Gerstner Jr.

Mr. Allen closes out his career on a sadder note. He entered the old American Telephone & Telegraph Co. in the spring of 1957, fresh out of Indiana's tiny Wabash College. He started out as one of more than a million rank-and-file employees of American Telephone & Telegraph and rose to CEO. A quiet loner and obsessive golfer, he had once hoped to stick around until age 65. He reluctantly agreed to shorten his tenure by two years to bring in Mr. Walter. Now he is leaving even earlier than that—and not entirely by his own choice.

The seeds of that humbling exit were planted four weeks ago in a weekend showdown between Mr. Allen and his directors at the Greenbrier resort in West Virginia. AT&T has for many years held annual gatherings for senior management at the Greenbrier, a plush retreat that counts among its features a hardened bomb shelter constructed at the height of the Cold War to protect Congress in the event of a nuclear attack.

On that weekend, Mr. Allen ultimately lost the faith of his biggest supporter and friend on the board, Walter Elisha, chairman of Springs Industries Inc. Mr. Elisha steadfastly defended Mr. Allen's much-criticized tenure as recently as two months ago. But that seemed to change at the Greenbrier, as Mr. Elisha mulled matters with board members, people close to the situation say. After briefly reviewing strategy on a Sunday afternoon, directors asked Mr. Allen to leave the room so they could discuss succession plans.

The AT&T chairman apparently hadn't expected to be cut out of the deliberations, and he angrily decided against waiting around. Shaken, he stormed out of the room and commandeered an AT&T van, one of several waiting to take directors back to their private jets. He ordered the driver to take him to the Greenbrier Valley Airport in nearby Lewisburg, W.Va., and the AT&T jet, leaving others to find their own way home.

An AT&T spokeswoman calls this version of events "ridiculous" and insists the meeting was "very cordial and went exactly as planned."

Meanwhile, the directors reflected on Mr. Allen's nine-year tenure and built a case against him rather quickly. The meeting took on the pall of a funeral as they solemnly discussed the Allen years, according to people familiar with the meeting. Mr. Elisha, through the AT&T spokeswoman, says Mr. Allen's "performance wasn't evaluated; there wasn't a review of the Allen years."

Another person familiar with the session, however, says directors slowly went around the room asking for one another's views. In the end, the newest board members—including George Fisher, chairman of Eastman Kodak Co., Kenneth Derr, CEO of Chevron Corp. and Ralph Larsen, CEO of Johnson & Johnson—said Mr. Allen had to go and relinquish his board seat to make way for a new leader.

Mr. Elisha, head of the search committee, and director Thomas Wyman, the former CBS Inc. CEO, began the discussion by retracing Mr. Allen's ascension and how he had been groomed for the top job, according to knowledgeable executives. The recap began with 1983, when then-CEO Charles L. Brown picked Mr. Allen, who was president of the Bell company in the Chesapeake Bay area, to be AT&T's chief financial officer. He quickly rose to No. 2 under the next CEO, James Olson—and suddenly became chairman when Mr. Olson died of a heart attack in May 1988.

Mr. Allen lacked technical training but soon took aim at a technical industry—computers—by mounting a hostile $7.4 billion bid for NCR Corp. in 1991. AT&T eventually ran up losses of about $10 billion on its computer efforts. Mr. Allen ultimately spun off NCR in the three-way split.

AT&T wouldn't comment on the Greenbrier meeting or the deliberations of its directors. But people familiar with the meeting say directors concluded the NCR debacle was one of Mr. Allen's major failings, not only because he didn't deliver on AT&T's primary growth strategy for the 1980s and beyond, but also because he let the core services business flounder from inattention and inadequate investment. As he poured billions into NCR—siphoning off money from the cash-cow long-distance business—he ignored pleas from his senior team to move into the hot area of wireless services. He only belatedly agreed to have AT&T acquire cellular giant McCaw Cellular Communications Inc.

Mr. Allen also presided over a brain drain, directors at the Greenbrier noted. NCR's senior team quit soon after the takeover and was replaced by AT&T executives who also left as NCR and Lucent Technologies Inc., the equipment unit, were spun off. Almost all of McCaw's original senior team quit, including founder Craig McCaw; former President James Barksdale, who now runs Internet-software pioneer Netscape Communications Corp.; Wayne Perry, a wireless dealmaker of the first rank, and Mr. Barksdale's energetic successor, Steven Hooper.

In addition, though others had brought Mr. Allen along, Mr. Allen didn't do the same, never grooming a strong No. 2 to succeed him. For eight years as CEO he refused to share power or mentor a No. 2. His de facto second-in-command, global-operations chief Victor Pelson, quit in 1995 after suffering a mild heart attack.

In October 1995, Mr. Allen named a president, insider Alex J. Mandl, but by the next spring Mr. Allen began to tell people he intended to stay as CEO for another three years. Rather than wait, Mr. Mandl quit in August 1996 to take a $20 million offer from Associated Communications Inc., a wireless company, to run its new wireless local-phone business.

Mr. Mandl's departure angered some directors who had hoped that AT&T finally had a succession plan. They urged Mr. Allen to find a No. 2 and heir. A search began, and AT&T soon had the chance to hire Mr. Armstrong until Mr. Allen stepped in.

The opportunity presented itself in August of last year. Mr. Armstrong got a call from two recruiters hired by Mr. Allen, Dennis Carey and Thomas Neff of the recruiting firm Spencer Stuart, according to people close to Hughes. The headhunters knew Mr. Armstrong had quickly turned a low-key supplier of satellite gear and defense systems into a satellite powerhouse with a thriving new consumer business, beaming hundreds of channels of crystal-clear digital pictures and sound to home-satellite dishes. Even stodgy AT&T had purchased a stake in Mr. Armstrong's impressive new DirecTV satellite service.

Intrigued by the AT&T overture, the Hughes chief told the recruiters he would be interested in talking about the job—but only if Mr. Allen would agree up-front that any deal would entail AT&T's CEO leaving immediately, said a person close to Hughes. Mr. Allen agreed to meet with Mr. Armstrong about a week later at New York's swank Four Seasons Hotel. It was their first face-off.

There, Mr. Armstrong talked about his tenure at Hughes and what he might bring to AT&T. Mr. Allen sat silently through most of the meeting but agreed to talk again with Mr. Armstrong at a later date, one Hughes insider says.

A few days later, Mr. Allen told the recruiters: No deal. He wouldn't leave immediately. Mr. Armstrong sent word back that this would be acceptable: "I'll give him three months while I go around, tour AT&T offices and meet AT&T people, but after that I take over." Mr. Allen never responded. "He just kept Mike hanging," the Hughes insider recalls.

Even more damaging, perhaps, Mr. Allen never mentioned the possibility of landing Mr. Armstrong to the AT&T board. This lapse was still a touchy subject as the directors discussed the succession last month at the Greenbrier.

Instead, Mr. Allen brought them Mr. Walter, the CEO of printing leader R.R. Donnelley & Sons Co. Mr. Walter was a hit with directors, who unanimously affirmed the choice. They promised the new hire that he would rise to CEO by January 1998. But analysts bashed the choice.

Eight months later Mr. Walter quit after behind-the-scenes lobbying by Mr. Allen to deny him the CEO's job. Mr. Elisha, ever loyal to Mr. Allen, unceremoniously branded Mr. Walter as lacking the "intellectual leadership" to run AT&T.

But Mr. Elisha and other directors decided they had to take control of the search this time. Mr. Armstrong's name soon emerged on the short-list, just as it had the first time around. This time the board didn't hesitate: If a deal worked out with the Hughes chief, he would enter as chairman and CEO "from day one," an associate says. Mr. Armstrong, who a year earlier had said Mr.

Allen could stay on for a few months, made much the same demand this month.

The AT&T board set just one condition: Mr. Armstrong would have to keep Mr. Zeglis as his No. 2 and agree to make the AT&T lawyer his heir apparent. The directors liked Mr. Zeglis for his grasp of industry issues and his smarts. Though they feared Wall Street would dismiss him as merely Bob Allen's crony, Mr. Zeglis had shown in the past he was his own man. He had strongly opposed the NCR deal despite Mr. Allen's pushing it, and he had pushed to buy McCaw despite Mr. Allen's resistance.

AT&T's board held intense final negotiations with Mr. Armstrong during the past week, and he came to a final agreement Friday. He and directors were hammering out minor details of his compensation and relocation package over the weekend. Mr. Armstrong's three-year AT&T contract could be worth more than $25 million, including stock options and funds that would have come to him had he stayed at Hughes, according to one person close to the situation.

Now Messrs. Armstrong and Zeglis will have to make some big decisions immediately. Numerous potential deals have passed AT&T by as it searched for its new leader. It failed to put together a $50 billion merger with SBC after protests from federal policymakers. Mr. Allen had to rebuff other potential partners that wanted to talk about a merger—including local-phone company GTE and Internet powerhouse WorldCom—because he was a lame duck.

Since then WorldCom has launched a $30 billion hostile bid for MCI, trying to wrest it away from its would-be owner British Telecommunications PLC, while GTE has tried to knock both out of the box with a $28 billion cash offer for MCI.

If GTE wins MCI, Messrs. Armstrong and Zeglis might have enough political cover to reignite talks with SBC. Or they could turn their sights on WorldCom, a less controversial choice because it isn't a Bell that grew out of the antitrust breakup of the AT&T empire. Getting WorldCom would give AT&T broad links world-wide into Internet services and in local-phone markets throughout the U.S.

"SBC and WorldCom are the two companies AT&T is studying most thoroughly as merger partners," one person close to AT&T says. SBC and WorldCom won't comment on their merger plans.

Mr. Armstrong might also make a play for his beloved Hughes Electronics, making AT&T once again the pre-eminent satellite carrier. For now, GM has made it clear that it isn't willing to sell the unit.

Joann S. Lublin contributed to this article.

Writers' Workshop

Talking Points

1) The opening paragraph personalizes AT&T as Ma Bell. How is this different from the other stories? What is the effect here?

2) The fifth paragraph sums up the background of this continuing news story. How effectively does it bring up to speed a reader who is unfamiliar with the story?

3) "The seeds of that humbling exit were planted four weeks ago." Look for other passages of descriptive writing in this story.

Assignment Desk

1) The world of the corporate boardroom is unfamiliar to some readers. Pick another setting that would be unfamiliar to readers and write a story about its culture and climate.

2) Writers frequently are reluctant to use too many abbreviations in stories, fearing their use will affect the pace of the writing. Rewrite this story without the abbreviations. How does it affect the story?

AT&T pins its hopes on Michael Armstrong

OCTOBER 21, 1997

NEW YORK—C. Michael Armstrong, who helped build IBM's overseas business before transforming Hughes Electronics Corp., stepped up to the biggest challenge of his career yesterday: restoring fading AT&T Corp. to its former glory.

AT&T's board, as expected, tapped the Hughes chief executive to be its new chairman and chief executive officer, succeeding Robert E. Allen, who will step down in 11 days.

An outgoing, high-powered sales executive who spent 31 years at International Business Machines Corp. before going to Hughes in 1992, Mr. Armstrong must improve AT&T's competitiveness, overhaul its culture, and push the company to new heights in the tumultuous trillion-dollar telecommunications world. If he fails, AT&T could fall far behind slicker, well-financed rivals.

AT&T packaged the announcement of its new CEO with the disclosure that it plans to sell its once-stellar Universal Card credit-card business and a customer-service unit. AT&T also posted third-quarter earnings that fell 15% from a year ago but managed to beat analysts' expectations.

Mr. Armstrong, 59 years old, will have to share power with a strong No. 2 who was his chief rival for the top job: Vice Chairman John D. Zeglis, an AT&T veteran. Mr. Zeglis was named president yesterday, but the company held open the post of chief operating officer. And while some people close to the situation said Mr. Zeglis had been tacitly assured he would succeed Mr. Armstrong, the new AT&T chief made it clear he isn't a mere caretaker in the top job and that no promises were made.

"There's been no discussion at all on that," Mr. Armstrong said in an interview following a packed news conference held to announce his appointment. "I don't think the board brought me in to govern—the board brought me in to lead." Mr. Zeglis praised his new boss as "the best operator in the world."

AT&T's brass took pains yesterday to present Mr. Armstrong's selection as a smooth transition of power, creating "the new team to lead AT&T into the next millennium." There were smiles all around, and flashbulbs popped furiously as Mr. Armstrong was introduced. But the tension in the hastily arranged New York news conference was extreme.

The new CEO grinned broadly, in stark counterpoint to the somber Mr. Allen, 62, who is leaving AT&T after 40 years, the past nine of them as CEO. The boyish-looking Mr. Zeglis, 50, sat to Mr. Armstrong's left, arms crossed, with a tense smile.

Investors, apparently endorsing the Armstrong-Zeglis team, drove up AT&T's stock price 5.1% in heavy trading. AT&T closed at $47.50 a share, up $2.3125, in composite trading on the New York Stock Exchange. "This is a great decision for the company," said Craig O. McCaw, who is said to be AT&T's largest individual shareholder with more than $1 billion in AT&T stock. "Mike Armstrong is an outstanding leader who understands technology, and John Zeglis knows the company and its challenges intimately."

Mr. Allen had passed on the chance to hire Mr. Armstrong as his successor a year ago, instead picking John R. Walter, who served eight months and left abruptly in July. This time around, Mr. Allen again opposed hiring Mr. Armstrong, instead endorsing his lieutenant, Mr. Zeglis. Yesterday, Mr. Allen, making possibly his last public appearance as AT&T's chairman, put all that aside.

"Some will ask, 'Haven't we seen this movie before? Why didn't we do this a year ago?'" Mr. Allen said at the news conference. "That was then, this is now." He told the crowd he supports the naming of Mr. Armstrong without "a shadow of doubt in my mind." The departing AT&T chairman will become chairman of the board's executive committee, in a largely titular role he will hold until February 1998, when he retires. Staying on the board beyond that, Mr. Allen said, would have been "potentially inhibiting to the new CEO."

Mr. Armstrong, spreading around some of the praise, also told reporters it was his idea to have Mr. Zeglis named president. "It was on Mike's recommendation that the board elected John Zeglis president," seconded AT&T board member Walter Elisha, who was chairman of the search committee.

At AT&T, Mr. Armstrong will need to attack strategic problems from Nov. 1, when he starts his job. As AT&T in the past year tried to articulate a strategy and find a new leader, its rivals moved quickly to form massive business combinations that aim to attack AT&T on four fronts: long-distance, local and wireless phone services, and the Internet.

AT&T is a distant third in Internet access after America Online Inc. and Microsoft Corp. And the five big Bell companies are girding to challenge AT&T in the residential long-distance market, AT&T's core business. Mr. Armstrong acknowledged the challenges but said it is too early to talk in specifics. "I haven't even walked in the door," he said.

Chances are the Harley-riding Mr. Armstrong has already sized up AT&T's situation and its senior managers. He entered Hughes as CEO right out of IBM, after learning that he wouldn't rise to CEO of Big Blue. Before taking command of the General Motors Corp. unit, he did a detailed analysis of his senior team. In short order, he fired managers who didn't make their numbers, gave Hughes a strong marketing plan for selling TV services to consumers, and laid plans to sell Hughes's giant defense business to Raytheon Corp.

Separately, AT&T's third-quarter net income dropped 15% to $1.22 billion, or 75 cents a share, from $1.43 billion, or 89 cents a share, a year earlier. Net income included a four-cent gain from the sale of the company's submarine-systems business. Revenue increased 1.1% to $13.38 billion from $13.23 billion.

Chief Financial Officer Dan Somers noted that net income from continuing operations of 71 cents a share actually beat analysts' consensus estimates of 65 to 66 cents because of slightly less spending than expected and other cost controls. He said he expects the same performance in the fourth quarter of 71 cents a share.

Long-distance revenue fell less than 1% to $11.7 billion in the quarter. The biggest decline was in the consumer market, where revenue fell 2.4% to $6.08 billion. Business-services revenue gained 1.9% to $5.62 billion. Revenue from wireless services hit $1.1 billion, a 10% increase.

Writers' Workshop

Talking Points

1) What overall impression does the story leave about C. Michael Armstrong? What devices does the writer use to create this impression?

2) Several news elements were included in this story: names of the new CEO and No. 2 for AT&T, the sale of a business unit, and corporate earnings figures. Note how the writer organized the story and reported these elements.

3) "But the tension in the hastily arranged New York news conference was extreme." How does the writer depict the tension in the news conference?

Assignment Desk

1) Write a profile of a successful local business leader.

A conversation with
John J. Keller

ALY COLÓN: In your stories about the changes at AT&T, you noted that the two principal players, Chairman Robert Allen and President John Walter, would not comment. Yet your articles offer rich detail about the roles they played and how they dealt with each other. How did you piece together that kind of insight and background on deadline?

JOHN J. KELLER: Well, it's a matter of constantly working your sources, and I have pretty deep sources at AT&T—executives who are now at other companies who used to work at the company and keep in touch with AT&T, as well as executives inside the company. And I think you have to rely on those people to point you in the right direction.

Often, you can't go with the story right away. You need to gather string so that you have enough critical mass to go with a story that's meaningful, and can give the reader enough perspective on what might be happening inside AT&T.

AT&T is an important company, not only to the industry, but to the economy. They're the most widely held stock in the United States. So there's a high degree of responsibility to get it right.

How did you cultivate those kinds of sources that keep you apprised of what's going on?

You keep in touch with these folks. You let them know that you care about them, you care about the company, you care about getting it right. And you don't only call them when you need something. You call them to see how they're doing, just to see how their work is going, what their frustrations are.

You call them to ask them for advice. "Did you see my last story? Was it on target? Did I make any mistakes? Do you think I'm missing something?"

A lot of times, I will get great feedback: "You missed that nuance about this executive change," or "the new technology that just went into the AT&T network." So they keep you on track.

But it's important to call constantly, not to be a pain in the neck, like some of their telemarketers who call you at dinner to try to sell you long distance service. But you keep in touch. You let them know that you're thinking about them, and that you care about their work.

Most people care about their jobs, too. When they see that you care about your job, they're often willing to help you out.

Do they express to you any fear about being identified as the source of information?

When someone thinks enough of the *The Wall Street Journal* to talk to me and take me into their confidence, they immediately achieve a very important status with me. I regard them right up there with my kids. I would guard their identity with my life.

I keep my notes under my own lock and key. And sometimes I don't go with things right away. I figure out a way to get the story out, and get it out as factually as possible, without it ever being traced back to a person or individuals. Usually, it's individuals because we don't go with fewer than two or three sources.

So there's a lot of having to fly under the radar when you cover something like this, especially a potential meltdown of a company. And you have to be very, very careful about protecting the people who talk to you. A lot of times you have to protect them from themselves. You have to be extra careful that that person isn't put into harm's way because they're trying to get you the right information.

How do you protect them?

Well, I give them the option of getting off the call right away. I tell them, "Look. I don't want that on my conscience, and I certainly don't want to do something that's going to harm you."

I try to reassure them that I will do everything possible to protect them. And I will not lie. But by the same token, I will take precautions to make sure they are not identified. I'll tell them to dial another telephone code to get around the regular system. Do everything possible so that they cannot be traced back to me. Call tracing goes on a lot. The phone system will capture the number even if you didn't get a connection. So the employer will have a record of every call that was made.

I make sure that they're not surprised by what comes out. And that goes for the companies I talk about, too.

I make sure the company knows exactly what I'm going to say about them before it comes out. I don't read them the story, but I tell them all the points that are going to be made in that story, and I make sure they have ample opportunity to respond to it.

Is there any approach that you think is especially useful to convince sources to be open?

Well, I try not to approach things from a cynical point of view. I think cynicism is dangerous. I think skepticism is OK. But I think you have to approach people from the point of view that they have a job to do, and you have a job to do.

A lot of times, the best people to approach are the middle managers, people at the lower levels of the company. Because the guys at the top say "do this," and then they have to go do it. And there's a lot of drama involved in that.

A lot of stuff has to go on to do that and get it done. A lot of memos have to go back and forth. Maybe some layoffs occur. Or maybe the company has to cut corners.

So those folks in the middle go through a lot of angst, and they're under tremendous pressure, because they have to please the boss, they have to get something done. They're the silent majority.

And they want to be heard. They want people to know that they're responsible for their company's success, that they're the ones who are carrying the load.

So we're both approaching our jobs in the same way. And I think if you do a good job of just talking about your story, and show them an appreciation for what you're covering, they get the idea that you're trying to get something out that's truthful, and that's important. That people will want to read about.

So on that level, I think you reach them. The other way to reach them is if they see a wrong that they want righted. They want to talk about it, but nobody will listen to them.

And you'll hear from that person, or you'll call that person one day, and you'll just hit it. And they'll say to you, "Guess what? My project was just cancelled." You take it from there.

How do you find those people?

You find them everywhere. You'll find them at conventions. You'll run into them in airports. You'll get calls from them. You'll get their names from somebody else who knew a friend who knew this guy at AT&T or MCI or the FCC. And you call them. You never forget the people you meet.

I have a database some people would kill for, and I keep track of people. I watch them as they leave their jobs and go somewhere else. I track their ascension, or descension, within a company. I keep track of their accomplishments. I keep track of when they talk about their families, and they want to tell me about their kids' soccer game.

Some of that is artificial. You're trying to sell this person on talking to you. But a lot of times you end up caring about some of the people you keep in touch with. You find out that they're not that much different from you.

I think that helps you. It makes you a better reporter. It makes you a better source gatherer. But it also keeps you in touch with people and what's important to them, which is really one of the reasons you're writing your story. You want people to care about the story you write.

I sense you care about depicting human interaction. They're not just numbers stories.

I think people want to see the story. They want to see the action when they're reading about it. There's a lot of drama in American business, going on every day behind closed doors. Most people don't see it. It's only the privileged few who see it.

People run businesses. People work for businesses, they manage them. Businesses often reflect the personalities of the leaders at the top.

AT&T had a lot of drama going on, because you not only had the insiders who grew up in the company moving into senior management and running it, but Bob Allen, who was the last CEO, brought in a lot of outsiders who were making a lot of changes to the company.

Tell me about the process you go through when you write a deadline story.

If you're a good beat reporter, you do a lot of preparation that will lead up to your being able to write a good story on deadline. It should almost not be a surprise to you when something breaks. You should almost be able to anticipate it. You should almost be able to conjure five different scenarios in your mind, in any given week, of where that company could go, where that guy could go, whether this guy could keep his job or lose his job.

It was evident that John Walter was running into problems at AT&T before he quit. I always knew that something could happen there. I knew that he and Allen weren't getting along. There was scuttlebutt about it.

The real issue at AT&T wasn't whether this guy or that guy would keep his job. The real issue was, "When is someone going to fix this company?" That is of paramount importance because of its importance as a company and as a stock. And you write that perspective into the story.

I basically wrote a story about a company in deep distress, with a leadership problem.

Tell me what took place, and what steps you took, the day Walter quit.

There was a board meeting that day at AT&T. I was in touch with AT&T to see if anything was going on, and the word that was coming back to me was, no, not much.

Late in the afternoon, the company came back to me and said, "John Walter has resigned. And we're going to have a director talk to the press shortly. You can call this 800 number."

Well, I don't think the interview began until 4:30. Our deadlines to hit all our editions is 5:30. I started gathering stuff together fast. I started mapping out what I wanted to know. OK, this guy's resigning. They don't have a CEO now. They've got to find a new guy to succeed Allen.

Does this damage Allen? You'd better believe it does. This potentially damages Allen with his directors, because he brought this guy in. He was picked by Allen, and now Allen is basically telling the directors that he's got to find another new guy. This is the second president to quit in a year.

So I start putting all this together, writing it down. OK, I've got a focus on that. I've got a focus on the fact that AT&T is running out of time here. It's got to get its house in order, and there's a tremendous sense of urgency. The company's got to get back on track. It needs leadership.

So by the time I go into the interview with the director at 4:30, I'm pretty much clear on what story I want to write. This guy quit. What are they going to do now?

And I want to know from the director why it happened, what are they going to do? Have they hired anybody to do the search? Is this guy going to get a fat pay-off? What happened behind the closed doors in the directors' meeting when this guy resigned?

At one point in the interview, this elicited an infamous quote from the director, Walter Elisha. He wasn't saying why they got rid of John Walter. He was being very vague about it. He wasn't answering the question. So finally I said to him, "Look. You've gone through two presidents now in a year. The company stock is having a lot of problems. Don't you owe it to your shareholders and to the public to let them know what happened here?"

And he said Walter "lacked the intellectual leadership to run AT&T." Well, a firestorm followed that quote, and it's haunted AT&T ever since, and it probably led to greater compensation for John Walter than he *would* have gotten.

It's very important to keep up the pressure during an interview. I mean, this guy came on the air with us, in general talking about, "Well, we just felt it was time for a change." Not really telling us what happened.

So you keep pressing, you keep prodding, you keep poking them. "Come on. Tell us what happened." You're never obnoxious, but you keep prodding them.

After he gave the quote about how Walter lacked intellectual leadership, I said something to the effect, "And that's it? That's why?" And then he decided he was going to expand on that.

He said, paraphrasing Mark Twain, "The difference between president and vice president is like the difference between lightning and a lightning bug."

That said a lot about their attitude towards this guy. They just felt he didn't have the guns to run AT&T. And they weren't going to tell us that at first. And he wouldn't have told us that unless we kept up the pressure on him.

So in the interview process, the key elements are...?

Tenacity, tenacity, and tenacity. You've got to stay on him. Don't let him steer you off point. They've given you the interview. *You* guide the interview. Don't let *them* guide the interview.

Be polite, but be firm. Because you have one thing in mind. You've got a story to write, and you want to find out what's going on.

In covering your beat, what's your goal?

You have to treat a beat like an obsession. You're never out of touch. I'm on my voice mail all weekend. People are calling me at home. When I'm on vacation, I'm constantly checking it. I carry a cell phone.

That's a good beat reporter. They're always in touch. They're always preparing. They're always gathering.

What other elements are important?

Competition is everything in this business. You know, it's one of the businesses where second doesn't count. If you're not breaking the story, you're last. And nowadays, that's not even enough. You're not king unless you break the story before anybody else, and you give the reader more perspective and more information than anybody else does.

So those are the motivators for me. Being first. Being in competition. Getting the full story out before anybody else does.

Give me an overview of your beat, of what you pay attention to.

You've got to be willing to do a lot of the grunt work.

I think it's extremely important for reporters to write about earnings, for instance. Each quarter, a company comes out with its earnings, and a lot of reporters don't like to do that. Well, it can be kind of dry, but each quarter, it forces you to keep in touch with the company you cover, and it forces you to keep an eye on each one of the company's units, which may report separately within that earnings report.

So to get the big stories, you often have to do a lot of the little stories. You should do your earnings and executive changes and keep track of them. It's very important.

Plus it gives you good sources, because you can follow somebody as they go to another company. Let's say one of your companies reports its earnings. You just can't quite put your finger on it, but you think you might be missing something.

So you call so and so. You say, "Look, we're completely off the record right now. But I'm looking at the company's earnings, and you used to work there. Does this sound right? Does this add up?"

And sometimes he'll say, "Yeah. It sounds fine." But sometimes he'll say, "Well, guess what. That's not exactly what happened there." Or something like that. A lot of times those people will help you fill in the missing pieces, or give you a little bit better perspective. It arms you with information. It makes you a smarter interviewer.

Do you think there is any significant difference between covering a business beat and covering other traditional beats?

Individuals, whether they're in government, whether they're in business, or whether they're running the New York Yankees, basically have the same ambitions and drives, and the same motivators. They want to do a rewarding job. They want to be rewarded for the job they do. They want to please the boss. They want to be the best, or be thought of as the best, and they invest a lot of ego in what they do.

But I think companies have secret societies. Each one has its own code. It's hard to crack the code.

MCI's code, as a genetic code, is a lot different from the genetic code at AT&T. AT&T's is based on protecting the monopoly here, ruling the earth in telecommunications. I mean, it's amazing what they used to own at AT&T. They owned everything. They had to give most of it up.

Their code is different at MCI, which is basically built on beating that monopoly, chipping away at it, breaking it up. You have to try to figure out where they are. Where they're coming from. And that makes it tough.

But in general, covering the people who run business, I think it's no different than covering someone in government. I mean, everybody has a Rosebud. Remember *Citizen Kane?* Everybody has something in their personality or in their background that motivated them or changed their lives, or led to some epiphany.

What role did your editor play in these stories?

Most times, I had an editor who was in constant touch with me, whom I kept apprised of everything I was doing, so that he would know how the story was developing. He might remember things that I said that I don't even remember.

There has to be a relationship with your editor. You can't fly solo when you're covering a beat. You have to keep your editor in touch with what you're doing, and it's impossible to get something out unless you're kind of flying in tandem.

Because a lot of times you'll have to send something fast and you can't really polish it. You've got to send it to them rough so you can get back on the phone and finish an interview.

So it's important to look at your editor like a partner, and for an editor to treat the reporter in that way. And I'm lucky to have editors here who do that.

The involvement can vary, but sometimes the editor will jump right in and say, "Why are we saying it this way? It should be said this way." Or, "Did we get to this guy? Did we give him a chance to respond? Have you heard from this guy yet? Do we have this adequately sourced?"

I'm the same way when I edit. Make sure that you've got two or more sources, all the time. Never one source. And always try to get someone who was in the room, not someone who heard from someone who was in the room.

That's extremely important. I can't tell you all the things I haven't written about because I was never able to source it that extra step. "Were you in the room?" "Well, no. But I can tell you; my friend heard it."

Well, then you'll find somebody who *was* in the room, and they'll say, "No, that's baloney. That never happened. It didn't happen that way." Or "You're missing a subtlety here," or "You're injecting something that didn't exactly happen in that way."

Tell me some of the lessons that you learned, maybe some of the things you might do differently in the future.

Well, I wish I had written a story that said, "Walter will leave." His days were numbered at AT&T. I like stories that tell the reader where something is headed.

They can make informed decisions about their stock. They can make informed decisions about their company, if they're working for that company. They can just be smarter readers by reading that story.

I often do that. I love doing strategy stories before anybody else does. Especially if I have it all nailed down, and I know where they're headed.

In "AT&T's Walter Failed To Court the Man Who Counted: Allen," I should have figured that out sooner, that John Walter wasn't courting Bob Allen properly.

And I know a lot about AT&T, but I wasn't getting that information out quickly enough. I found it out and I had a lot of the evidence. But I didn't really start to get smart about the evidence I had until I had to write that story. I wasn't being tough enough on the information I had. I'm saying, "Oh, they'll work it out. You know, this is just growing pains."

Well, they weren't working it out and I wasn't willing to take that extra step, and say, "This guy is toast."

So how do you work with yourself to not be cynical, but still be tough enough to be looking in that direction?

I think each time something happens that causes you to reassess the way you approach the story, it makes you a little bit smarter. There have been times when I've been burned, where I've been lied to by companies.

I never forgive a lie. When you're doing a story, and the company knowingly misleads you, that's really hard to forgive.

To me, that's unforgivable, because I'm not supposed to lie to a company. Would they excuse me if I lied to them? If I told them I'm not going with something, and then I just hit them with a story that was unflattering, would they forgive that? No way. And they'd put all their people on notice not to trust me.

So at the end of the day, this is a game of trust. Each time something like this happens, it just makes you a little smarter, and makes you remember, "Well, I've got to go back and ask them a second time," or "I have to ask them in a different way."

And the particular thing that you'll do next time?

...is to say, are you sure you've looked at everything the way you should have looked at it? Are you sure you've examined the information you have, the interviews and other stuff that you've put together? Are you sure you've covered all your bases? Are you sure you're not missing something? Are you sure you've assessed this guy's role in the right way?

Do you know that I'm still asking questions about Walter? He's not even at AT&T any more, but when I run into people who might know something about him, I ask them about him, and about his role, and about what happened there.

Even if I'm not going to write about it. I want to know. I want to know whether I got it right. I want to know whether I've been fed a line by the company.

And will that cause me to go back and write a story that changes what I've said? No. But I'll tell you one thing. It puts me on guard the next time I deal with them.

What do you enjoy about deadline writing?

I just enjoy the adrenaline rush of having to write a story on deadline. With a big story, you're on the spot. You've got to deliver the story to the editor's desk. They want a good story. And you know you have to deliver, and for God's sake, you're delivering for *The Wall Street Journal.*

So there's all this pressure to get it done, to get it right. It's the process of being on the spot, and having to deliver. It's almost like—not to make light of this—but it's almost like you feel you deliver a Page One story on deadline, and you go home that night feeling, "Well, wow. This is like great sex." You did it.

It's a wonderful feeling. It means you have to pull together everything you've learned. It's just a wonderful, wonderful thing for me.

Is there anything about the stories that you've done that you think is important to explain, to help people understand?

Well, I think there is one thing. I remember one time I made a visit to AT&T, and AT&T officials took me to the archives. They had this big building where they store all the mementos of the empire.

They took me through this building and there in a cage was the desk that Alexander Graham Bell sat at when they made the first transatlantic call. And over there was the first Princess phone.

And I was looking at this and saying, "My God. This is history here. There's the piece of Telstar, the first satellite put up by this company. There's the transistor. It won the Nobel Prize for its developers."

The AT&T guys went into this refrigerated room, and brought out this little thing in a blister pack.

They opened up the blister pack, which was just kind of carelessly fashioned with some Scotch tape. And inside was this little book. Alexander Graham Bell's lab book.

There in detail was every step of his experiment, and "Watson, come here. I need you" written down, in quotes, exactly as he said it to Watson.

I couldn't believe it. I said, "This is really something! This is like seeing the moment that high tech developed." Because before that you had Western Union and its low-tech telegraph.

AT&T rose up and just kind of drove development in the country. Bell Labs was the source of a lot of technical breakthroughs and a lot of new things that today we take for granted.

So I'm looking at this lab book, and I'm saying, "Wow, it all came from that." And then they went in and got out Watson's book, and we all had a chuckle over it, because Watson had a slightly different quote about what Bell had said to him.

The AT&T guy looked at me and said, "So. Which one do you think history went with? The boss's quote. The boss's book."

There was a tremendous sense of history there. The way you write those stories, you look at them to see what impact they are having on this grand institution that was responsible for so many of the things we take for granted today, that helped open up the world to communications. And you think about how you can use this to write that story in a way that touches people.

It also helps you recognize the start-up of future AT&Ts. Because, after all, at the time AT&T came about, it was like a gnat on the butt of Western Union. Western Union was the biggest telecommunications company in the world. They ruled.

So you really should try to have a sense of the importance of what you're writing about. This is more than just some search for a new CEO. This is AT&T or IBM or Coca-Cola. These grand icons helped build modern America.

With your knowledge, and the background you've acquired, and the experience you've had, you prob-

ably could be a Wall Street analyst, possibly making a lot more money. What keeps you in journalism?

Well, the temptations are always there. And some of us get calls a lot, and offers of big money. I mean, obscene amounts of money. I've chosen this. There's a tradition here at the paper. It's more than a hundred years old. I'm part of something bigger than me, and people have died for the right to do what I do.

It's a great feeling of tradition and also, you're helping people. You're telling them about what's going on, and I think that's very gratifying.

I must say I'm well compensated by the *Journal*. They've always been very good to me. But I didn't go into the business to make money. I never did. I went into this because I like to do it. I have fun doing it. And I'm endlessly fascinated by the people I get to meet and the stories I get to write about.

That being said, I could end up doing something else someday that's equally gratifying. This is a dynamic world we live in.

The Philadelphia Inquirer

Barbara Demick

Finalist, Deadline Reporting

Barbara Demick covers the Middle East for *The Philadelphia Inquirer.* She got her first taste of foreign reporting in Bosnia, covering the war from 1993 until 1997 as the *Inquirer's* Eastern Europe reporter. She lived for much of this time in Sarajevo, in one neighborhood that she later used for her book, *Logavina Street: Life and Death in a Sarajevo Neighborhood.* Demick grew up in northern New Jersey. She graduated from Yale University with a degree in history and was a Knight-Bagehot Fellow at Columbia University. Her first newspaper jobs were with the *Hudson* (N.J.) *Dispatch, The Jersey Journal,* and the *Dallas Times Herald.* She landed a job in 1986 covering retailing for *The Philadelphia Inquirer's* business section and later moved to the Wall Street beat and to Washington before going overseas. Her foreign reporting has won the Polk Award, the John F. Kennedy Award, and was a finalist for the Pulitzer Prize. She has also written for *New Republic, MORE Magazine, Barron's,* and the *Village Voice.*

Demick tells the story of the West Bank village of Zurif, a suspected haven for Arab terrorists, and the collective price it pays for the continuing warfare with Israel. Weaving a tapestry of details, voices, and history, she helps an American audience try to make sense of a senseless conflict.

Inside a center of terror

MAY 1, 1997

ZURIF, West Bank—And so another of the stone houses of Zurif was turned back to the dust of the land.

It was 6 a.m. last Wednesday when Israeli army bull-dozers rumbled through the village's dirt roads and ex-peditiously plowed into the house of Jamal Al-Hur, a suspected terrorist. Loud-speakers awakened residents with warnings not to venture out of their homes. While children gaped curiously from behind barred windows, sleepy adults sipped their morning tea and vowed to get even.

"It doesn't matter if they demolish all the houses in Zurif. We'll rebuild them ourselves," declared Asaad Qadi, 52, a member of the village council. "Zurif will not be so easily defeated."

Zurif is a dry and destitute village of 12,000, perched on a barren hilltop 10 miles southwest of Jerusalem. Little in its appearance distinguishes it. But it has become notorious in the Israeli press as a lair of terrorists—members of a cell of the Islamic militant group Hamas.

The trouble started March 21, when a son of the vil-lage, Mousa Ghneimat, blew up himself and three Israeli women in a Tel Aviv cafe.

Then, two weeks later, authorities found the body of an Israeli soldier buried outside the village. The Israeli government blames Zurif residents for kidnapping and killing the soldier, as well as for the murders of seven Israeli civilians who have been ambushed on nearby roads in the last year and a half.

In all, 11 Israeli deaths and 49 injuries have been blamed on Zurif residents.

As retribution, the Israeli army has arrested about 30 young men and demolished four houses of suspected terrorists. It has also effectively turned the village into an open-air prison, prohibiting all 12,000 residents from traveling outside Zurif. And it imposes frequent curfews, when residents are forbidden to leave their homes.

"Somebody made a mistake and now thousands of us are being punished," complained Qadi.

But there is little sympathy for Zurif in Israel, where scores of civilians have been killed in Hamas bombings at bus stops, restaurants and shopping centers, and where Israelis are united in fear of terrorist attacks. A right-wing member of the Israeli Knesset recently called for "wiping the village of Zurif off the face of the earth."

No one here seems to deny the guilt of the arrested residents. In this traditional and deeply patriarchal society, the older men deplore the killing of Israeli women and children. On the other hand, they portray the attackers as patriots defending the Palestinian cause.

"These kids are murderers, but they didn't do it for nothing," Qadi said. "I'm considered a moderate around here, but the way the Israelis behave toward us, I'm now asking that children throw stones at the soldiers."

The latest round of attacks on Israelis has been inspired by construction on a 6,500-unit Jewish settlement, known as Har Homa to the Israelis, on land coveted by Palestinians in East Jerusalem.

Although Zurif is not directly affected by the settlement, residents here can identify with the land dispute. Zurif, at the very edge of the West Bank, lost two-thirds of its agricultural land when the lines dividing Israel proper from the West Bank were drawn at the end of the 1948 war. More land was confiscated by the Israeli government after the occupation of the West Bank in 1967.

Along with the land, Zurif lost its wells and springs. It suffers from chronic water shortages, and today can grow only grapes and olives. More than one-third of the village's original residents have left over the years; indeed, there are so many living in Jordan that they have established a village there called Zurif. The remaining residents mostly work as laborers in Israel.

"This used to be just a simple village. People were satisfied cultivating their land and tending their animals. There were no killings, no roadblocks, no terrorism," said 65-year-old Mahmud Hamidat. "What is left for us now are just these empty hills and our own humiliation."

Zurif is visibly poorer than many other West Bank villages, its arid streets choked with dust and rubble and lined with half-completed, cinder-block houses. There are no telephones, no sewers, no indoor plumbing. Electricity arrived just two years ago.

The closure of the village has deepened the poverty and resentment. Residents have been unable to get to their jobs in Israel, and merchants have had difficulty getting milk, vegetables and fruit past the army checkpoint into the village. While other Palestinians also have been barred from entering Israel proper for the last month; Zurif residents haven't been allowed to travel elsewhere in the West Bank.

Yesterday, Israel began easing the restrictions for thousands of Gaza and West Bank residents and said the closure would be further eased in coming days—except for Zurif, which will remain sealed.

"I can't go to school," complained Heitham Abu Fara, a 21-year-old chemistry major at the University of Bethlehem. "I'm afraid of flunking. A group of us tried to sneak through the hills on foot, but they caught us and sent us back."

Zurif residents complain that the closure has cut off food, money and medical care. On April 12, a 60-year-old man died of a heart attack as he waited to get through an army checkpoint and go to the hospital in nearby Hebron, villagers said.

Another complaint is that soldiers are shooting holes through the metal cisterns in which residents collect precious rainwater. Indeed, most of the cisterns are pocked with bullet holes.

"When the kids throw stones and they don't catch them, the soldiers get frustrated and shoot the water tanks," said shopkeeper Mousa Balladya. "Look, I don't approve of what these people did, killing women and children, but I don't think it's right either to have collective punishment for the whole village."

An Israeli army spokesman said the incident in which the man died at the checkpoint was under investigation, as it is the policy to let emergency cases leave the village. The spokesman said the army had heard nothing about the shooting of water tanks.

Israel says the tactics of collective punishment and home demolition are useful deterrents: They make it clear to would-be attackers that such actions put their family, friends and neighbors in jeopardy.

It is rare—though not unprecedented—for an entire village to be closed like Zurif, said Avi Benayahu, spokesman for Israel's Defense Ministry, who added: "Zurif is a special case."

In truth, Zurif has been at war with Israel for most of the last half-century. During the 1948 war, Zurif villagers were held responsible for killing 25 Israelis trying to take supplies to an isolated enclave in Gush Etzion. In the mid-1980s, several villagers—including members of the same Ghneimat clan as the Tel Aviv bomber—were imprisoned for the murders of five Israeli hikers and backpackers. The Ghneimats are one of the largest clans in Zurif, accounting for more than 2,000 people.

In the 1980s, the killers were connected with a militant unit of Palestinian leader Yasir Arafat's Fatah organization. But since Fatah has become more mainstream, village elders say, the angry young men of Zurif now identify with the more combative Hamas movement.

Those rounded up in the recent series of arrests included several well-established Zurif residents. One is grocer Ibrahim Ghneimat, 39, a local Hamas leader. Another is a building contractor, Jamal Al-Hur, 27, whose house was demolished last week.

The most infamous of the Ghneimat clan is Mousa Ghneimat, 28, who was blown up along with the three Israeli woman in the cafe. Although Ghneimat was killed by the blast, Israeli security now believes that he had meant to flee the cafe but the bomb detonated prematurely.

Ghneimat's second-floor apartment was demolished by the Israeli army three weeks ago, and his widow and four children are sleeping in a green tent pitched on the roof of a poultry shop. His parents and siblings live in an adjoining two-room apartment, where the women do their cooking on an open fire in the stairwell.

"We are just poor, simple people. God help us," said Zina Ghneimat, 52, as she clutched a school photograph of her late son. "I am illiterate. I cannot tell you why my son did what he did. I don't understand these things.

"He was never involved in these political factions. I believe he was used by other people."

Mousa Ghneimat's 18-year-old brother, Khalid, said Mousa might have been motivated by the constant humiliation of living under the occupation.

"I suppose I'm proud of my brother. He sacrificed himself for his homeland," said Khalid. "He chose his way. As for me, I don't think I would sacrifice my life to kill innocent people. I'm not ready to give up my future."

Lessons Learned

BY BARBARA DEMICK

At the risk of sounding callous, I'll make a confession: For Middle East reporters suicide bombings are a staple of the beat. They happen with depressing frequency, so much so that we can almost cover the stories in our sleep.

I moved from Berlin to Jerusalem in March 1997. It was a mere six days later that I got my first suicide bombing. A Palestinian had strolled nonchalantly into the crowded patio of a Tel Aviv cafe, where he blew himself up. Three people were killed along with the bomber. I jumped in the car and drove from Jerusalem to Tel Aviv, about an 80 minute trip. By the time I got to the Apropos cafe, the dead and wounded had been taken. The entire scene, I must admit, was a pale shadow of what I'd seen in Sarajevo, where I'd covered, among other horrors, a mortar shelling of an outdoor market that killed 68 people in the blink of an eye.

I felt I couldn't convey the horror of the Tel Aviv bombing without meeting the people who were intimately involved. So two days later, I attended the funeral of one of the victims. Anat Rosen Winter was a lawyer and a young mother. She had been drinking an iced cappuccino at the cafe, her eight-month-old daughter beside her table in a stroller. The photographs of the bleeding baby being carried out of the cafe were carried in newspapers around the world. It was as evocative as the famous picture of the limp baby carried out of the Oklahoma City bombing. I was the only foreign journalist who bothered to attend the funeral and Anat's friends and relatives were surprisingly eager to talk to me. They told me that Anat had been a staunch supporter of the peace process, deeply committed to giving the Palestinians a state of their own. For the family, the tragedy of Anat's death transcended the personal: As her body was lowered into the grave, people wept for the predicament of the nation along with the loss of the individual. I couldn't help but cry at the funeral.

But what about the bomber? What kind of person can walk into a cafe and detonate a bomb next to a mother and baby? For journalists covering violence, the perpetrators are usually more interesting than the victims since they presumably made a conscious choice. Mousa Ghneimat was an intriguing figure because he didn't fit the profile of a suicide bomber. He was married with four children. He spoke fluent

Hebrew and worked frequently in restaurants in Israel. He came from the West Bank, a village called Zurif that had been the birthplace of numerous terrorists over the preceding decades.

In the aftermath of the bombing, the Israeli army closed the checkpoints around Zurif to effectively keep the village's residents in and the journalists out. The West Bank is laced with dirt paths so a persistent journalist can almost always figure out how to get around the checkpoints. A week later, with the help of a translator who knew the back roads, I got into Zurif and spent a day talking to the late bomber's mother and some of his neighbors. The story that resulted described the long cycle of violence emanating from Zurif and the Israeli responses that, it seemed to me, were ultimately counterproductive in stanching terrorism.

Zurif residents complained that they were suffering from collective punishment. The closure of the village meant that 12,000 people were effectively under house arrest. Humiliation was the word they used to describe their predicament. The late bomber's mother, Zina, a 52-year-old illiterate peasant, served me coffee in the part of the family's house that hadn't been demolished. She said she couldn't bear to watch television after the bombing because she felt so bad about the Israeli mother and baby. Yet she viewed her son's suicide as the act of a heroic martyr who would be rewarded in the afterlife for his sacrifice. Most of the villagers I spoke to in Zurif felt the same way. It was abundantly clear that Mousa Ghneimat wasn't an anomaly. There were plenty of other young men in Zurif who vowed they would do the same. Although I left Zurif with sympathy for the predicament of the Palestinians, it was clear enough why Israel needed to keep the entire village closed off.

What did I learn from covering the Tel Aviv cafe bombing? I suppose I reacquainted myself with one of the cardinal rules of journalism: Follow up your stories. On the Middle East beat, with so much fast breaking news, yesterday's bombing can rapidly fade in interest and seem like ancient history. The first-day story might be the big bang—it was literally the case with the Tel Aviv bombing—but the subsequent reporting can be far more rewarding and revealing.

Hartford Courant.

Lynne Tuohy

Finalist, Deadline Reporting

Lynne Tuohy of the *Hartford Courant* has been a full-time reporter for 21 years, and has covered the Connecticut legal system for nearly two decades. Her beat includes coverage of the state Supreme and appellate courts, death penalty and other high-profile trials, and legal issues. Her awards include the Polk Award and American Bar Association's Silver Gavel Award for team coverage of a state police telephone taping scandal.

Tuohy, 42, joined the *Hartford Courant* in 1984, after spending six years at the *New Haven Register*. Before that, she worked at the *Springfield Valley Advocate* weekly, and *The Daily News of Newburyport,* Mass.

Her coverage of a murder trial that reported on forensic technology and trial strategies at work was an ASNE finalist for deadline writing in 1988.

Covering the high-profile case of "Dr. Doe," the young physician-in-training infected with AIDS by a needle stick while treating a patient, she reports the news and uses the storyteller's craft to tell a larger tale of one victim's fight to find meaning in tragedy.

Physician who got HIV
from needle wins record verdict

DECEMBER 18, 1997

NEW HAVEN—Just minutes after the jury began its deliberations Wednesday in the landmark case brought by 35-year-old "Dr. Doe" against Yale University School of Medicine, Dr. Doe sat in a nearby room and declared victory.

"I've won." It seemed a curious statement for a woman whose doctor predicts she will die of AIDS in less than 10 years, and whose own career as an internist was derailed when she pricked her thumb on a needle she had just withdrawn from an AIDS patient as a 25-year-old, first-year resident at Yale.

But she is the same woman who declared at age 6 that she wanted to be a doctor so she could help people. By suing Yale for negligence in failing to adequately train and supervise her in its residency program, she hoped to bring national attention to the issue of proper training and precautions to reduce the thousands of accidental needle stick incidents.

No jury verdict could take that away, just as no jury verdict could ever make her "whole," she said.

"Money can't compensate me for what has been lost and what will be lost," she said. "Most people don't have to confront their own mortality at age 25, to look at life and wonder what your legacy will be."

When the jury asked for a calculator after barely three hours of deliberations in the landmark case, it was tantamount to a verdict. Dr. Doe's legacy was being cemented in numbers.

The jury obviously had found the renowned medical school negligent. Two questions remained. What value would the jury assign to Dr. Doe's lost earnings, medical bills, the children she would never have and her painful road to premature death? And what portion of the blame, if any, would they assign her?

Make that three questions. Did anyone have a calculator?

In a courtroom overflowing with lawyers, reporters and their briefcases, only one person had a calculator:

Dr. Doe's mother. She dug it out of her black purse, handed it over to the sheriff and watched as it disappeared into the jury room.

Twenty minutes later, the jury emerged without the calculator, but with the numbers. They awarded Dr. Doe $5,297,000 in economic losses—those tallied for past and future lost earnings and medical expenses. They awarded her $10.5 million for emotional and physical pain and suffering. Total damages: $15,797,000.

The jury then deducted 22.5 percent—the portion of the blame they assigned Dr. Doe. They later said it was a compromise between the half who felt she was 20 percent to blame, and the other half who felt the number should be 25 percent.

The total damages assessed Yale University— $12,242,675—is believed to set a new record for personal injury jury awards in Connecticut.

Her attorney, Michael P. Koskoff, said the jury's award is significant beyond its size.

"The important thing about the money is to make programs around the country realize it is cheaper in the long run to train people properly," Koskoff said. "It sends the message that you can't skimp when it comes to human lives. You can't skimp when it comes to the lives of these interns and the patients they're treating."

As the verdict was read, Dr. Doe remained expressionless until it was accepted by Superior Court Judge Patty Jenkins Pittman. Then she broke into a broad grin.

"We did it," she said softly to family members and reporters who flocked around her as the jury returned to the deliberations room. "Hopefully we've sent a message, loud and clear, you've got to train people. We got 'em!"

Her mother, who had sobbed and trembled through some of the more graphic medical testimony of what likely lay in store for her daughter, tearfully embraced her youngest child. "I'm so proud of you," she said. In the next breath, she said, "I want my calculator back."

"I'll buy you one," replied Dr. Doe, displaying the sense of humor her family and friends marvel at.

That the jury found her partly to blame for the needle stick incident disappointed, but did not surprise, Dr. Doe, whose identity has been masked to protect her privacy and her career teaching and practicing occupational medicine at an unidentified university.

"Do I feel I had any fault in this? No. Did I stick myself with the needle? Yes," she said. "Perhaps it made it easier for them."

Attorney William J. Doyle, who represented Yale, said the college would appeal.

"We all feel for Dr. Doe and her family. It's impossible not to," said Doyle. "But we strongly disagree with the jury's verdict. The consequences of Dr. Doe's needle stick presented a very sympathetic case, and I'm afraid that sympathy carried the day."

Doyle said the verdict does nothing to change the outstanding reputation of Yale's residency program.

Jury foreman Joseph Zigmont would not comment on the jury's deliberations, other than to say, "It was a tremendous responsibility. We tried to do a good job."

Dr. Doe came to Yale's residency program in June 1988 after winning awards for her performance at the University of Chicago School of Medicine. On Aug. 18, 1988, she had been instructed by a senior resident to insert a catheter into an artery of a patient dying of AIDS at Yale-New Haven Hospital's intensive care unit.

Dr. Doe had performed the complex procedure only once successfully, two days earlier, under the supervision of that same resident, Dr. Alison Heald. Doe erroneously believed it was all right to keep the needle in hand after it was withdrawn, in case it had to be reinserted to reposition the catheter in the patient's artery. Heald had not corrected her. In fact, Heald employed that same technique herself.

Expert witnesses who testified during the trial said the needle should have been disposed of immediately, and under no circumstances should it ever be reinserted into the catheter.

Koskoff and co-counsel James Horwitz, in final arguments to the jury after nine days of testimony, said Yale failed to formally teach proper procedures to either Dr. Doe or to Dr. Heald, failed to assess whether Dr. Doe was competent to perform the procedure she was ordered to do and failed to adequately supervise her.

No supervisor was present when Dr. Doe, reacting to a gush of arterial blood that spurted from the patient, covered the catheter with her right thumb to stem the blood flow. Her thumb landed as well on the needle she held in her left hand, alongside the catheter opening.

Blood tests in mid-November confirmed she was HIV-positive. She learned of the diagnosis by phone while she was working a rotation in a ward filled with AIDS patients.

"If there's any legacy I want to leave, it is that an incident that was utterly preventable has been brought to [people's] attention, and everyone who follows me will be given protections I was not given. My legacy will be to prevent illness."

Lessons Learned

BY LYNNE TUOHY

Never turn your back on a jury.

The only thing predictable about juries is they will do whatever most vexes the lives of the reporters covering them.

If you arrive a little late to court on a Monday morning because you *know* the jury is scheduled to have three hours of testimony read back, that will be the morning one juror doesn't show up and a mistrial is declared.

If you dash from the courtroom to phone in a verdict to an anxious editor, the newly convicted murderer will choose that moment to hurl a water pitcher at the jury foreman who just pronounced him guilty.

If you leave court a few minutes early because the jury is deadlocked and the judge has announced he will instruct the jurors the next morning to try to reach a compromise, all hell will break loose. One juror will sit obstinately outside the deliberations room and refuse to join his colleagues, proclaiming himself browbeaten and harassed. Mistrial.

These examples are not hypothetical. Having fallen victim to the first, I was around to witness the second and third.

There wasn't a similar dramatic twist to the conclusion of the Dr. Doe case, but the jurors did return a verdict in the complex negligence case much sooner than expected.

Throughout the two-week trial, I had been setting up and plotting an interview with Dr. Doe—the plaintiff whose life changed radically when, as a Yale medical school intern, she stuck herself with a needle she had just withdrawn from an AIDS patient.

The jury began its deliberations at 12:15, and I began my interview with Dr. Doe minutes later.

I had lobbied to speak with her at the earliest opportunity. She declined to be interviewed before the case went to the jury. I had anticipated there would be no verdict after a scant half-day of deliberations, and my intention was to use the interview as the basis for the next day's story, a profile.

I always try to have some strong story in the works to run during deliberations, to mine that period of suspense when the case is a jump ball that can go either way. In this case, that period was short-lived.

I had finished the interview with Dr. Doe and was talking with one of her sisters when the jury requested a calculator.

That was tantamount to a verdict. Clearly the jury had found Yale liable and was tallying the damages.

It was 4:20 p.m. and time to regroup.

The verdict would come back that day and would be carried on two or three cycles of local television news before the *Courant* rolled off the presses. In high-profile cases, a morning paper is seldom going to deliver the "news" of the verdict. This is both liberating and challenging to the reporter covering the trial. I don't always have to write a straight news story, but what I write has to be compelling enough to hold readers beyond the verdict's bottom line.

I set out to exploit what I had that no one else had: Dr. Doe's own take on what this verdict would and would not do for her.

When I interview people, I always note what surprises me, figuring readers might react the same way. I was startled when she began our conversation by proclaiming victory.

The trial had featured graphic testimony about how AIDS would ravage her body; she feared the dementia most. Her doctors testified that she would be dead within 10 years. She had testified about her heartbreak at the prospect of a life without children of her own.

There was no doubt Dr. Doe was suffering a terrible fate. It was anything but certain the jury would lay the blame for that on Yale. Yet here she was, waxing triumphant. The lead gelled. It reflected her spirit, while reminding readers of the awful price she paid for this victory. It put the verdict in perspective.

I included the calculator in the story because it added drama and, later on, humor, when Dr. Doe's mother insisted on getting it back.

The story ends with Dr. Doe's assessment of her legacy. The quote is taken not from her breathless, post-verdict comments, but from the interview done hours earlier, while the jury was still reaching its landmark verdict.

Pittsburgh Post-Gazette staffers who worked as part of the team covering the Klan rally: Ervin Dyer, LaMont Jones, James O'Toole, Dennis B. Roddy, Lawrence Walsh, Michael Fuoco, Tom Birdsong, Robert Dvorchak, Milan Simonich, Monica Haynes, and Jonathan Silver. Not in the photo: Mackenzie Carpenter, Bill Schackner, Jan Ackerman, and Lillian Thomas.

Pittsburgh Post-Gazette
Team Deadline Reporting

The staff of the *Pittsburgh Post-Gazette* knew it would be a tense and potentially explosive day when the Ku Klux Klan marched through the city's downtown, ostensibly to reclaim the streets from criminals. The newspaper assembled a team to cover the day's events and, like the rest of the city, braced for what was to come.

But the preparation that preceded the march began long before Robert Dvorchak sat down late on the afternoon of April 5 to pull together the day's reporting in a seamless narrative. The newspaper made use of reporter Dennis Roddy's knowledge of white supremacist groups, an expertise he had developed after covering smaller hate groups in the past.

Roddy was able to help the staff size up the threat that the march posed to the city as the *Post-Gazette* journalists struggled with the question of whether they were playing into the hands of the publicity-hungry Klan by dedicating so many people to the march. There were people urging the newspaper to ignore the Klan altogether. But with the convergence of a professed hate group and a number of counter-demonstrators— some prepared to meet violence with violence—the newspaper decided to err on the side of more coverage, not less.

Dvorchak sent reporters out with two dominant thoughts: "We don't know what's going to happen. There's a potential for this thing to just fizzle and be much ado about nothing, or it could turn out to be a worst-case scenario. So we've got to be prepared." He also asked that the team give him "a sense of what people were feeling, what they were talking about, and some of their own feelings, some of what they were experiencing...because you're out there on the streets."

What followed was award-winning prose: rich, telling detail; a strong sense of place; resonant voices from a range of locations and perspectives; and a clear, unfolding narrative that weaves background information and spot news together so that the reader hardly knows where one ends and the other begins.

Pittsburgh Post-Gazette staffers who worked as part of the team covering the Klan rally were Jan Ackerman, Tom Birdsong, Mackenzie Carpenter, Robert Dvorchak, Ervin Dyer, Michael Fuoco, Monica Haynes, LaMont Jones, James O'Toole, Dennis B. Roddy, Bill Schackner, Jonathan Silver, Milan Simonich, Lillian Thomas, and Lawrence Walsh.

—Keith Woods

Face-off with hatred

APRIL 6, 1997

The hooded face of hatred and intolerance appeared Downtown yesterday, and the Ku Klux Klan's racist message was met with name-calling, stone-throwing, scuffling, counter-rallies and prayerful pleas for unity.

Although friction between opposing factions approached a flashpoint, and the potential for violence hung in the air, the Klan rally on Grant Street ended largely without incident. Three arrests were reported by a heavy force of city and county police clad in riot gear and body armor.

Thirty-nine Klansmen in robes or storm-trooper uniforms gave white-power salutes and delivered similar speeches laced with racial taunts and profanity from the steps of the City-County Building.

But a chain-link fence and police barricades on Grant Street separated them from about 3,000 raucous onlookers who shouted back their own obscenities and delivered middle-finger salutes.

Two in the crowd were arrested for throwing rocks, and a third person was charged with disorderly conduct and failure to disperse.

On a drizzly day when the Klan and its Nazi symbols appeared, messages of a far different nature resonated from elsewhere in the city.

A rally for unity drew 3,000 people to Market Square, hundreds more jammed St. Mary of Mercy Church on Stanwix Street for a Mass and ecumenical prayer service, about 200 members of a group called The Concerned Black Citizens held a teach-in at Westinghouse Park in North Point Breeze.

Anti-Klan rallies sprang up spontaneously.

The ugliest incident occurred at Cherry Way and Fourth Avenue, just a few hundred feet from where Klan members spoke.

Six Klan supporters—five men and a woman—were spat upon, shoved and taunted before police stepped in to protect them. One of the supporters was sprayed in the eyes with pepper spray, apparently by someone in the crowd, before they were driven away in an ambulance.

"We saw today the very best and very worst of Pittsburgh," Mayor Murphy said after the Klan rally ended shortly after 3 p.m. "I've never felt that kind of revulsion."

Police Chief Robert W. McNeilly Jr., whose forces were responsible for the security of both the Klan and the onlookers, breathed a sigh of relief.

"We survived," he said tersely.

The Indiana-based American Knights of the Ku Klux Klan, one of dozens of Klan factions in the United States, initially said it wanted to march in Homewood, a predominantly black neighborhood. Then the Klansmen settled on a rally outside the City-County Building.

Most Klan rallies are designed to show a presence in a town, sometimes to recruit new members.

Yesterday's rally, said Pennsylvania Grand Dragon C. Edward Foster, the main force behind the rally, was simple.

"Our ultimate goal was to stir up the white revolution. To cause enough hate and dissension so they'd riot down there.

"We hope they burn the place down."

They didn't.

THE DAY UNFOLDS

Shortly after 9 a.m., paramedics and police SWAT team members gather in a parking lot near the City-County Building to prepare.

Paramedics review procedures for washing pepper spray out of afflicted eyes and brief each other on anti-riot techniques. They also don bulletproof vests and gas masks.

The SWAT teams assemble outside their old headquarters on the Boulevard of the Allies near Smithfield Street. A bomb-squad trailer is parked outside while police put on their body armor and gas masks while checking their weapons and plastic handcuffs.

A little more than an hour later, at St. Mary of Mercy, people more concerned with the spiritual than the confrontational gather.

The Rev. John O'Toole celebrates Mass for more than 500 casually dressed men, women and children in a church that can hold 850.

The faithful don't seem to mind the television and newspaper photographers walking down the side aisles.

As the Mass progresses, a lone police car is parked on Fourth Avenue beside PPG Place. Across the street and toward Market Square, four police officers chat idly. Their riot helmets and a water bottle sit atop a garbage receptacle, against which lean four long riot batons.

The crowd at Market Square is light—the Pittsburgh Coalition to Counter Hate Groups' counter-rally won't begin for another 50 minutes, but people of all ages, races and ethnicities are starting to gather, holding placards and staking out spots next to a stage.

After the Mass lets out at St. Mary, more than 400 people stick around for an ecumenical prayer service conducted by the Christian Leaders Fellowship, an organization representing 11 major denominations.

"Racism is an evil that must be rooted out of the church and every aspect of our community," the organization says in a statement read by Bishop Alden Hathaway of the Episcopal Diocese of Pittsburgh.

"As spiritual leaders, we must speak out without reservation against any effort that promotes racism, hatred or intolerance in any form, especially when this is done by those who identify themselves as Christian, such as the Ku Klux Klan."

The clergy conclude the service by singing, "Let there be peace on Earth," a hymn that ends with the words, "and let it begin with me."

THE PEACE IS THREATENED

Anti-Klan demonstrators mill around a fenced-in parking lot across Grant Street from the Klan roost. Police hope the cage, as some call the enclosure, will keep Klan members far apart from their detractors.

One of the first people to arrive inside the fence, 135 feet from the steps of the City-County Building, is Chuck Grodes, 49, of South Fayette. Like everyone who follows him inside, he is checked for weapons by police holding chirping metal detectors.

On the chain-link barrier are signs that say: "Warning, Do Not Climb Fence! Violators Will Be Sprayed With Mace."

Grodes recalls a black friend during his Vietnam days as he denounces racism.

"I didn't look at it like black and white. He saved my ass. He was my brother. In combat, you don't have time to hate a guy. We were like family."

In the same hour, the mayor heads Downtown, first for a final look at police preparations and then for an appearance at the anti-Klan event at Market Square.

Along Grant Street, Murphy works his way among the waiting police officers shaking hands and offering thanks.

"I hope we're overreacting," he confides to one.

Murphy's public day began tethered to a rope held by a member of the Pittsburgh Explorers Club. He rappelled down the face of Mount Washington, grabbing rusted beer cans, decaying cups and the odd champagne bottle.

It was part of the annual cleanup the club organizes to scour the Pittsburgh landmark, a reminder that many Pittsburghers would spend their day demonstrating engagement with their city in ways that have nothing to do with opposition to, or support for, the Klan.

"I'd rather be doing this than what I'm going to be doing the rest of the day," he said with a glance back at the cliff.

After a change of clothes, Murphy heads to the DoubleTree Hotel for a political meeting with labor leaders.

Less than a mile away, more people are milling around outside the Fourth Avenue entrance to the enclosed observation area than have gone in.

There are young black men with dreadlocks and braids; one is dressed in a blue pinstripe suit. Young white women with black lipstick and pierced brows, noses and ears, and young white men in black pants and T-shirts all are wearing "Stop Racism" stickers.

Several members of the Anti-Racist Action group from Detroit are there, too. Rebecka Helton, 20, observes that Pennsylvania Klan members seem to be more openly racist than those in the Detroit area.

She turns toward some young women wearing T-shirts depicting Confederate flags who've turned their backs to Fourth Avenue.

"Why are you hiding?" Helton shouts to them. The women turn and curse at her.

Derek Johnson, 25, a photographer accompanying the Detroit contingent, predicts, "There's going to be some trouble today."

A young black man stands in the street outside the entrance to the cage.

"I came down here because I hate the Ku Klux Klan," he says. He won't enter the cage, he says, because the hand-held metal detectors used by police at the entrance would stop him cold.

Inside Kaufmann's a block away, a black security guard and a white clerk at the pastry counter discuss the Klan.

"Have you ever seen one of them in costume?" asks the clerk, a woman in her 50s.

"I've never seen them except on TV," says the guard, a much younger man who gives his name as Jonathon.

The clerk describes the store as "dead" for a Saturday. Jonathon, who occasionally pulls weekend duty, says foot traffic seems about normal.

He resumes his post near an entrance to the shoe department. Several other doors are covered by uniformed security people.

"It's a shame that they've got to do this," Jonathon says of the store's management.

Outside the store, a family of five decked out in Penguins sweaters notices the overwhelming police presence on street corners. On the way to the Penguins' 1:30 p.m. game against the Ottawa Senators, the family stops to have a word with four officers at Smithfield Street and Forbes Avenue.

A beat officer whose name tag says "Carnahan" tells them he's hoping for heavy rain. Nothing better than a downpour to cool a crowd running on adrenaline, he says.

Carnahan, who declines to give his first name, says he doesn't necessarily think police are in for a long afternoon. "We really don't know what to expect," he says.

At Fifth Avenue and Smithfield Street, 30 or so anti-Klan marchers zip along, many carrying signs that say, "Absolute KKKrap."

Ben Zimmerman of Farmington waves a placard that says, "White sheets hide red necks."

"We came to Pittsburgh today because we believe all men were created equal," Zimmerman says.

KLAN ON THE MOVE

By prearrangement with Pittsburgh police, Klan members take the Pennsylvania Turnpike to Exit 5, Harmarville, and their vehicles pull into a lot behind a Giant Eagle. They arrive at 12:45 p.m.

C. Edward Foster, Pennsylvania grand dragon of the American Knights of the KKK, can't find the undercover police officers assigned to the group. He decides he's been tricked.

He picks up a cell phone and calls Sgt. Mona Wallace of the police intelligence unit. Where are his contacts? Foster demands.

She directs him to a truck nearby, where two undercover officers await. The caravan follows the officers to the Pittsburgh Public Safety Training Academy on Washington Boulevard in Highland Park.

Foster and his entourage had left the village of Walston, just outside Punxsutawney, Jefferson County, a few hours earlier. Their first destination was the Sunrise Inn in Monroeville, where a group of out-of-state klansmen had stayed overnight.

About noon, as some robed Klan members leave the motel, some of them jaw with customers of a Burger King nearby.

"One person that wasn't (a Klan member) and one that was started running off at the mouth," says an employee of the restaurant.

A state trooper shoos the Klan members toward the turnpike before the confrontation can escalate into a fight.

Monroeville police characterize the standoff as a "slight incident."

But the mood of the rest of the day had been set.

EAST OF TOWN

For the 200 people gathered at the "Black Family Day Teach-In" at Westinghouse Park in North Point Breeze, it was more pep rally than protest.

The gentle flapping of the red, black and green African-American unity flag and the steady beats of the 10-member Imhotep drummers filled the air.

A stream of speakers, from community organizer Emma Slaughter, who pushes for building a black cultural museum in Homewood, to civil rights lawyer Leroy Hodge, who urges economic and political awareness, lends its own rhythms to the breezy, drizzly afternoon.

The crowd, clad mostly in wind suits, sweats and T-shirts, feasts on an array of political empowerment messages—register to vote, start your own business—but also on salad, cookies, fruit and fried chicken.

Bariki, an organizer who goes by her first name only and is a member of Concerned Black Citizens, which sponsored the teach-in, says the day was one to focus on "the plight of the African in America."

"We should be aware of the Klan's devastation through history, but more importantly we're here to mobilize independent and free-thinking African-Americans."

Politics wasn't always on center stage. The teach-in was a way for everyone to get into the act.

Eight young girls from Homewood's Sankofa Rites of Passage program drill team march; men from the Nation of Islam rap.

Councilwoman Valerie McDonald stops by. She had earlier visited the anti-Klan rally in Market Square.

"It was good to get away from the Klan and get back into the community. I like the messages of unity here."

Dora Martin visits with her two children, Jaymie, 8, and Malcolm, 5.

"With the Klan in town, you wouldn't know it was Pittsburgh 1997. You'd think it was Selma 1963," she says. "I want my kids to know their history, but I also want them to know that they have a future."

DOWNTOWN PREPARES

Pittsburgh Coalition to Counter Hate Groups rally organizer Barney Oursler is checking preparations, lining up the speakers and coordinating his team. "The hard work is going to be after today," Oursler says.

A cheer erupts a few minutes later as about 40 people from the North Side march toward Market Square. Overall, the noontime atmosphere is festive as about 3,000 people—young singles, couples and families—listen to the first of 50 speakers.

They include representatives of the city and county, the state Legislature, religious organizations, community groups and labor unions.

The mood all afternoon is reminiscent of a family reunion as old friends kiss, hug and shake hands.

The mood is far different nearer to Grant Street.

A 17-year-old boy from the South Hills—he won't give a name—turns up in a black T-shirt with a swastika and "Weiss Macht"—white power—emblazoned on it. Alyson and Laura Finney, sisters from Mt. Lebanon, also have come to support the Klan. Alyson is wearing her "grim reaper" pendant, and Laura is wearing a T-shirt with a Confederate flag.

For a few minutes, Alyson talks a tough game. Black people, she says, are inferior.

The first confrontation begins. Alyson is spotted by a group of anti-Klan protesters, who confront her.

"Y'all get the hell out of here!" shouts Elmer Hyatt, a black man from Wilkinsburg.

"I'm allowed to stand here if I want to, right? Why should we get out?" Finney says.

Angry words go back and forth, and Finney turns around to discover that her cohorts have melted away into the crowd.

"You know what I'd like to know?" George Spratley, a North Side man, asks Finney. "What are you going to do when you go to heaven and you find out God is a black man?"

"I guess I'll go to hell," Finney says.

Police SWAT Team Cmdr. Dom Costa eases his way into the growing clot of angry people and quietly breaks it up.

On Fourth Avenue near Oxford Centre, about 30 people, black and white, primarily young, mill about.

Their numbers are dwarfed by the police officers in riot gear. Half a block away, at Cherry Way, five county police officers atop horses stand at the ready.

On Forbes Avenue, at the other entrance to the cage, the scene is nearly a mirror image of what is found on Fourth—police in riot gear, deputies with metal-detecting wands, paramedics standing in front of the Allegheny Building.

More people trickle in. Most are young. They are black and white and Asian, casually dressed in T-shirts and jeans, peasant dresses and sandals.

Even in this melting pot a few stick out. One man wears a blond Mohawk haircut and has numerous piercings in his nose, ears, lips, tongue and eyebrow. One woman has aqua-colored hair, another purple. A few of the men sport shoulder-to-fingertip tattoos.

At 12:08 p.m., Cornell Womack of the Grant Street Anti-Klan Coalition leads a group of people onto Forbes and begins a chant: "What do we want?" "Justice!" "When do we want it?" "Now!"

A few minutes later, some in the anti-Klan group begin chanting to those inside the viewing enclosure, "Come out of the cage."

Now there are several hundred people near the cage entrance on Forbes. It begins to drizzle. The chants continue.

In front of the City-County Building, McNeilly, the police chief, huddles with Deputy Chief Charles Moffatt as Assistant Chiefs William P. Mullen and Nate Harper scurry about. Forty officers from the Community Oriented Police unit, in riot gear, line a fence separating the cage from Grant Street.

On both Forbes and Fourth avenues, police horses, wearing tiny shields to protect their eyes, stand ready.

Lt. Daniel Quinlan walks the fence line, chatting and laughing with spectators in the cage. He ignores the insults occasionally hurled his way.

In the midst of all this, a frail, ancient woman with a cane inches her way up Forbes and onto Grant, through the buffer zone and right under the noses of the police.

She can't speak and appears to be deaf as well.

She scribbles her name, "Helen Jean," on a pad for a questioner.

What is she doing in the middle of this?

She scratches out her answer: "71-D Hamilton Bus."

Paramedics take the woman out of the security zone.

CHERRY WAY

On Forbes Avenue just outside the gated-in area shortly after 1:30 p.m., a Klan supporter in a blue shirt ventures into the anti-Klan crowd and flashes a Nazi salute. He quickly retreats toward Cherry Way amid shouts from several anti-Klan demonstrators. "Don't you stick that in my face!" one man shouts.

On Cherry Way and Fourth, a big crowd gets angry when it spots six people with shaved heads standing among them.

Dozens of people begin spitting at the six. Sixteen SWAT team members with helmets, shields and automatic weapons are only feet away. They sit tight.

The crowd, black and white alike, shouts "KKK out! KKK out!"

Young people advance on the six, spitting and threatening. A few people throw punches. A heavy-set Klan supporter is hit in the eyes with pepper spray.

Finally, after 90 seconds of mayhem, the SWAT team steps in to protect the Klan sympathizers. They form a protective shield around them and hold the crowd at bay.

Two anti-Klan people taunt the SWAT team. One shrill blond man drops to his knees in front of a rifle-toting officer.

"Shoot me," the man says. "You know you want to. You know you want to shoot me."

The officer stands still and grim-faced. He says nothing.

Sgt. Paul Minella, a command officer, says the six Klan supporters are not under arrest. Rather, they are under police protection, at their request.

Golfball-sized chunks of asphalt fly and pedestrians scatter as helmeted police walk two men, both in handcuffs, past a jeering crowd on Fourth Avenue near Cherry Way. Shouts of "KKK!" by a small group of Klan supporters outside the fenced-in pen are drowned out by a larger crowd yelling "Whose streets? Our streets!"

One of the men in handcuffs exchanges taunts with the crowd while standing at Fourth and Cherry, waiting to be removed by police along with the second handcuffed man. Additional police arrive. Traffic moves slowly through Cherry Way within several feet of the disturbance. Traffic backs up on surrounding streets, including Wood and the Boulevard of the Allies.

About 2:20 p.m., a police SWAT armored assault vehicle rumbles up the Boulevard of the Allies toward Cherry Way with its lights flashing to remove the six who have been under SWAT team protection.

An older man yells curses at the six as they step into the sanctuary that will drive them far away from this angry mob.

"You should let us kill them...suckers," a young man says to a SWAT team member.

The mood is nasty. People are grouped along sidewalks tightly because Cherry is open to pedestrian and car traffic. People are sticking their cameras right into the faces of foot patrol officers in riot gear, snapping away. There are several young black men wearing black bandannas over their faces. People are shouting anti-police slogans.

SEND IN THE KLAN

At 1:10 p.m., Klansmen arrive in a staging area away from the City-County Building—police won't say where—and are checked for weapons.

They bundle up their robes and costumes and pile into a green police bus. Foster and Imperial Wizard Jeff Berry ride in a police wagon. The caravan makes its way Downtown, and the vehicles pull into the main yard of the old County Jail.

The Klansmen follow police and deputies through hallways and stairs of the old jail, across the Bridge of Sighs into the County Courthouse and through a warren of halls. They stop near the sheriff's office to put on their robes.

Then they go down a series of stairs and through a tunnel that runs below Forbes Avenue, and surface in the City-County Building.

The roar and rumble of anger flashes off the brick and stone walls inside the canyon of Grant Street as the first Klansman steps outside. The hooded and robed specter walks up to the city-supplied lectern and begins to speak.

Nothing comes out. But he is booed and jeered from across the street nonetheless.

He fiddles with dials and knobs below the lectern and tries again.

Silence, still.

The Ku Klux Klutz walks back into the building to fetch Foster, who promptly accuses ZOG—that's Klanspeak for "Zionist Occupation Government"—of tampering with the volume.

Thirty hooded Klansmen roll out the front door of the building, along with three in helmets and storm-trooper uniforms with swastika armbands, and six young men dressed in a combination of jeans, combat boots and an occasional bandanna over the face. One is wearing a hockey mask.

Henry Clement, neo-Nazi from New Jersey, waves a red, white and black flag bearing a swastika. He's wearing a German-style army helmet, black outfit, combat boots and a ski mask.

Klansmen raise their left arms—some opt for their right—in a salute.

"White Power!" they shout.

The crowd surges forward, and the security fence 135 feet away begins to rock. It holds, to everyone's relief, as blacks and whites taunt the Klan to come closer and take off their hoods.

"You know what?" Murphy says as he looks down from a low roof at One Oxford Centre, a tight smile on his face. "I'm glad we did everything we've done. I am so glad."

Gesturing toward the police commanders standing behind the row of riot-equipped police, Murphy says, "This is exactly what they said to us: You need a strong fence."

Murphy ignores the light rain that darkens his suit as the Klan's rants drag on. Around him, some officers document the scene with still and video cameras. Others peer through binoculars, then radio colleagues on the ground, directing them to scattered rock-throwers and troublemakers.

Among the items being thrown—apparently for symbolism—are soda crackers. "Keep an eye on the guy in the red cap."

"It's the guy in the white suit. He's two-thirds of the way along the fence. If the deputies walk forward, they'll run right into him."

In the ensuing hour, dozens of stones will fly. An orange makes its way to the first step. McNeilly is hit by a flying dinner—a container of stir-fried rice.

Foster steps to the microphone: "We are the American Knights of the Ku Klux Klan—mad, bad and dangerous to know."

Imperial Wizard Jeffrey Berry of Indiana, a self-styled minister, offers a prayer: "We pray that no violence will break out, but if it does, let it be."

Brad Thompson, grand dragon of the state of Indiana and second-in-command of the American Knights, breaks into a slur-laced invective against blacks, Jews, gays and foreigners. The crowd is now in a lather.

"You people hate what you do not understand," Thompson tells them. "I hate what I do understand. That is the difference between you and me."

Then, as if it were simply part of a nightclub act, Thompson steps back and speaks, almost as an aside, to the furious protesters.

"We get pretty emotional up here, people. Relax."

The security fence is still shaking. Police are ordered to take out pepper-spray canisters. At Oxford Centre, police officers monitoring the crowd try to figure out which way the spray will drift if it's used. Abruptly, the crowd eases up. The spray won't be used as police and sheriff's deputies inside the fence calm the crowd.

Steve Bowers—his real name is Stephen Nastasi, son of a Philadelphia store owner—is introduced. He is the hydra, or second-ranking Klan officer in Pennsylvania, and head of the neo-Nazi Adolf Hitler Free Corps.

"I'm an American Nazi and I hate everybody," Bowers shouts.

The strangely attired Clement is introduced. He is the second-ranking Nazi in the Adolf Hitler Free Corps, and he promises the crowd a race war.

"I am here because I hate your guts. I'm here because I worship your death," Clement rasps. "We are eager to participate in this holy race war. This is the beginning of the apocalypse."

More stones fly. A rock glances off the upper stairs of the building. Foster steps to the microphone: "The (deleted) who threw this can meet us out back."

At this point, county police with gas masks on their faces form a wedge and force their way to the fence closest to the speakers. They arrest one man for throwing stones, and the crowd cheers.

Foster announces there is something wrong with the microphone and suggests that Jewish agents in the city are tampering with the sound system.

Of an estimated 100 or more hurled objects, one finally finds its mark. A black-robed Klan "nighthawk," or security officer, is hit in the shoulder. He adjusts his hood and the speakers go on.

With their permit expiring at 3 p.m., Foster closes the proceedings. "Let's pack it up. We're out of here," he says.

It ends like comic opera. Clement, the jumpy storm trooper in a ski mask, rushes to the microphone.

"Hail Jefferson Davis!" he shouts. "Hail Nathan Bedford Forest," who founded the Klan in 1865.

A pair of robed nighthawks grabs the still-shouting Clement by the arms and pulls him back inside.

IT'S OVER

Across the street, police begin to hustle people out of the fenced-in area.

"The rally is over. The permit has expired. Please leave the area," a county officer says through a bullhorn.

Costa and city police Sgt. David Allman breathe sighs of relief.

"I had a bad feeling about today. It could have been ugly," says Allman, who has been relaying orders from headquarters to his troops on the ground. "The Klan stands for nothing but hatred and evil."

Costa, outfitted in full riot gear, praises his officers and the demonstrators who mostly have kept their emotions under control.

Murphy comes down from his perch and points to the rocks thrown by the crowd. The projectiles sit at the feet of the statue of the late mayor Richard S. Caliguiri. The statue was wrapped in black plastic while Klansmen spoke.

Much court wrangling during the past week had been over the distance city police sought to put between pro- and anti-Klan forces. The final settlement reduced the buffer from 200 feet to 135.

"Is the police photographer here?" Murphy asks. "We ought to get pictures of these stones so if they come back, we can go into court and show why we want 200 feet."

Moments later, he walks to the steps where a swastika had flown earlier in the day. With an aide, he carefully pulls away the black wrap from the Caliguiri statue.

Grant Street is quiet and empty once again.

This story was reported and written by staff writers Mackenzie Carpenter, Robert Dvorchak, Ervin Dyer, Michael A. Fuoco, Monica L. Haynes, LaMont Jones, James O'Toole, Dennis B. Roddy, Bill Schackner, Milan Simonovich, Jonathan D. Silver, and Lawrence Walsh.

Citizen's groups fight against hate

APRIL 6, 1997

By Jan Ackerman

The region's fight against hate groups didn't begin when white men came to town dressed in bed sheets.

In Monroeville, a racial hate flyer circulating at Gateway High School two years ago prompted formation of a local group that tries to fight racism at its roots.

In the Allegheny Valley, an incident in which a black teen-ager was beaten by white thugs in Harrison brought the Alle-Kiski Community Relations Council into existence.

Some Washington County residents formed a task force in 1989 when racial incidents erupted around the Mel Blount youth home in Buffalo. The Washington-based Committee for Racial Equality continues to operate, one of the oldest groups of its type in the state, said William Lacey, one of the group's founders.

"Our mission is to eradicate racism within ourselves and within our community," Lacey said. "It is a 24-hour job."

Out of both subtle and blatant incidents of discrimination and hatred across Western Pennsylvania, citizens' groups have sprung up to sponsor seminars, education programs and church services. They bring in speakers and try to encourage dialogue.

Yesterday, members of some of these groups, under the banner of the Pittsburgh Coalition to Counter Hate Groups, gathered in Market Square to hold a rally to counteract the Ku Klux Klan rally at the City-County building on Grant Street.

Leaders of the groups say that standing up against the Klan is an easier mission than getting people who don't consider themselves biased or who don't think about the issue to acknowledge and deal with their own prejudices.

"As long as we talk about this guy from Punxsutawney, we don't have to make excuses for our own biases," said Ray Firth of the Monroeville Race Unity Forum.

Firth was referring to C. Edward Foster, a grand dragon in the American Knights of the Ku Klux Klan, who lives in Walton, near Punxsutawney, Jefferson County, and was to lead the Klan in its first Pittsburgh rally in about 70 years.

The Pittsburgh Coalition to Counter Hate Groups, the umbrella organization that organized yesterday's counter-demonstration in Market Square, has been fighting all kinds of hatred for about 19 years, said Barney Oursler, a co-founder.

The coalition passed out banners and signs saying, "Not in Our Town." That theme is based on a video that tells the story of residents in Billings, Mont., who joined together when their neighbors were under attack by white supremacists.

In Western Pennsylvania, hate does talk in isolated incidents that continue to plague communities and erupt in school districts, where the young have learned hatred from the adults around them.

Last fall, six students were suspended from Slippery Rock High School in Butler for using racial slurs and for harassing the half dozen black students who attend school there.

In October, a Derry couple was forced off the road and their car was damaged in what police said was a racial attack. In November, volunteers joined in to re-paint the Resurrection Church in West Mifflin after satanic obscenities, swastikas and white power symbols were painted on the church.

In 1995, a teacher at Trinity Middle School in Washington County received a 20-day suspension on charges that he used a racial slur referring to a black student. That same year, some schools in Washington County were plagued by racist incidents, including black puppets with nooses around their necks and Ku Klux Klan cards slipped into student locker vents.

Firth said the flyer circulated at Gateway High School in March 1995 prompted high school students to demand that adults in the community take some action.

The flyer included a copy of a Pennsylvania Game Commission logo and a message calling for hunting minorities.

Firth praised the school district for its quick response to the incident. Four white Gateway students were suspended and the school district outlined plans for programs to heighten sensitivity to racial issues.

Those programs could be tested: Foster has said he wants to hold a Klan rally at the Gateway School District later this year.

In northern Allegheny County, the Pittsburgh North Anti-Racism Coalition was formed after a local peace group decided to explore relationships between economic downturns and racial problems.

What the group found was that blacks didn't feel entirely welcome in the predominantly white North Hills. At the same time, whites feared that life in the North Hills wasn't typical of what their children would experience when they moved to areas with more diverse populations.

"Our concerns are that as things go, (racism) in the North Hills is more covert than overt," said Mary Sheehan of McCandless, a spokesperson for the Pittsburgh North Anti-Racism Coalition.

The coalition recently confronted the North Hills school board when it passed a resolution asking the government to pay for the cost of educating children who live in homes owned by the U.S. Department of Housing and Urban Development.

The coalition believes schools should support a mandated HUD plan that would create housing opportunities in Allegheny County's suburbs for people who used to live in a Braddock housing project.

"When hate talks, we have the right to say no," said Anita Fine of New Kensington, a spokeswoman for the Alle-Kiski Community Relations Council.

Fine said the council, which sponsors seminars and educational programs on all forms of discrimination in the Allegheny Valley, came into existence after a 14-year-old black youth was attacked in Harrison in 1992. She said his jaw was fractured and he was blinded in one eye.

The attack was so "horrific," Fine said, that a group of residents placed an advertisement in the local newspaper vowing not to tolerate racial hatred in their community. She said so many people wanted their names printed on the ad that the group had to place a second ad to accommodate the signers.

Unity thrived at Market Square peace gathering

APRIL 6, 1997

By Jonathan D. Silver

Banners fluttered, voices boomed and unity thrived yesterday afternoon in Market Square as about 50 speakers denounced racism and preached tolerance during a tranquil anti-Ku Klux Klan rally that drew about 3,000 people.

Contrasted with the charged atmosphere on Grant Street where the Klan rallied, and that on Cherry Way and Fourth Avenue, where a scuffle broke out and tensions ran high, Market Square was the picture of serenity and as festive as a country fair.

There were blacks, whites, Puerto Ricans, Sikhs, Muslims and Jews standing side by side. Priests dressed in collars stood watching the panorama unfold along with families, white bikers and spikey-haired punks.

A group of young black men with faces partially covered by black bandannas who joined the rally toward the end identified themselves as gang members, said Barney Oursler, a rally organizer.

Peppered by a spring drizzle for much of the four-hour gathering, the diverse crowd of all ages, races and ethnicities cheered, held signs aloft, clapped and yelled anti-racist slogans as speaker after speaker ascended to a stage in the square's northwest corner, drawing roars of approval from the crowd.

"Hate and bigotry does not create one job," said Lou Gerard, secretary treasurer of the United Steelworkers of America.

"If what they stood for wasn't so serious, they'd be humorous," said Allegheny County Commissioner Bob Cranmer, who called the Klan a "last gasp."

"They are dead, but racism and hatred aren't," Cranmer said.

"The message today is to reject the message of that crowd up on Grant Street," said Congressman William Coyne, D-Oakland. "They are spewers of hate, bigotry, intolerance. That's their heritage, all they know."

A banner strung behind the stage read "Not in Our Town"—the slogan of the Pittsburgh Coalition to Counter Hate Groups, which organized the rally—with a red swastika printed on a black background.

Placards sprouted from the swell of people, the signs bearing slogans such as "Peace," "Rx: Justice," "Don't Hate, Relate," and "In the Dark We All Look the Same."

From Mayor Murphy to local politicians, clergy members to academics, special interest activists to community leaders, each of the speakers stepped beneath a white canopy and fed the hungry crowd with words that galvanized. Their speeches lasted several minutes and ranged from messages of tolerance to political rhetoric.

They challenged the crowd, and themselves, to not be satisfied with speaking out against racism only during the rally, but to carry on the struggle in the future.

"What you say here today, you have to take it into tomorrow and the next tomorrow and the next tomorrow, and don't forget, because the Klan won't," said Lavera Brown, one of the rally's organizers and the first speaker.

At the front of the stage, Debi Goldberg and Bill Murphy took turns signing to the crowd.

Small groups of police officers—31 in all—wielding long batons blocked off all entrances to Market Square and kept an eye on the crowd, stepping in only a few times to calm down a drunk man and stave off a beggar from harassing Murphy as he went to speak.

"The hard part is to change this city," said Murphy, guarded by two plainclothes police officers. "The boardrooms and the political power structure, the universities and the employers."

Then Murphy asked everyone in the crowd to say hello to a stranger standing nearby. Everyone did, black and white people shaking hands, greeting one another and breaking out into broad smiles.

There were other politicians in the crowd, including City Council President Jim Ferlo and council members Sala Udin and Valerie McDonald.

Chancellor Mark Nordenberg of the University of Pittsburgh was there, as was Tim Stevens, president of the local branch of the National Association for the Advancement of Colored People.

But easily recognizable names and faces were only a component of the crowd. From the Hill District, the North Side, Penn Hills and neighborhoods throughout Pittsburgh and beyond, demonstrators and everyday people straggled into Market Square.

About 2 p.m. a white man with long hair and a black man with a colorful knit cap climbed up on a pair of planters near the stage and hoisted a banner that read, "New Kensington, Pa./Give Peace a Chance."

"He's a white biker. I'm a black Muslim. I didn't like whites and he didn't like blacks, and we grew to love each other in two years," said Charles Turner, "My car broke down," he said, starting to explain how the two met.

"I took him home," said his friend, Gary Walker, 32, finishing the sentence.

One of the last—and most dynamic—speakers was Carnell Womack, spokesman for the Campus Coalition for Peace and Justice.

"We want, as an organized body, to demand that this Klan mentality be wiped out from our city!" Womack thundered.

"White sheets only do not a Klan member make!" Womack shouted. "They can lurk in the shadows of respectability, and in the name of public safety, destroy the fabric of community life!"

Writers' Workshop

Talking Points

1) The first section of "Face-off with Hatred" summarizes the events surrounding a Ku Klux Klan rally in Pittsburgh, and the counter-rally and demonstrations the rally sparked. What picture does this summary portray? How is it supported in the rest of this story and in the other stories in the package?

2) Following the introductory section, the story switches from past tense to present tense. Is this effective? Discuss possible reasons for such a switch in voice.

3) In "Unity Thrived at Market Square Peace Gathering," the reporter writes: "Market Square was the picture of serenity and as festive as a country fair." What details are used in the story to support this statement?

4) Objectivity is the goal of news stories. Are these stories neutral about the Klan? About the counter-rally? Can you detect biases or sympathies in the tone of the stories?

Assignment Desk

1) Note the use of racial identification in these stories. When is it necessary to identify someone's race or ethnic background? Interview editors at a local newspaper about their policy on racial identification.

2) How many official sources are quoted in these stories? What range of other residents is included? Rewrite a version of these stories without using the voices of residents, and another without including official sources. How are these stories affected by those changes? List ways to include the voices of everyday residents in your stories.

Recalling deadline with
Robert Dvorchak

KEITH WOODS: Let's go back as far as the first word that there would be a Klan march, and some of the early planning meetings that you might have been a part of. Walk me through some of those things chronologically.

ROBERT DVORCHAK: First of all, there was an atmosphere in the city that dates back a couple of years. A motorist was stopped by suburban police, and he ended up dead. His name was Jonny Gammage. He was a cousin of a Steelers football player. It was a pivotal moment, and it crystallized people's feelings on racial issues, and police, and all kinds of things.

So there's a racially charged atmosphere, because Jonny Gammage was black, all the police officers were white. None of them has ever been convicted of any wrongdoing, although everybody seems to be unanimous in the sense that if you were stopped for a traffic violation, you shouldn't end up dead seven minutes later if you're in police custody.

So that basically heightened everybody's racial awareness.

Now, unrelated to that, you have the KKK, which has an element in Pennsylvania, and particularly western Pennsylvania. They had been seeking a permit from the city to march in a predominantly black neighborhood called Homewood. There had been a certain number of killings and crime that happened on Formosa Way.

The KKK wants to march in a predominantly black neighborhood to essentially say, "We're going to take back the streets. We're going to clean up crime in this area." But really, what they were doing was agitating racial tensions, which are already high.

The city is thinking, "We can't allow that to happen." So they fought it. When you fight a permit, it no longer is a racial issue; it becomes a First Amendment issue, and you have people getting involved on both sides.

Now, the KKK is looking at its own situation, and it says, "Well, rather than just march on Formosa Way, maybe we can have a bigger impact if we have a general demonstration in the city."

So they changed their tactics, too. And again, the city fights it. The mayor takes a position that we don't want the KKK in our city, and he's got a lot of popular support on that view. But the courts are saying, "They have a legitimate right to have their views espoused, no matter how repugnant they are."

So a permit is granted for them to have a demonstration downtown.

Now, this leads to all kinds of things. People are protesting the Klan presence. Some people, who support the Klan, are geared up for this. Other people, including the NAACP, asked the media, "Why don't you just ignore these people and they'll go away?"

You know, that may be a nice thought, but that's not the way things work in the real world. It would just be impossible for a news organization to ignore something that had so many elements to it. And this is all leading up to April 5, 1997, when the Klan demonstration was going to be held.

So you have an atmosphere in the city that's just roiling. The Klan is coming. There are supporters of the Klan; although they're in the minority, they are there. There are people who are repulsed that the Klan is coming, and hope to fight them and take them on. There are those who say we can't stop the Klan from coming and giving their message, but we can do something that shows that the city and the residents condemn what they're saying, and we'll have counter-meetings, counter-demonstrations, counter-events.

Can you characterize some of the conversations within the newsroom about how the newspaper would cover it? As it was unfolding, what kinds of plans were developing?

I mentioned that there were some who were saying, "If we just ignore it, it will all go away," which is unworkable. So now the question becomes, *how* do we cover this?

There was very vigorous debate through the week as we reported on some of the developments: the Klan getting its permits, and then the counter-demonstrations, and so forth. Whether we should have played these things as prominently as we did on Page One or were we just being used by the Klan to get their message out?

Essentially, we were looking at a situation that could have been a flash point for violence. There's a lot of hatred on both sides. Everybody hates the Klan. The Klan hates everybody else.

So, in a sense, we had to prepare for it almost like the police did, or the way an army would. We'd say, "Here's the situation. It could potentially escalate. We'd better be prepared. We can't just do the normal thing here."

It would be safe to say that the overriding thought was, "Well, if we're going to err, we're going to err on the side of caution, and have maybe too many people out there instead of being caught short and not having enough, and then having to react."

So you debated within the newspaper how to cover it. Can you go a little bit deeper on that, and talk about what people were saying, and where people were coming from?

There were people who said, "Wait a minute. We're overreacting here. We're playing right into the Klan's hands, because all these people want is publicity, and what we're doing is giving them the publicity they deserve, so we're being used as the mouthpiece for the Klan."

They said, "You're not going to need that many people to cover what essentially is a demonstration. Why do you want to do it that way?" What did we end up with? I think 11 people, plus photographers.

Those were the key arguments against it. One, you're playing into the Klan's hands just by being a mouthpiece for them and getting their point of view across, and two, it's just too much. It's overkill.

The counter-arguments, though, are, "We're not going to report just what the Klan is saying. We want to say: What is the message coming out of the rally for unity? What's the message coming out of the ecumenical service? What about the teach-in that the Concerned Black Citizens are having? Let's be at all of these places, and then let's see what develops."

How did you navigate through the cross-racial conversations that invariably must have come up?

I can tell you this was probably the most nettlesome issue there. Those arguments were heard and considered and we said, "Yeah, look. We appreciate your point of view."

But also there was a complexity in the sense that one of our reporters, Dennis Roddy, had written about militia groups and right-wing groups before. He had developed some contacts within the Klan, and he had written some stories about the Klan in Pennsylvania leading up to this. He said, "Look, we're not just reporting what the Klan is saying. Let's see who these people are. Let's look at some of these figures and see what kind of background they come from."

Dennis was able to establish that the leader of the KKK in Pennsylvania had a criminal record. So we were able to get beyond the face of the Klan, the hood of the Klan, and get into some of the body and substance of who these people were, which seemed to be the breakthrough.

When did that breakthrough come in the process?

This really does come later in the week. The rally was held on a Saturday, and I'd say up until Thursday and Friday, there were still a lot of heavy feelings on both sides on how this was all going to happen.

And I think one of the other arguments was, "Well, look. It's a fluid situation. We really don't know what will happen, but things can happen. We had better be prepared."

Did all of those concerns influence how these stories ran, how long they were, where they ran in the paper, any of those kinds of things?

At least indirectly. But, as I said, I think as the stories were reported leading up to the rally, almost every one was played on Page One. The idea was, "Rather than shrink from this, downplay it, or try to turn away from it, if we're going to shine a spotlight on this, let's shine the light this way."

Talk about the importance of teamwork in putting this together.

The team itself was set up ahead of time. I'm playing a dual role, in the sense that I know I'm doing the overview, but I also know that I need to be out on the street to get a real feel and a real sense for it.

My word to everybody before they went out was, "We don't know what's going to happen. There's a potential for this thing to just fizzle and be much ado about nothing, or it could turn out to be a worst-case scenario. So we've got to be prepared."

Now, if it's a journey into the unknown, my marching orders to everybody were, "Just be alert. Pay attention. Make sure you give me all the detail you can find, about whatever specific location you're at; give me detail, little subtle nuances."

I wanted them to give me a sense of what people were feeling, what they were talking about, and some of their own feelings, some of what they were experiencing, because when you're out on something like this, you're a detached observer, to be sure. That's the way reporters are trained. But you're also part of it, because you're out there on the streets.

My theory on these things is that when you're painting a picture with words, the richness of the story comes in the fine detail, not in the broad strokes. So I wanted those little pinpoint details that would bring things into focus.

One of the important keys that made this work was the diversity of the team that was assembled. We had men and women. We had black reporters and white reporters. We had a political writer following the mayor. We had our right-wing extremist expert. We had a police reporter who has a rapport with the police department and their organization, so he knows about their planning and what they hope to do. And then we had the urban affairs people and general assignment people.

So there was a definite mix of people who were assigned to both beats and general assignment, and different levels of expertise, but that's exactly what we wanted and needed to cover the story.

I note that you told people to pay attention to what they were feeling. When you send people out on a story like this, it really doesn't matter who you are or where you've come from, this kind of story invariably will have some kind of profound impact on you as you're watching it—even if it's just that you're afraid of what might happen. I wonder how you tapped into that over the course of the day?

Some of that comes from personal experience. I've been to a lot of things over the course of my career. You know what it reminded me of was the day before a battle.

I was in Desert Storm, and I ended up on one of those infamous ground combat pools that everybody talked about. So I'm living with the 82nd Airborne Division, and before the ground war starts, I'm sleeping in this little hole in the ground that I dug myself in Iraq.

So I knew, from that point on—if I didn't know it before—that when you're involved in something like this, you actually become part of it, and rather than fight that, you can tap into it.

When you're writing or reporting on these things, I think the key ingredient is to tell people what you saw. What you heard. What you felt. What you sensed. It won't work any other way.

Now, we're at the start of the day. You've given them those marching orders, and you're out there yourself. How are you bringing all of this together? Tell me how the day unfolded.

We had an editing team in the office—the managing editor, a desk editor, and some assistants. So we're in touch, either by cell phones with each other, or we know where everybody's going to be, and they're also in touch with the office. So it's like a little command and control set up.

The important thing was before we went out was to make sure we kept a good log. If something is going to happen at 9:30 a.m., make sure you note the times, the place, and the background on that.

There was a time line that was becoming apparent. Some events are happening earlier than the Klan rally.

Some people are gathering just before the Klan rally, and then there's the Klan rally itself. So we were able to get some sort of organization during the day, just by the way the events unfolded.

Some of these reports were being funneled back to the office, and they're keeping a log, and we're all keeping our own individual logs out there.

Are there details that came back to you, that really just struck you as the kind of winning thing you were looking for?

Well, we held a debriefing meeting where everybody who was outside, and everybody who was inside, the editors who were monitoring the TV and the radio traffic and so forth, all sat down in a room and said, "Well, what was it like? What happened? Everybody tell me the thing that struck them the most." That really helped to form the umbrella for the day.

You say, "What we need is an overview, a big picture of what happened, and then we have to explain what happened during the day." A decision was made to do it chronologically as much as we could because there are obviously some overlaps, no matter what happens.

And I think it was natural for it to be explained chronologically. I think it captured an ebb and flow to the day on how some of the things developed, how tensions would tighten, and then relax, and then tighten again, until ultimately there was a confrontation, and then how everything just receded.

One of the dangers in doing this kind of reporting is, if you're not out enough, if you didn't have that force out there all over the different places, you might have come back with a story that reported more on the brink of disaster and less on the normalcy that was happening elsewhere.

Exactly. I thought that was the critical element to why this thing worked, was that we had enough people out there to see these things, and to experience them themselves, and not just listen to what the police were telling us. We were able to see what was happening.

We had all these police dressed in riot gear, and fences set up, and buffer zones, and the Klan's coming. There's going to be demonstrations against the Klan. There are people who are just curious as to what's happening. There were people who were downtown who have normal business. It's a Saturday. They're shopping or whatever. And they're going to be downtown anyhow. So you have all this mix of things.

One of the things that came out of this postmortem meeting was the little old lady who was just going to get her bus. She's got a rhythm to her day. All she's doing is walking to her bus stop to catch the bus. And she's oblivious to everything that's happening around her. She just comes walking through.

I remember when they told me that, I said, "That's exactly the kind of thing that's going to bring this story alive. That's exactly the kind of thing that we need to tell the story."

What kinds of things did you learn from this experience that you want to tell other people?

Well, I think I'll go back to the military analogy again. You know, what a soldier sees from a foxhole is a very specific area in front of him or her.

So I don't have any idea what's going on in Kuwait City, but I sure do have a real good grasp of what's happening here. So rather than try to have everybody see the overall picture, I said, "Give me your snapshot. Give me that picture you're seeing in front of you."

And when I have that, I can put each one of those snapshots together, and when I look through the album, I can say, "OK, now, I have an overall picture."

I think as we were unwinding, as the copy was being put into the layout, and before the paper was out, we were saying, "Well, maybe we did overreact," or "Maybe we did have too many people." But boy, it was good to have them out there.

Recalling deadline with

Dennis B. Roddy

KEITH WOODS: Talk a little bit about what you brought to the story.

DENNIS B. RODDY: In early 1995, there was some kind of inexplicable rally in a town called Meadville, and we noticed a brief Associated Press article saying that all these people had turned out to hear a critic of the Clinton administration. When I started calling around, I realized very quickly that this had been one of those right-wing militia meetings that we'd heard rumblings about.

Because of that, I started keeping track of various right-wing groups, right-wing alliances, and inevitably, you start running into some of the stranger offshoots, such as Christian Identity, and the World Church of the Creator, and people with all sorts of fairly unsavory racial theories.

And then eventually, you start to read, and you cross-check, and you see how many of these people had also been in the Klan. And as it turns out, when the Klan decided they wanted to hold a rally in Pittsburgh, it didn't take too much backgrounding to figure out where some of the theories came from, you know, which Klansmen might be Christian Identity members, which guys were also neo-Nazis.

That was the remarkable thing about this Klan group. When we heard that they wanted to march, they said, "Why don't you do a profile of this Foster guy?" And Ed Foster [Pennsylvania grand dragon] was quite confident there was going to be no problem being profiled, because the only criminal record that was really worrisome to him was a conviction on indecent assault.

In their motorcycle days, he and some other guys raped a girl, killed her dog, and then set fire to her car. And he was sentenced so long ago that he seemed to be fairly shocked that I had been able to locate a usable record. What he hadn't considered was that I would be able to locate the prosecutor who would remember vividly such a crime in a small town.

So anyway, I went out to profile Foster, and one of the first things we noticed was that he had some Nazi regalia around there, and we pretty much determined that he wasn't simply a Klansman, but that his branch of the Klan was affiliated with a Nazi group called the Adolf Hitler Free Corps.

And I found out that the leader of that was a fellow who had started another Klan organization years back, and had been a member of David Duke's organizations. I called him and I realized we really had two profiles here, two guys with connections to groups that have, in the past, been accused of violence.

So we just kept piecing things together, and what I found was, of course, there were all the old interconnections. I mean, these guys had associations with this red-neck museum down in the Carolinas. They had affiliations with other Nazi groups, and in the case of Steve Nastasi, I found out that he was a contributor to and member of the organization that grew out of the old Populist Party—a breakaway group called the American Nationalist Union—and had been writing for their publication under his other name. Nastasi had been the leader of the Adolf Hitler Free Corps that had affiliated with Foster's branch of the Klan, also under a pseudonym.

These connections aren't unusual in these groups. But the problem is, they're just so hard to assemble and put together, so that you know all of the players, and you know which Klan group is fighting with which Klan group. These organizations have a shelf-life of about 18 months before other people get angry, or somebody else wants to control the organization, and they break away, or they splinter. I mean, one of the reasons they're in the Klan is that they can't get along with people.

So the trick was to do all of this and still get these guys to talk to me. There was a period of about a week where I was the meat dish on their hotline, calling me an agent of ZOG. And from covering the right wing, I knew that that meant Zionist Occupation Government.

They cast around trying to find something on me. Somebody called me up and said they had seen some flyer with my picture on it; my face in a crosshairs. It took them about a week to cool down, and they clipped my stories out and put them in their scrapbook.

And that was the other very worrisome thing. There was the reality that we are also their oxygen source. These guys love the publicity.

So I guess the debate that was going on at the newspaper about whether to give them the coverage or not resonated with you.

Oh, yeah. I was called by the city editor, who said, "We want you to do this profile." And there were very, very deliberate steps that I took. I said, "Well, first of all, I will go out and interview people and I will find out if they really are serious about doing this rally—if they're really doing this, or if this is a publicity stunt."

I said, "We need to find out who they are, and it needs to be something that gives them scrutiny beyond the 'So-and-so says he's not a racist, but he just loves his own race,' kind of pablum that these guys pass off, and that I have seen reporters bite on." I've seen reporters just take this at face value.

So I went out and I found the record. I found the prosecutor. I found the judge. I found all the people who knew about Foster as a rapist and Foster as a terrorizer. I found the people who had fired Steve Bowers from his job as a security guard at Villanova when they realized he was heading a neo-Nazi Klan organization. I found the records of the Hitler Free Corps members who were arrested for beating the daylights out of some poor soul down in suburban Philly.

I found all of these things, and then I went back to the newsroom and I said, "OK, now we have this information. Do we still want to do a story, and what are the ramifications?"

If this had been something we had to turn around in a day, I don't know how we would have done it, because there was so much deliberation about how much publicity, and what kind, to give these guys.

And we finally decided that we had enough to show, not simply that they intended to march, but that they were going to be a big problem for this area in days to come.

So we did the story, and I got clobbered in the letters to the editor. Absolutely clobbered. People, usually sanctimonious liberals, writing about what a scaremonger I was, or how I was playing into their hands, or how we were being cynical and profiting on the misbehavior of these guys. It was as if nobody had really *read* the story; they just had seen that we *did* a story. It was as if nobody had actually looked and seen that what we were doing was warning the community not simply that there was an active Klan here, but that it was a particularly insidious Klan, and that it was headed by people capable of, and with a history of, violence.

I mean, if we had not done that story and there had been violence, people would have called us irresponsible.

Right. You're almost in a Catch-22.

Yeah. You really are. And you're also aware that these Klan guys do love getting publicity. They really do.

Even if it's bad?

They would prefer neutral publicity. What newspaper do they think is going to give them a favorable story? I mean, the most they're hoping for is something they would consider fairly neutral, and there was no question that there was nobody on our staff who was sympathetic to the Klan. And I made that clear to them going in.

The other thing I found out is you have to play very straight with them; you don't try to chumbuddy these guys along. They know I think they're nuts. Ed Foster knows I think he's a bundle of trouble, and that I wouldn't want him living next door to me. And you know, he's agreeable to the idea that he wouldn't want me living next door to him, either. But that being said, if you play straight with these guys, generally, they're like everybody else.

Yeah. Now, take me to the day of the march. You're out there. You've got the assignment to be on the other side of the fence. What's it like?

The federal judge who ordered the city to grant them the permit to hold the rally had said the city was under no obligation to put anybody on the other side of the fence, and in fact, everybody else had to be somewhere else. So we actually had to argue with the police and get a police commander to countermand his underlings' decisions, and let us be up closer to the Klan.

Prior to that, I went behind the fence to start working the crowd and to try to figure out who was who, because we were very concerned that some of the anti-Klan groups had a reputation for being as violent as, or in some cases, more violent than, the Klansmen themselves.

A few thousand people came to confront the Klan. And one of the first things I did was I started looking for things that would signal racist groups there. In this case, it wasn't too darned hard. I mean, I found one kid with a swastika shirt.

But I found a young woman who, as it turns out, had lived in my neighborhood at one time. I said, "What are you doing here?" And she had come to support the Klan. One of the demonstrators, who I think was more amused than alarmed by her, said, "Well, what are you going to do when you get to Heaven and find out God's a black man?" And she said, "I guess I'll go to hell."

So I got some tremendous interplay between these two groups that showed what the gulf was, and I just basically wrote it up as straight narrative.

While I was over there, I saw the old lady who was on the way to get to her bus. I thought, "Oh, my God." This is either an assassin disguised as an old lady, or it's an old lady who somehow, inexplicably, got through there.

And I went up to talk to her, and she touched her mouth and ears, and I realized she could not speak. Basically, my first thought was, "I've got to get her out of here." It would just be intolerable if she got hurt, with so many people around aiming to protect half the world. So we wrote notes back and forth, and she had trouble writing, too, but I said, "What are you doing here?" And she wrote down a number and letter—she wrote down 71D. And I said, "Hamilton bus?" And she nods and writes down "71D, Hamilton bus." She was just going to get her bus. The paramedics who were on hand quickly moved her out of there and got her to wherever she had to be, I hope.

Then I went back up to the other side, and that's when the Klan came out, and that's also when people started throwing rocks, and small batteries, and pieces of pavement they were able to pull out of the parking lot. Just a ton of stuff. And the problem was that reporters were between the Klan and the demonstrators, so we actually were the ones who were getting hit with stones more frequently than they were hitting Klansmen.

From there, it was sort of like covering the citizen comment portion of a municipal meeting, except in hell.

Can you give readers some tips, something that you've learned from this experience beyond the "Be prepared" part, which obviously seems to be huge for you.

I guess I learned that the strongest reporting has a very clear narrative to it. You start somewhere and finish somewhere. It's good to have an inverted pyramid to start with, to give people a sense of it. But if you're really going to put people in the place, you need to be able to tell the story from start to finish, and in many ways, what I learned by this is that there is a way of writing that is almost cinematic.

If you look at the reporters as cameras, you realize you want to set up cameras from every possible angle to really give a sense of what's going on. And you're simply changing perspectives. You're changing from the anger of the crowd, to the hatred of the Klansmen, to the concern of the police, to the befuddlement of the old lady who somehow wandered right into the middle of it on the way to get to her bus.

If you're taking on something this big and intend to be comprehensive, you've got to treat your reporters, in many ways, as camera units, and have everybody give their narrative and then splice it together, like you're splicing film. If they write it so that you can see what's happening, and hear what's happening, then you're really splicing together a movie narrative.

The Boston Globe

William Doherty

Finalist, Team Deadline Reporting

William Doherty is a legal writer for *The Boston Globe.* He was born and raised in Boston and graduated from Boston College and Suffolk Law School. He joined the *Globe* in 1972 from the *Boston Herald-Traveler.*

Doherty returned to reporting last year after 10 years as an assistant metro editor. He has also been a member of the Spotlight Team, the *Globe's* investigative unit. But most of his career has been spent covering state and federal courts and legal affairs.

From the start, the case of the British au pair on trial in a Massachusetts court for killing the baby in her care was *The Boston Globe's* story. When the judge made a startling 11th hour decision to sentence her to time served, Doherty and *Globe* staffers Don Aucoin, John Ellement, and Brian MacQuarrie had just a few hours to report and craft a well-organized deadline account that anticipated and answered readers' questions about the latest twist in a puzzling case.

Finding no malice, judge gives Woodward freedom

NOVEMBER 11, 1997

Louise Woodward, the 19-year-old British au pair who faced life in prison for the death of a baby in her care, walked from a Cambridge courtroom to freedom last night after a judge reduced her murder conviction to involuntary manslaughter and sentenced her to 279 days—the time she already spent behind bars since her arrest.

In a day filled with delays and drama, Judge Hiller Zobel used his power to correct what he called a "miscarriage of justice." While the teen-ager may have been "rough" with 8-month-old Matthew Eappen, the judge wrote, she did not act with malice—a key element of second-degree murder.

"After intensive, cool, calm reflection, I am morally certain that allowing this defendant on this evidence to remain convicted of second-degree murder would be a miscarriage of justice," the judge wrote.

The ruling—and Zobel's sentence—touched off a new wave of emotions in the trial, which has been televised live worldwide and has made international headlines.

Cheers erupted from crowds outside the Cambridge courthouse and inside a pub in the teen-ager's tiny hometown of Elton, England. Patrons there joined millions of others watching the live broadcast of the judge's decision.

But the rulings also sparked cries of outrage. Last night, more than 75 people called the *Globe,* most of them to say they believed Zobel's ruling was an injustice to baby Matthew.

While defense lawyers said they were pleased with the outcome, prosecutors said it "trivialized" Matthew Eappen's death. Meanwhile, one juror said Zobel's decision to set Woodward free was "a complete injustice."

Zobel could have sentenced Woodward to up to 20 years in prison for the death of the baby, who slipped into a coma Feb. 4 after a skull fracture and brain hemorrhaging. "In selecting the sentence here I do not denigrate Matthew Eappen's death nor his family's grief," Zobel said.

Before announcing the sentence, Zobel asked Woodward if she wanted to say anything. "I just maintain what I said at my last sentencing—that I am innocent," she said.

Vicky Woodward, 18, Louise's sister, told reporters yesterday that a joyous and stunned Louise phoned her in Elton shortly after the sentence, according to early editions of several London newspapers.

"She was expecting to get 10 years in prison, so she couldn't believe it," Vicky Woodward is quoted as saying, according to the *Sun,* a London tabloid. Louise, she said, was "just looking out over Boston from her hotel room, she was eating Ferrero Rocher chocolates."

Last night, media representatives and state troopers congregated outside the Harborside Hyatt Hotel at Logan Airport, where Woodward and her parents, Gary and Susan Woodward, were reportedly spending the night. Hotel officials refused to comment.

Though Zobel's ruling ultimately set her free, Woodward showed little reaction as the sentence was imposed. Her parents embraced, and her father appeared to cry.

Prosecutors and defense attorneys alike said they will appeal, and Woodward agreed to stay in Massachusetts pending the outcome. The state probation department will keep custody of her passport.

At a press conference after yesterday's hearing, Elaine Whitfield Sharp, one of Woodward's lawyers, said her client wants to indulge in the simple pleasures of freedom after nine months in prison. All she wants, Sharp said, is "to walk to the end of the corner. To catch a bus. To buy a Coke. To make herself a cup of tea. To be a free person."

At a separate press conference, Middlesex District Attorney Thomas F. Reilly said Zobel's decisions "sickened and saddened" him. "I don't believe there was any justice for Matthew Eappen in that courtroom today," Reilly said. The 279 days Woodward served, he noted, were only a few days longer than Matthew's brief life.

Reilly said the Eappens were "devastated."

"Say a prayer for them," he said. "They were victimized once, and they were victimized again" by "an incredibly bizarre series of events."

Meanwhile, Barry C. Scheck, the leader of the defense team, said the attorneys' strategy, and the testimony of their medical experts, will provide a pattern for others who may stand wrongly accused of child abuse due to shaken-baby syndrome.

In his decision, quoting Oliver Wendell Holmes and John Adams, Zobel wrote that the jury's verdict should be overruled in "the interests of justice."

In his view, Zobel said, Woodward was frustrated by her inability to quiet Matthew's crying. The evidence showed she was "a little rough" with the baby and acted out of "confusion, inexperience, frustration, immaturity and some anger, but not malice."

"The roughness was sufficient to start (or restart) a bleeding that escalated fatally," the judge wrote. "This sad scenario is, in my judgment, after having heard all the evidence and considered the interests of justice, most fairly characterized as manslaughter, not mandatory-life-sentence murder."

At a 3 p.m. sentencing hearing, prosecutor Gerard T. Leone Jr. argued that Woodward should serve between 15 and 20 years in prison for Matthew's death. "The defendant has not acknowledged doing anything to Matthew Eappen that would equate with manslaughter," Leone said. "The defendant has never, never shown any remorse for the killing of Matthew Eappen."

But defense lawyer Andrew H. Good urged Zobel to release Woodward with credit for the time she already served at MCI-Framingham while awaiting trial. The fact that Woodward maintained her innocence, Good argued, should not be held against her.

After the statements, Zobel took a 25-minute recess, then announced his sentence: time served.

The 17-day trial, which ended Oct. 30, touched off a heated public debate on the issues of child care and working parents. Both Eappens are physicians.

Prosecutors alleged that Woodward violently shook and slammed Matthew, fracturing his skull and causing fatal bleeding. But the defense claimed the injuries were perhaps three weeks old, and began to bleed again that day, probably when the baby was slightly jarred.

After Zobel announced the sentence, Leone asked the judge to delay releasing Woodward until the state could file an appeal. But the judge rejected the request, effectively setting Woodward free.

If the manslaughter option had been available to the jurors, they might have selected it, Zobel said—not as a compromise, but because it matched one view of the evidence.

Zobel described that view: that Matthew had a pre-existing blood clot and Woodward handled him roughly, with excessive force that caused fatal rebleeding and death.

But the jury never had a chance to consider manslaughter. In a major gamble, defense lawyers persuaded Zobel to exclude the lesser charge as an option for the jury. Confident that Woodward's testimony and their medical evidence was strong, the defense adopted the "all or nothing" stance, hoping to avoid any compromise manslaughter verdict.

Zobel instructed the jury that the only options were to acquit Woodward or find her guilty of first- or second-degree murder.

At a press conference last night, Whitfield Sharp proclaimed: "Louise is innocent. Louise is free. And Louise thanks all of you who continued to believe in her through the darkest days of her life."

John Ellement, Ellen O'Brien, and Judy Rakowsky of the Globe staff and Globe correspondent Josh Trudell contributed to this report.

Lessons Learned

BY WILLIAM DOHERTY

Courtrooms often serve as stages on which our moral values are played out.

But the emotional appeal of the Louise Woodward trial and the gnawing social issue at its center—the child-care dilemma in dual career families—topped any of the hundreds of trials I have covered during the past 25 years.

From that first day in February when the *Globe* broke the news that a baby in Newton, Mass., was in critical condition and his au pair had been charged with abusing him, the paper devoted enormous resources to reporting the story.

We had reporters in the courthouse every day and used our ties to sources in the courthouse, the prosecutors office, and the defense team to complement the daily trial coverage.

But we also went beyond this standard fare: We examined au pair agencies, asked specialists unassociated with the case to evaluate the medical evidence, cast a critical eye on the media coverage, and analyzed how the young au pair came across on television.

The day Judge Hiller Zobel reduced the verdict and set Woodward free was the most dramatic twist in the trial.

His decision in the morning to reduce the verdict from murder to manslaughter was applauded by many. But later in the day, when he released her with 279 days served, he was almost as widely criticized.

The judge released his written opinion in the morning on the Internet. But when a power outage delayed the transmission more than an hour, clerks rushed to make old-fashioned paper copies.

Hours later, at 3 p.m., Zobel was back in court, setting Woodward free.

During the trial, the judge held daily off-the-record briefings sessions for reporters. He answered questions about procedure and the law and tried to explain the American justice system to the large delegation of British press.

Although the judge was talking, the lawyers in the case were not. Before the trial started Zobel warned them about court rules, which restrict what attorneys can say about a case. They interpreted it as a gag order and clammed up.

Woodward's parents also were silent during the trial, as least for the American press, as was the au pair, Louise Woodward, herself.

The night of the jury verdict Zobel offered jurors a chance to return to the courtroom to answer reporters' questions in return for not being chased by the press in the days ahead. They declined to do so.

Zobel sealed the names and addresses of the jurors for their protection. But some who were located afterward talked about the verdict. More outspoken were several alternate jurors who did not agree with the verdict of the deliberating jurors.

Besides the main story, our ASNE entry explained to readers what the legal basis was behind the judge's decision. We examined why the prosecutors felt the judge's decison was hypocritical.

The defense team, while applauding the decison, vowed to appeal to get any conviction thrown out. The Eappens were stunned; Louise's hometown of Elton, England, rejoiced. We captured the conversation in the community after the change of verdict.

The Internet sites where the judge posted his decision became clogged and stopped working for periods. We told the readers why. And we interviewed former judges who disagreed with one another as to whether the sentence was appropriate.

Chicago Tribune

Louise Kiernan

Finalist, Team Deadline Reporting

Louise Kiernan is a reporter on the *Chicago Tribune*'s metropolitan news staff and runs its urban affairs team. Since she joined the *Tribune* as an intern in 1992, she has reported from Northern Ireland, covered Princess Diana's funeral, worked on the Sunday magazine staff, and contributed to the newspaper's features, commentary, books, and travel sections. Her urban affairs reporting has focused on social policy, including welfare reform and children's issues. She was one of the principal reporters for the *Tribune*'s "Killing Our Children" series, which was a finalist for the Pulitzer Prize in 1994 and the grand prize recipient of the Robert F. Kennedy Award for reporting about the disadvantaged. She also won the *Tribune*'s writing award for 1997.

When a hometown Catholic boy named Francis George was appointed Chicago's new cardinal in 1997, Kiernan and *Tribune* staffers Ron Grossman, Peter Kendall, Steve Kloehn, Dave Newbart, and Graeme Zielinski produced a comprehensive profile that traced his rise through the church hierarchy and gave vivid glimpses of the man behind the priest's collar.

From 1st grade, a man made for the cloth

APRIL 9, 1997

In first grade, Francis George was the kind of kid the nun asks to play the priest for the class demonstration of Mass.

And he was the kind of kid who had not only figured out how to pronounce the Latin, but had already memorized most of the prayers.

From the bungalow on the Northwest Side where he grew up, the path that brought Francis George home again to Chicago as the city's new archbishop was a long and meandering one. It spanned six decades and much of the globe.

But, in another sense, it seemed a short journey for this boy who always knew he wanted to be a priest and didn't let anything, not even the polio that crippled him as a teenager, slow him down.

In the press conference Tuesday that introduced him to Chicago, George referred to a few lines from a T.S. Eliot poem that expressed this sense of homecoming. They read: "And the end of all our exploring/Will be to arrive where we started/And know the place for the first time."

George may have arrived back where he started, but the place is getting to know him for the first time.

The people in Chicago will learn these things about him. Francis George is an intellectual man who speaks four languages and during his summer vacations, sits in a boat in the middle of a Michigan lake and reads.

He is a well-traveled man who was once deported from India and tailed by secret police in Eastern Europe. And he is a loyal man, who still invites that first-grade teacher and the childhood friends who call him "Frannie" to the ceremonies marking his quick advance through the church hierarchy.

He is a funny man, too, who, when he was once asked in a newspaper quiz what his favorite clothes were, answered: "Usually black."

Of course, as befitting an archbishop, he is, above all, a spiritual man. There is a story people who know him like to tell about that.

When he was installed as bishop in Yakima, Wash., where he served for six years, he warned his parishioners about his bad leg. Because he wears a brace, he said, he might occasionally stumble.

"I will fall from time to time," he told them. "And I just ask you to pick me up and let us continue on."

Francis Eugene George was born on Jan. 16, 1937 at St. Elizabeth Hospital to Francis and Julia George. His older sister, Margaret Mary, was almost 6.

The family moved from the Southwest Side to Portage Park when Francis was a toddler. George's father was an operating engineer for Chicago's public schools. His mother worked at an advertising agency until she had her children.

They lived in a red-brick bungalow at 6121 W. Byron St., just two blocks from St. Pascal Church, a white ethnic and working-class parish.

Both parents were active in the church. Francis served as an usher and Julia was a member of the Altar and Rosary Society.

George went to the parish school, St. Pascal's Grade School, 6143 W. Irving Park Road. His first-grade teacher, Sister Rita McCabe, remembers asking him to demonstrate Mass to his classmates.

For the lesson, Sister Rita, a member of the Franciscan Sisters, set up her desk as an altar. She asked George to come up and play the role of the priest.

"He could pronounce the Latin prayers and knew many of them by heart," she recalled. "Actually, he knew almost the whole Mass."

"I think he was the smartest little boy who ever went through my classroom," said McCabe, who is 80. "I think he has always had a calling. His mother did, too. I know she always felt he would be someone special in the church."

His friends thought so, too. He always talked about becoming a priest.

He taught Dick Wermich his Latin prayers to become an altar boy. Frances Ryan—Sister Frances Ryan—felt their shared interest in the religious life kindled a friendship. He practiced Mass on the neighborhood youngsters.

Still, he was a regular kid. He was a member of the "Byron Street Gang," a handful of boys who hung around together, playing baseball in the street and riding bikes.

Friends envied "Frannie" for his bike, a strange cross between a wagon and a bicycle called an Irish Mail. They dubbed it the Franarang.

George wasn't even out of grammar school when his hopes of becoming a priest were almost crushed. At 13, he contracted polio. The disease left him with a pronounced limp and a full brace on his right leg.

He missed at least four months of school. When he returned, he managed to keep his position as first in the class and graduated from eighth grade as class valedictorian.

He decided he couldn't go to Quigley Preparatory Seminary in Chicago because it was too hard to make the bus trip on crutches.

Instead, he went to the now-closed St. Henry Preparatory Seminary in Belleville, which was a boarding school.

"The polio may have struck for a reason," said his sister, Margaret Cain, who lives in Grand Rapids, Mich. "That's when the polio struck, when he was praying to God (about where to study). It came like an answer."

He attended high school and two years of college at St. Henry's, which was run by the Missionary Oblates of Mary Immaculate, the religious order he would later join.

After Sister Rita McCabe left St. Pascal's to teach in the South, she remained George's friend. As he got older, she hoped to persuade him to join the Franciscan order.

She arranged for him to spend two summers working with Franciscan priests in the black communities of Nashville. "He seemed to really like the experience, but I didn't succeed," she said.

George entered the Oblates' order in 1957 and made his vows four years later. In 1963, he was ordained as a priest at St. Pascal's.

From St. Henry, George went to Our Lady of the Snows Seminary in Pass Christian, Miss., also now closed, and the seminary of the University of Ottawa in Ottawa, Can.

At the University of Ottawa, where George received a bachelor's degree in theology, Rev. William H. Woestman, a professor of canon law, remembers the 20-year-old student as a "Renaissance type of person."

"He is not an easy person to debate with because he is very intelligent and is quick to point out where people are wrong...but he does it with great kindness," said Woestman, who taught George in a seminar.

George spent a great deal of time in the academic world and thrived there, teaching and learning at a furious rate over the years.

He earned a master's degree in philosophy at Catholic University in Washington, D.C., and a master's degree in theology from the University of Ottawa.

He taught philosophy at the Jesuit-run Creighton University in Omaha and at the Oblate Seminary in Pass Christian.

And, at Tulane University, where George received a Ph.D. in American philosophy in 1970, he produced as his dissertation the headily titled: "Society and Experience: A Critical Examination of the Social Philosophies of Royce, Mead, and Sellars."

It was an exploration of the three leading American philosophical movements in the early 20th century, according to the professor who chaired George's dissertation committee.

In 1973, George moved to St. Paul, Minn., to serve as head of the Oblates' central province, which covers nine midwestern states. There, he is remembered as an engaging conversationalist, a bright man who liked to talk about plays, books, opera and movies.

After just 18 months, he was named the order's vicar general, its second-in-command, and moved to Rome.

As vicar general, George traveled widely, visiting the countries where the order's members perform their work, said Rev. Edward Carolan, the order's secretary.

"He is a very good, holy man," Carolan said. "He is a very well-read intellectual, very up on theology, an ardent reader and a very personable man."

George spent 12 years in the Vatican, from 1974 to 1986. Then he moved back to the United States to become the coordinator of the Circle of Fellows at the Cambridge Center for the Study of Faith and Culture.

This Catholic think-tank was established by Cardinal Bernard Law of Boston to study the relationship between the Catholic faith and American culture. There, George cemented relationships with prominent officials and thinkers in the American church.

George's circulation in those circles created some trepidation when he was named the bishop of Yakima, Wash., in 1990.

What would a bureaucrat from Rome do in a diocese of 64,000 whose population was more than half Hispanic and included many migrant workers?

The answer came quickly. Soon after his Sept. 21 installation, George left for Mexico, where he took a three-week crash course in the country's culture and language.

He made bringing together the diocese's Anglo and Hispanic populations a personal mission. He persuaded the two communities to worship together in the same churches and opened up diocesan jobs to qualified Hispanics.

In time, he forged a close relationship with the diocese, although it was never completely free of friction.

Guadalupe Gamboa, the Washington state director of the United Farm Workers union, said he felt George had some trouble relating directly to the migrant workers.

"He was a very intelligent man. Originally, I think he understood the plight of the farm workers on an intellectual level but not from the gut," said Gamboa.

Over time, though, the bishop became more sensitive and set up a series of dialogues with migrant workers, Gamboa said.

In general, very little controversy marked George's tenure in Yakima. He consolidated the Catholic schools under a superintendent. The diocese eliminated its debt, got five new priests and saw its population of Catholics increase by 6,000.

George did not have to deal with the much larger questions of the church, although by intellect and temperament he is probably more suited to them.

Instead, he was a bishop in the most pastoral sense of the word, trying to mend the small rifts that frequently occurred in the diocese.

"In a quiet diocese like this one, there are few issues that break down on liberal and conservative," said Rev.

John Murtagh, pastor of Holy Family Church in Yakima. "We're just trying to survive, to grow some apples and some wine. Liberal and conservative really don't mean much here."

George still tends to think in terms of the larger church, or the universal church. He adheres closely to the teachings of Pope John Paul II and wrote the thesis for one of his doctorates on the pope's view of inculturalism—how different cultures get along.

In Yakima, people marveled at the man who wrote lofty articles and kept tall stacks of books on his floors or tables or anywhere else there was space.

"He's a thinker, a theologian," said Monsignor Perron Auve, who was George's first chancellor at the diocese but now is pastor of St. Andrew's Church in Ellensburg, just north of Yakima. "His mind-set is very close to John Paul II. He thinks the way the pope thinks about most if not all of the issues in the church."

It came as little surprise, then, when just last April, George was appointed archbishop of Portland, a diocese that covers all of western Oregon and includes 304,000 Catholics.

One of the most controversial issues in Oregon is doctor-assisted suicide because the state has passed the country's only law permitting it. Although the law has been tied up in court since its passage, George wasted no time in fighting it.

At his installation ceremony, he denounced abortion, infanticide and suicide, saying they were "sins against the God that gives us life."

In the 10 months he worked there, George earned a reputation as a friendly and tireless leader.

In the Portland archdiocese, where about 70 percent of the Catholics aren't church members, George saw his role as a missionary.

"At receptions, he's always the last person out the door," said Rev. Paul F. Perry, the archdiocese's vicar general.

Although his parents died in the mid-1980s, George periodically returned to St. Pascal's and kept in touch with a number of his childhood friends.

When he became the first person from the parish to be named a bishop, the church invited him back to say Mass.

They went to see him, too. Friends from St. Pascal's attended his installations in Washington and Oregon. Some traveled to Rome last June for the pallium ceremony, which recognizes archbishops named to their sees in the previous year.

At the ceremony, the pope did not make George kneel to receive the pallium as archbishops usually do.

"As a sign of his care," said Rev. Ronald Metha of the Yakima diocese, "the pope deliberately got up from his chair so Archbishop George wouldn't have to kneel and get back up. He knew that would be painful for him."

George remains close to his sister and her husband, James, and vacations with them in Ludington, Mich., where they have a summer home.

Above the couple's couch in Grand Rapids, they keep a painting of the Holy Family George did at the age of 15. Tuesday was his sister's birthday, and she thinks her brother might have arranged the announcement date as a special present.

"He will teach the faith and the truth; that's his responsibility," she said. "The people of Chicago are lucky."

Lessons Learned

BY LOUISE KIERNAN

For about four months, I became what can only be described as a handicapper of Roman Catholic hierarchy.

After Chicago's much-beloved archbishop, Cardinal Joseph Bernardin, died in November 1996, reporter Steve Mills and I were assigned to figure out who would be his successor.

So we set about learning everything we could about the church and its likely candidates for the Chicago post.

We found out that one bishop liked to play computer Scrabble; that another reportedly forced out a college instructor whose teaching conflicted with his own conservative beliefs; that a third was such a charmer he talked Pope John Paul II into visiting New Jersey.

We learned what day of the week the news usually came and how the chosen candidate was notified of his appointment. We analyzed the chances of the country's prominent bishops by birthdate, size of diocese, and purported chumminess with the pope. We traveled to the cities of the leading contenders. We scoured their church newspaper columns for clues.

Just about anywhere else, this process might seem like overkill. But not in Chicago. Here, the archbishop is more than a religious figurehead. He is politician and power broker, with a pinch of pop star thrown in.

For weeks, local gossip columns tossed about prospects' names like so much confetti. We got news releases from far-flung church officials proclaiming their utter lack of interest in the post.

And when a little-known archbishop from Oregon arrived at O'Hare Airport on April 7 amid rumors of an impending announcement, the local television stations carried it live.

When we got confirmation later that night that he was, indeed, the one, my heart sank.

It was someone we knew almost nothing about.

Francis George, the archbishop of Portland, had made our list, but just barely. We had nothing more on him than a handful of newspaper clips and a photocopied biography.

That's the first lesson: Be prepared, but be prepared to be unprepared.

We sent reporters to most of the places where Francis George had lived or worked: Washington, Oregon, downstate Illinois, and Chicago's Northwest Side. My assignment was to work the phones and write the story.

Our months of groundwork proved useful in some respects. We knew what information to look for and where to find it.

Sure, "Frannie" George was a good kid, but how good? Nice? Come on, even serial killers' neighbors describe them as nice.

And smart? Virtually everyone we talked to said Francis George was smart. But that said nothing.

We needed stories, anecdotes, examples. That's the second lesson: Get details.

I tracked down the Tulane University professor who served as chairman of George's dissertation committee. The title of the young priest's dissertation? "Society and Experience: A Critical Examination of the Social Philosophies of Royce, Mead, and Sellars."

That said smart.

We knew what pictures Francis George drew for his high school magazine, what he wore to play pretend Mass, what the migrant workers in Yakima didn't like about him. So what?

We needed the theme that defined this man's life, that said who he was and what that meant for Chicago.

That's the third lesson: Focus.

I read through everyone's notes and highlighted the interesting bits, looking for patterns. One thread emerged.

Francis George was an intellectual and spiritual man, yes, but not a contradictory or even particularly complex one.

He was, at heart, a kid who had wanted to be a priest so badly he wouldn't allow anything, not even polio, to stop him.

The story had its bones. Now we had to flesh it out.

Throughout the afternoon, I kept refining and revising drafts as more information came in. Moving up a detail here. Cutting out a mediocre quote there.

That's the fourth lesson: Write early and often.

The editing process must have been painless because I don't remember it. By 9 p.m., we were done.

And the final lesson?

Come in a little late the next day.

"The Legend on the License" revisited: A note from the editor

In a 1980 essay, John Hersey, the reporter and novelist—his nonfiction classic *Hiroshima* is a skillful example of narrative reconstruction—drew an obvious but important distinction between journalism and fiction.

"There is one sacred rule of journalism," Hersey said. "The writer must not invent. The legend on the license must read: NONE OF THIS WAS MADE UP."

The year after Hersey's essay, "The Legend on the License," appeared, Janet Cooke, a young reporter for *The Washington Post,* was awarded the Pulitzer Prize for "Jimmy's World," a graphic story that explored the life of an 8-year-old heroin addict. The paper was forced to return the prize when it was discovered Cooke had invented the child, along with various facts on her own résumé. Certainly not the first example of fabrication in the history of journalism, the incident sparked a firestorm of criticism and soul-searching in the newspaper business. It also ended the career of a promising young writer.

Nearly two decades later, the Janet Cooke case remains a cautionary tale for reporters and editors about the perils and penalties of fabrication. Unfortunately, it hasn't stopped it from happening as events in the spring of 1998 demonstrated.

In May, the *New Republic* fired Stephen Glass, a young associate editor, after learning that he had fabricated characters and quotes in 27 of the 41 articles the magazine had published in the last few years.

Then in June, *The Boston Globe* reported that it had asked for and received the resignation of one of its metro columnists, Patricia Smith, after she admitted fabricating people and quotations in four of her columns. Earlier in the year, Smith's work had been honored with the Distinguished Writing Award for commentary/column writing by the American Society of Newspaper Editors. She was also a finalist for the Pulitzer Prize and had won a national reputation as a powerful poet, writer, and role model for writers. Subsequently, the *Globe* asked ASNE to rescind the award and the editors' association agreed. "There is no place in journalism for fabrication of any kind," the society board said in a statement.

Since then, *Globe* editor Matthew V. Storin said, in a note to the paper's readers, "in addition to the four columns in which Smith has admitted fabrications, (we) have found 20 more for which we cannot document the identities of individuals mentioned...the *Globe* will ask Smith to cooperate in a review of 28 columns from 1995 that also have been questioned." None of her columns submitted for the ASNE Award or the Pulitzer apparently contained any fabrications, Storin said.

As a result, the columns by Smith that were initially honored do not appear in *Best Newspaper Writing 1998,* where they were to have been published. This marks the first time in the award's 20-year history that a winning writer has been stripped of the award. Sadly, it is not the first instance of fabrication by a journalist; in fact the Smith case was one of several highly publicized instances of unethical behavior by journalists that surfaced in the spring of 1998.

The journalistic crimes of Stephen Glass and Patricia Smith and the issues they have already raised about media credibility, racism, shoddy editing, and a decline in standards will be much-debated. For the readers of *Best Newspaper Writing,* the cases remain an object lesson for every journalist. The ASNE's journalism contest and the series of books it spawned has always been and will always be about excellence in writing and the reporting that underlies it. *Best Newspaper Writing* honors literary grace but never at the expense of accuracy and honesty.

Journalists who want to invent characters, dialogue, or scenes can always write screenplays, short stories, novels, or in the case of Patricia Smith, compelling poetry. Those who choose journalism must always remember—and live by—The Legend on the License. When they ignore it, they betray not only themselves but their readers, every other journalist, and anyone who admires the power of journalism to inform, educate, and inspire.

"As anyone who has ever touched a newspaper knows, that's one of the cardinal sins of journalism: Thou shall not fabricate. No exceptions. No excuses."

Those are Patricia Smith's words, written in her final column for *The Boston Globe*.

Christopher Scanlan
July 1998

SCRIPPS HOWARD NEWS SERVICE

Dale McFeatters

Finalist, Commentary

Dale McFeatters is a senior editor, columnist, and editorial writer for Scripps Howard newspapers. He decided at age 5 to go into the newspaper business after accompanying his reporter father to a fire that destroyed the city's largest railroad station. McFeatters has been with Scripps Howard in Washington, D.C., since 1969, first as regional reporter for the *Birmingham Post-Herald* and later as a member of the national staff, assistant managing editor/news, and managing editor of the 50-person bureau. He came to Washington from his hometown newspaper, *The Pittsburgh Press,* where he was a general assignment reporter. He has reported nationally and internationally for SHNS and now specializes in economic, national security, and foreign policy issues, and writes a regular column. McFeatters graduated from Colgate University. He and his wife, Ann, Scripps Howard's White House correspondent, have two sons and a daughter, all teen-agers.

In "Dr. Jekyll and Ms. Hyde," he delivers the familiar lament of the parents of teen-agers with a blend of irony and analogy that makes his particular misery an experience that feels universal, touching, and funny.

Dr. Jekyll and Ms. Hyde

NOVEMBER 6, 1997

My daughter loves me deeply for two reason: I have a driver's license and credit cards. When she is not in need of them, her communications to me are limited to "Go away" and "Leave me alone."

Not that I see her that often, usually just twice a day, when she appears briefly in the morning, emanating a scent so powerful it seems to have visible rays, and slightly less briefly at dinner, a meal she tries to get through as quickly as possible to minimize the time she spends actually face to face with her family.

She goes directly to her room and closes the door. Generally, there are two ways I know she's home. The den ceiling is leaking from one of her interminable showers. And the phone never rings. It never rings because she's always on it, and, thanks to call waiting, can ration other family members' use of the phone.

Under duress, she will admit to having parents but she does not want the fact widely broadcast. If I must be seen in public with her, it is in only one capacity: chauffeur. She and her friends have perfected the art of pretending I'm invisible...and deaf, which I soon will be if I don't regain control of my car radio.

Something awful happened to my charming, studious, thoughtful daughter at age 12. I would call it a Dr. Jekyll and Ms. Hyde situation, but since she's turned 13 it's been all Hyde. Hyde, you'll remember, was the weird, crazy one.

Her older brothers were easy. Boys don't grow up; they just grow bigger. Other parents had warned us that girls are great for the first 10 or 11 years, which she was, but it all gets paid back when they turn 12 or 13, which it is.

One mother advised, "Don't sweat the small stuff." Well, like what? "Hair, for example."

The hair. Our daughter has lovely, natural, light blonde hair, the color a lot of women pay a lot of money to have. For some reason, this color wasn't chic enough for junior high school and, after a sleepover with her cronies, the hair turned orange, not the orange of an Irish carrot-top but the kind of neon, unnatural orange used to color life rafts so they can be spotted from 30,000 feet up.

It will wash out, we were promised, and the orange did start to fade after a couple of months. Then came the Halloween sleepover. Now her hair is purple, the deep, rich purple of an automotive finish and one that will last just about as long, according to the label of the jar her mother confiscated. At least her whole head is purple. One of her friends opted for stripes.

The color will be ideal for the eighth-grade homecoming dance, one of those social events that requires D-Day-like planning among her friends, largely to huddle in a heaving mob and scream over the music while hormones blow through the gym lights like fog.

Sometimes in the course of my chauffeur's duties, a boy is pointed out as meeting an exceptionally high standard of hunkiness. My thought, which I keep to myself, is invariably the same: "Well, if you get tired while dancing with him, you can always rest your chin on his head."

My female colleagues are deeply sympathetic, generally describing the age as "difficult" or "terrible." But in seeking to be reassuring, they invariably achieve the opposite by reminiscing about their own alarming instances of misconduct when they were 13.

They always conclude by saying, "She'll grow out of it. They all do." I don't doubt she will survive her adolescence; the larger question is, will I?

Lessons Learned

BY DALE MCFEATTERS

A columnist's offspring, for the sake of both the children and the readers, should be used sparingly, but my daughter's purple hair was too much. If I have to suffer this kind of aggravation—the dye job happened while my wife was out of town—I figured to at least get a column out of it.

The subject violated one of the accepted rules of good column writing: Write what you know. I was, and remain, baffled by adolescent females. At dinner last night, she spoke twice: Disney World is boring; she wants to take up boxing.

The column proved easy to write—no lack of material—and something of a relief. I wouldn't say "cathartic" because it elicited helpful predictions of disasters yet to come: "Wait until she gets her driver's license." "If you think that's bad, try tattoos and body piercing."

A co-worker, whom I like but with whom I share little in common, sent me a note saying he found the column "very comforting. It's easy for the parents of these Miss Hydes to think we're all alone. I'm really happy there are others like you experiencing the same intense misery."

And I suppose that's what a good column does.

Tracey O'Shaughnessy

Finalist, Commentary

Tracey O'Shaughnessy grew up in Lexington, Mass., where her father worked as a printer for *The Boston Globe* and her mother worked as a cabaret singer. She attended Lexington High School and The American University in Washington, D.C., where she majored in French and journalism. After an internship with Gannett News Service, she went to work as a reporter for the *Norwich* (Conn.) *Bulletin* and then returned to Washington to write features and general assignment for the *Potomac* (Md.) *Almanac*. She stayed there nearly 10 years, winning awards for her column and leaving as assistant publisher. She came to the *Waterbury Republican-American* in 1994, where she now works as Accent Editor, writing two columns a week and feature stories in addition to her editing responsibilities. She attended Georgetown University in pursuit of a certificate in theology and now attends Wesleyan University, where she is studying for a master's degree in Liberal Arts.

For the columnist, everything is grist, even a vacation. In this column, O'Shaughnessy introduces us to her special spot—a Nantucket lighthouse at dawn—and unfolds a series of reflections that illuminate the need we all have for rest, reflection, and the inspiration that a beacon can furnish.

Finding sanctity
in a lighthouse

AUGUST 31, 1997

NANTUCKET—Sankaty Lighthouse is at the far west end of Nantucket, just outside of Siasconset, where roses cloak small, gray cottages in an aromatic embrace. The lighthouse sits on a sloping ridge on this long, crescent-shaped island, and beside it sits a lonely metal swingset, whose splintery seats sway creakily in the breeze. In the past, signs led tourists to the stately old beacon, but I notice they are gone this year, as though Sankaty Light, as it is called, is reserved for those devoted enough to know the secret passage through Bayberry Lane, up the slow incline that leads to the crest of Sankaty Light.

I come here every year on my bicycle, usually in the early morning hours when Nantucket is asleep and the infamous Nantucket fog blankets the island, lending an air of mystery and nobility to the cobblestone.

It is just early enough to imagine that the island is mine and I am of the island, a native Nantucketer who knows its heather and moors and the tiny footpaths that lead to its still, salty ponds. It is a silly conceit. The island, though pacific and restful in the summer, is harsh and desolate in the winter and demands more of a hearty soul than I have to give. But for the morning, I indulge my fantasy and pedal through the thick, moist gray dawn toward the lighthouse. It is about seven-and-a-half miles through empty, glinting gray paths. Depending on the wind, it can be a rather arduous ride, indeed. But I have with me the symphony of the birds, who have been up longer than I and whose verbosity echoes through the heather and wild roses that overlay the island. If I push myself, I will reach the lighthouse just as the sun dapples through the fog and paints the harbor a brilliant, saffron yellow.

I make this ride every summer, sometimes twice, which leaves my thighs ruddy with wind and effort, quivering with exertion and memory. It is a devotion of sorts. The lighthouse and the untrammeled streets that lead back into town are a kind of altar at which I pay annual homage. It is a confessional of sorts, a large, airy, imposing penitential pew where I reflect on the year past and make oaths that may dissolve like the fog by this time next year. But I make the passage alone and with hope. Activity holds enlightenment and oceanic opportunity for reflection.

That is what a vacation should be about, not merely indolence, but inspiration. Yesterday, I saw a woman on the beach, talking heatedly into a cell phone, hands on the hips of her Ann Cole swimsuit, barking out commands into the plastic box. It reminded me of a radio report I recently heard about a man who consults with executives who are workaholics and find that today's technology is their panacea, that drug that enables them to get their fix of work without wingtips or office politics. The consultant makes his living telling such people how to vacation. How to vacation? Good heavens, have we really come to that?

I want to tell the woman with the cell phone to throw it into the cold Atlantic and walk aimlessly along the sloping beach as the tide goes out. It is curious that although we vacation with others, our best moments are those we have alone. Most epiphanies occur not among those we love, but when we are alone with our thoughts, unmoored and unconnected to the outside world. In those alone moments we gather the fortitude and faith that give us the strength to be together.

I know I am close to Sankaty Light when I reach an old wooden houseboat, dry-docked in the sea grass, as if forgotten. Ironically, the boat is called Memory. Nantucket is thatched with bike trails like this one. And I hear from my innkeeper that another such path is being constructed along the road to Polpis and Quidnet, which will link up with the path from 'Sconset, providing a long and intense ride for masochists like myself.

I greet the news with ambivalence. I am glad for the new path, which will allow me safer passage from 'Sconset back to town. But a wonderful desolation exists in this corner of the island; it is where they grow cranberries and great, green ears of corn and lettuce. Along the pond of Quidnet, regal blue herons lord with majestic silence over their briny pastures. My intrepid riding along the side of this lonely road allows me to glimpse them in their slow, elegant repose. I feel an unjust sense of proprietorship over this area; I can't help it,

I don't want it to be shared. Silly, I think, and futile. But silliness and futility are what vacations are all about.

As it turns out, I am not alone on the road to Sankaty. I see mothers with strollers, a few gangly runners and a biker or two. All of them are headed to the lighthouse; it is a marker, a touchstone. It is like a child's game: go up, touch the lighthouse, run home. This beacon is the turning point of one's constitutional.

For the most part, lighthouses like this one have been stripped of their romance; no longer is there a hope of a human inhabitant stoking tea inside, offering shelter, succor and clipped conversation. Today, Sankaty Light, like most lighthouses, is computerized, and emits a pulsating, mechanized heartbeat that, nevertheless, inspires a satisfying serenity. And so all of us are mesmerized and attracted to it.

We all need a beacon of this sort. Perhaps it is to remember that there is an end to the road, or that there is an eternal candle; that there is always an always. I think about the early morning journey all of us have taken to the lighthouse. Like monks with their matins, we all pray silently to the same God, but each of us gathers from him a different sort of inspiration. Perhaps it is not so bad that a different bike path will extend to the lighthouse. All of us need such a touchstone.

More importantly, we are hungry for the long and lonely road that leads to it. We will need to revisit it often, in our memories when days are less sunny and auspicious than this.

Lessons Learned

BY TRACEY O'SHAUGHNESSY

I have always thought that writing a potent political column seemed a glamorous sort of work. I grew up reading *The Boston Globe* and reveling in the piquant put-downs of poetic politicians, wishing one day I would be able to mimic such rhetoric.

Somehow, however, the requisite interest in politics eluded me; the more I read of it, the more weary I became. The whole rigmarole of politics seemed like repeat season on television. And yet there seemed a universe of worries, fears, dreams, desires, and epiphanies that captivated me and that I wanted to explore. I grew up a rather thoughtful and somber lass and catalogued my ever-rambling reveries in a series of journals which, if ever found, would certainly condemn me to a psychiatric ward. Although writing did not come naturally to me, the desire to write, to articulate, and to explore was incessant. The practice of trying to understand what I was thinking and draw from it some philosophical conclusion was as inherent as (it seemed to me) it was annoying.

When I turned to column writing, I used those same muscles. I used my own private contemplation to point out some universal concerns. Initially, I found all of this repulsively self-indulgent, but the more I wrote about my experiences, the more common they became and the more readers seemed to identify. As the daughter of a cabaret singer, I was used to seeing people mine their own personal lives for the amusement of others, and I often wonder whether that peculiar background was my biggest influence in writing "Sunday Reflections."

Of course, not all of my columns are enlarged journal entries. Every now and again, I do get a chance to sound off socially, using those piquant pejoratives I admired so, and admire still. But time and again, what readers say they enjoy most are my columns about my life in this wild and woolly world of ours. I have thought about this and believe it says less about me than it does about the world in which we now live, where community is strained. The more insulated we become, the more estranged we feel from one another, the more we need the honest conversation of strangers to give us the illusion of proximity. The more newspapers can do that, the more we will inhere in the readers' lives.

The most important lesson I can say that I have learned from writing the column is that those stray, seemingly parenthetical thoughts, considerations, concerns, and anxieties that one person has are not so very different from those that occupy the minds of the rest of us. And the thought that one person's thoughts, to paraphrase Emerson, can mirror a universal truth, is comforting to reader and writer alike.

The Miami Herald

Leonard Pitts Jr.

Finalist, Commentary

Leonard Pitts Jr. was born in 1957 in Orange County, Calif., and entered the University of Southern California at the age of 15 under a special honors program. He graduated summa cum laude four years later with a degree in English.

Pitts was a stringer and then the editor of *Soul,* a pioneering national black entertainment tabloid. His work also has appeared in the Los Angeles *Herald-Examiner, Oui, Musician, Billboard, Essence, TV Guide, Parenting,* and *Reader's Digest.*

Pitts also wrote for all-news radio stations KFWB and KNX in Los Angeles, was the co-creator and editor of *Radioscope,* a black entertainment radio news-magazine, and wrote for Casey Kasem's Top 40. In April 1991, Pitts joined *The Miami Herald* as its pop music critic and won an award from the American Society of Sunday and Feature Editors. In 1992 he won the National Headliner Award and became a general columnist for the *Herald* and Knight Ridder News Service. In 1993 Pitts was a Pulitzer Prize finalist in commentary and won the Green Eyeshade Award and the NABJ Award of Excellence. In 1997 he won second place for serious commentary in the Green Eyeshade.

Weighing in on the death of Princess Diana, Pitts is the columnist as a voice of conscience. With anger and bitter eloquence, he forces us to take an unflinching look at the price we all pay when fame becomes "a public body search."

We wanted too much, and paid a horrible price

SEPTEMBER 1, 1997

How many pictures of her do you suppose there were? Thousands? Hundreds of thousands? A million?

How many do you suppose would have been enough? How many before photographers and editors and people like us said: This is sufficient. This satisfies our need.

At this writing, the shock of Princess Diana's death in Paris is still fresh. There is still a numbness from this latest cold reminder that life is chance, not guarantee. And yet already, one sorrow surfaces distinct from the others: the manner of her death.

The black Mercedes in which she rode led a high-speed motor chase to escape pursuing photographers. It crashed. And just like that, she was gone. Just like that, she was dead.

It seems a grisly object lesson, its ironies sharp as razor blades. The paparazzi chased to death that which justified their existence, paid their bills and, not incidentally, made some of them wealthy. The goose who laid all those golden eggs lies dead, and there is blood on the hands of her exploiters.

And already, the people are righteous in their anger, outraged at this latest excess of "the media"—a catch-all excoriation that draws no distinction between the *National Enquirer* and *The New York Times.* A television newsperson doing a stand-up report hours after Diana's death was called a "scavenger" by a passerby.

But the hypocrisy of the people is transparent. After all, the photographers who chased Diana into that tunnel weren't badgering her on a whim, bore her no enmity. Rather, their pursuit was based in the sure knowledge that any pictures they took would find favor with magazines and newspapers and thus, with readers around the world who could not get enough of this woman.

Fame makes scavengers of us all, then. Even Diana herself was in on the deal, willing when necessary to use her celebrity toward her own ends. She used it to win sympathy, used it to mold public opinion in her battles with Prince Charles. And yes, she used it, too, to bring attention to the hungry, the sick and the suffering.

She used it, it used her. Her fame was symbiosis and incest, a handshake with the devil.

But she did her best with it, lived her life to the whir and click of the shutters. She entered a room and brought with her a sudden electrical storm, flashes of light and patches of shadow with photographers yelling, leaning in, elbowing one another, trying to capture her. For us.

And you have to wonder, how much more of her did we really need? What amount of pictures would have done the trick? How much closer did we want to be?

We'd attended her wedding, watched her bear children, seen her marriage crumble, heard secrets she whispered to friends. We knew about her eating disorders, her infidelities and insecurities. We saw her sweating in the gym.

We were not this intimate with our own families and friends. Yet we wanted more. Always, more.

Once upon a time, fame seemed one of life's nicer perks, something that raised you above the common run of women and men. Now it is a public body search, the camera lens a proctoscope. We confuse fascination with intrusion, human interest with trespass. Our descent into voyeurism has been so steep and so deep that we now know the underwear preference of the president of the United States and may soon learn about the physical characteristics of his penis and testes.

We know everything about everybody. All it has cost is their dignity. And ours.

Now it seems to have cost one woman her life.

Yet one doubts the object lesson is learned even at that price, even as we remember how a shy, coquettish girl smiling on the arm of her husband became a woman always ducking, running, seeking a lonely place where voyeurs could not intrude. Until finally she fled into a tunnel on the banks of the Seine, still racing for that lonely place she never quite found.

It is said that after the crash, with the vehicle twisted and steaming, with blood leaking, bodies torn and Diana dying, a photographer stood over the mess taking pictures.

Just one more, luv. One more before you go.

Lessons Learned

BY LEONARD PITTS JR.

We were shocked. *Everybody* was shocked. It was one of those moments when time and breathing suspend themselves and you glance from eye to eye, seeking words that would make madness make sense.

Princess Diana...dead? Not possible. Not believable.

And the shock brought with it a dawning sense of highly personal loss I found hard to understand. How could it feel personal when she was someone I'd never even met nor even had the slightest interest in?

Granted, when Magic Johnson announced that he had the virus that causes AIDS, when the news flashed that Marvin Gaye had been shot to death, there came this same insane sense that somebody I knew had been lost. But then, at least, the reaction carried some tiny grain of logic. I had followed and admired these men for years. By contrast, the way I felt about Diana caught me by surprise. I had no idea she meant anything to me until the very moment she was gone.

It was while I was in the midst of grappling with all this that the phone rang "I know you're still technically on vacation," said the boss, "but..."

Five minutes later, I was banging away on the keyboard, trying to sum up a sudden maelstrom of emotion, while at the same time keeping one eye on the clock as it raced toward a deadline just a couple of hours away.

Now you want to know what I learned from it? Geez-criminy! I don't know!

Well, maybe that's not quite true. I learned—or perhaps more accurately, re-learned—that sometimes a columnist's best work owes as much to the heart as to the head. I wrote three more pieces about Diana, all of them cooler in their reflections than the first. Yet I wasn't as happy with any of them.

I also learned—or, again, re-learned—that time is of the essence. The holy deadline is our friend, at least some of the time. Because a ticking clock has a way of squeezing a maddening babble of emotion down to the meat of the thing. When you don't have time to niggle and natter, to stare at the ceiling, ponder your navel, or consider competing approaches, the burst of writing that results often has to it a purity and a clarity you might not otherwise achieve.

The most important thing I learned, though, has little to do with writing. Diana's death—and I still think this is true,

regardless of the revelations that have come out since then—
is a cautionary tale about the tabloidization of American media and the increasing price of fame. Our interest in this
woman created an industry too influential for her own good.
And ours. Camera crews chased her, image-besotted people
lived through her, the machinery of celebrity gorged itself on
her, and even the ivory towers of American journalism found
themselves forced to attend her, or else be left behind by
readers more interested in her marital difficulties than in the
possibility of a NATO expansion.

Now she's dead. Time and breathing have unlocked themselves, life moves ahead. And you glance back and wonder:
What was that all about? And was it really, truly worth it?

Mike Jacobs
Editorial Writing

Mike Jacobs is editor and vice president of the *Grand Forks Herald.* He was born in Stanley, N.D., and graduated from the University of North Dakota with a bachelor's degree in philosophy and religious studies. He joined the *Herald* as state capitol correspondent in 1978, and served as St. Paul correspondent, editorial writer, city editor, and managing editor before he was named editor in 1984. He previously worked as a reporter for several North Dakota papers, including *The Forum* in Fargo and *The Dickinson Press,* and was managing editor of *The Morning Pioneer* in Mandan and the *North Dakota Union Farmer.*

For its coverage of the 1997 flood, the *Herald* was awarded the Pulitzer Prize for public service "for its sustained and informative coverage, vividly illustrated with photographs, that helped hold its community together in the wake of flooding, a blizzard, and fire that devastated much of the city, including the newspaper plant itself."

Jacobs is a regular contributor to his paper's editorial pages, as well as writing a column on birds. But when the Red River surged past its banks and then over the sandbag dikes hastily erected by townspeople, his commentary became an almost daily presence. His editorials speak with the compassionate voice of someone who shares his neighbors' pain while never losing touch with the journalist's responsibility to report the news.

—Christopher Scanlan

The day that changed everything

APRIL 20, 1997

Our hometown will never be the same. How could it
ever be? The catastrophe that has struck Grand Forks
calls everything into question. All of our plans and
projects will be re-evaluated in light of the enormous
events of April 1997—ice and water and fire.

Our relationship with the river has changed. Of
course, our river has flooded before, several times cata-
strophically. But it has never delivered such a stunning
blow. In the last week, the Red River has been an inex-
orable force, and its current tore at our levees and our
lives. In neighborhood after neighborhood, the water
found its level, and in most, it was well above the level of
our daily lives, in our homes and in our consciousness.

Grand Forks has sustained deep wounds, and there
will be scars. On Saturday evening, as we write, the
river continues its historic rise and fire is tearing at the
heart of downtown. Thousands of buildings are immersed. Several of the town's most historic structures
are alight. There is no apparent power that can save
them. These buildings were part of our past.

The *Herald*'s buildings may have been among them.
We can't know. Water keeps us from our usual workplace. We are producing this edition at a UND computer lab. The loss of these structures—unwitnessed by
most of us—was among the unexpected, dramatic moments of our community's catastrophe. Our notions
about ourselves must also have changed. Thousands of
us found the strength of character to help selflessly,
even heroically. As our homes were destroyed, we reminded each other that "It's only stuff," and that "So
many others have it so much worse."

We must have wondered, all of us, whether any
community anywhere had ever suffered so much, and
yet we know that others have. Miraculously, we have
been spared loss of life. Marvelously, we have found
friendships we didn't know about, as strangers came to
offer labor, called to offer shelter, reached out to offer
strength. Could it have been so in any other town? Yes,

perhaps. But never on such a scale in our hometown. And it is in that spirit, from that indomitable strength, that our hometown will go forward. It is going to be a difficult time. Let us begin this morning.

Today, we remember another community not unlike our own—geographically isolated, demographically homogenous, chronologically mature. Rapid City, S.D., was devastated by a flood in the early 1970s. The heart of the town was destroyed. Rapid City remade itself, embracing the stream that struck it. Now, Rapid City is among the liveliest cities of the Plains, economically successful and culturally unique. This is the status that Grand Forks has long sought, most often successfully. Can this be our city's destiny? It is certainly our city's opportunity.

Writers' Workshop

Talking Points

1) This editorial seems more like a speech, rallying readers to support one another and their community. What language does the writer use to encourage readers?

2) The writer wrote this editorial without knowing the full effects of the disasters on the newspaper. How does it affect the tone of the editorial?

3) This editorial is full of emotional language and images. How does it serve as a catharsis for readers who are facing the same destruction?

Assignment Desk

1) The *Grand Forks Herald* won the Pulitzer Prize for public service for its coverage of the disasters that hit the area. Read those articles to see what inspired the editorials.

2) Write an editorial based on dramatic events in your community that encourages positive action.

A cruel blow, a tough recovery

APRIL 21, 1997

Good morning.

This is the second day after disaster.

For the *Herald,* the disaster grew worse—unbeliev-ably—when we learned our newsroom, circulation and finance departments and Handy Mail, a subsidiary business, were destroyed in the fire. For those of us who write and edit the *Herald,* this blow is a cruel one. Our remodeled building was especially fine, the work of Schoen and Associates, and the envy of newspaper people who saw it.

The physical structure is only part of the loss. The past was lost, too. The *Herald's* archives were de-stroyed. For decades, librarians here have clipped the newspaper, recording the comings and goings of the mean and the mighty, the haughty and the humble. For decades, beginning with W.P. Davies, editors of the *Herald* have kept a file of important dates in the com-munity's history. Jack Hagerty kept it up, and I have tried to maintain it. Some issues may be salvaged on computer or on microfilm at UND. But everything else is gone. Unrecoverable. In my office was a file of news-paper etiquette, ranging from proper dress to proper use of language, that M.M. Oppegard compiled. It, too, is gone.

The *Herald,* however, is not gone.

We are working tonight in the public school in Manvel, a community whose people have taken us in, offering everything from food and lodging to bed sheets and telephones. This is our second emergency newsroom. The flood chased us from our first, on the UND campus. We are deeply grateful to the people of Manvel, and to officials of the university, as well.

Our gratitude, and the gratitude of the entire com-munity, must go out to so many other people. We at the *Herald* learned how beneficial it is to live close to a major military installation, as firefighters from Grand Forks Air Force Base, joining the city fire department and others, struggled to contain the blaze that destroyed our place. Their efforts failed, but not because they didn't try.

The city learned, too, what an invaluable institution the National Guard is. Guardsmen showed up in my neighborhood when the emergency dikes were laid. And they were in Grand Forks Sunday, when I left the city, directing traffic, protecting property, holding down the fort.

These are only two of the public institutions that have served us well in this crisis, and will serve us well in our recovery.

The loss at the *Herald* is not limited only to the past. Much potential was lost. Ryan Bakken lost the text of a book he is writing about the incredible winter we survived together. The text was in his computer; a printout was in the briefcase I abandoned on my way out of the building.

Past and potential. All lost in the present.

But the *Herald* has begun to rebuild. Against large odds, we have succeeded twice in producing a daily edition of this institution, which has lived in, loved and wrestled with Grand Forks for more than a century.

This is Day Two of our life after the disaster; it is Year 118 of our enduring relationship with Grand Forks.

In the days to come, this newspaper will discuss what must be done to rebuild our town. One part is to help us keep our voice. That is what we have succeeded in doing; it is what we will strive to do, tomorrow and in the time to come.

Writers' Workshop

Talking Points

1) The writer starts this editorial with the words, "Good morning." Yet it's not a good morning for the newspaper or for the community. Why would he choose these words?

2) The writer uses some powerful alliterative phrases: "the mean and the mighty, the haughty and the humble." Look for other alliterative passages in these editorials.

3) The newspaper's losses mirror the losses in the community. How would readers react to the shared sense of loss?

4) The editorial challenges readers to "help us keep our voice." What is that voice? How could readers help keep it?

Assignment Desk

1) The editorial sets forth the mission of the newspaper. Write a similar editorial stating the mission of an organization or group.

2) The writer raises the question: What is the newspaper? What's his answer? Ask local journalists to answer this question.

Future is as big a challenge as river

MAY 3, 1997

One thing must be clear to anyone who wanders around our cities:

How hard we worked to save them.

The sandbag dikes run for many blocks along the river. The clay dikes run for many miles.

And still, we lost.

It is hard to accept this bitter truth, even two weeks after the dikes broke and the city was flooded.

How hard we worked.

How hard we fought the rising water.

How confident we were we would turn it back.

All of this contributes to the shock of losing, the sense of disappointment, the well of anger, the sense of grief.

It is vital that we understand that all of these reactions are normal. We have suffered a trauma as deep as any community. It was unimaginable before it happened, and we will be shaking our heads about it for many years to come.

The river was a challenge, and we rose to meet it. Throughout the days leading to the crisis, we rallied ourselves to fill more sandbags and make more sandwiches. We felt the community drawing together, and we celebrated it. Together.

We lost that battle. The river was bigger than we were, even all of us together.

Now, we need to hear the voice that propelled us in the days that we fought together. That voice told us two important things. The first was our community was important enough to fight for, and we had to fight together.

Nothing that has happened has changed these truths. Events have only made them starker.

These are very special places.

Before the flood, these were cities with character. Neighborhoods were distinctive, each with its own identity and the loyalty of its residents. Downtown was lively, with galleries, stores selling all manner of collectibles, great restaurants, night spots, apartments.

These supplemented commercial centers spread around our cities, serving customers from a huge geographical area. The same for our hospital. Our university.

The preceding paragraph is written in the past tense. It has to be. Our cities are damaged, and we don't know what the future holds.

One thing we do know, however, and that is that the future depends on us.

We need to bring the same determination, the same confidence, the same spirit to our effort to rebuild Grand Forks that we brought to the effort to save it.

We lost once, but the loss need not be permanent. We can succeed. Together.

Then, decades from now, the pain will be replaced by pride in how hard we worked to regain what the river took from us. We will be winners then.

Writers' Workshop

Talking Points

1) The writer repeats the word "how" in the beginning of the editorial. How powerful is the effect?

2) Does this editorial look more to the destruction of the past or to the hope of the future? How does it balance the two?

3) What sense of the area does this editorial give you? How would you describe the community?

Assignment Desk

1) Write an editorial praising a positive aspect of your community.

Even a deep well of patience can run dry

MAY 9, 1997

Some thoughts while stripping a basement:

- We are not what we own.

If we were, we'd all be much less than we were a month ago—and each of us knows we are stronger, more generous and more patient than we were.

- Patience is not inexhaustible.

The mood in our town is getting testier as junk piles up on our berms and we learn it will take weeks to get attention from an electrician.

Our cities need to do something about both of these situations. Whatever limits have been imposed on haulers and electricians must be re-examined.

- Not knowing is the worst thing.

We all learned this while the floodwaters were rising, and the truth hasn't changed. It's good the cities have defined what areas must be cleared for a floodway. There'll be controversy about the proposal, of course. That's healthy. At least now we have something to react to.

We all want answers, and we want the answers to be consistent and fair. Above all, we want the talk to be plain. Frustration with formal answers and bureaucratic jargon is on the rise—and contributes to a feeling of impatience and alienation our cities can't afford.

Someone—Mayors Stauss and Owens, perhaps—needs to deliver a lesson in courtesy and plain talk to every officer of every government agency in town. The vast majority of them are doing heroic work, but there are a few of the other kind.

- Humor helps.

All over town, wags have attached signs to their piles of garbage, or they've arranged things in a way that brings a little smile. Or, they've made up jokes to share with one another. One of the new ones suggests a new state motto. It would be, "North Dakota: Land of four-season disasters (Blizzard, flood, drought and poor hunting)."

It's not true, of course, but it's worth a smile.

▪ We get by with a little help from our friends.

All across the towns, friendships are cemented by working together, and new friendships are made when people reach out to help one another.

▪ Charity is real.

The Red Cross truck came by with a woman from West Virginia and a man from New York. They offered hot drinks, a hot meal, snacks and a little conversation—every bit of it financed by people who probably never gave us a thought before our flood.

▪ Neighborhoods matter.

People who happen to live in adjacent houses have become neighbors, concerned for each other and ready to offer help.

Grand Forks and East Grand Forks have always had strong neighborhoods. The flood has made them stronger.

▪ We're all in it together.

No one among us can wonder, "Why me, Lord." In this flood, it's not you and me. It's all of us. Together.

Writers' Workshop

Talking Points

1) The writer initially gives the impression that this editorial is a collection of random thoughts. How does he do that? Is there really a deeper theme to the editorial?

2) The editorial refers to the frustrations that members of the community face in their cleanup efforts. Are the issues to which he's referring clear to readers? Is additional information needed to explain the situations residents face?

Assignment Desk

1) The writer was inspired in this editorial by his own cleanup work. Take a personal experience of your own and write an editorial about the universal lessons to be learned.

The *Herald*'s first commandment: Never hold the news

MAY 20, 1997

The *Grand Forks Herald* is a newspaper. Our business is to present truthful information of interest. That is why we chose to publish the Angel's name.

We thought about it, and we agreed that there is more than one side to the question. We recognize a right to privacy. We're also sensitive to the fear that publishing the name might endanger other charity.

Still, as journalists, we could not withhold information of interest that we knew to be true. To do that would have violated the *Herald* newsroom's first commandment, which is "Never hold the news." We hold that as our first commandment because we believe printing the news is part of the bargain we have made with the community. We'd be breaking the bargain if we didn't print the news.

Until the weekend, the *Herald* had no interest in seeking the Angel's identity, but the nature of the story changed when the Angel, Joan Kroc, arrived in Grand Forks and her presence was made known to us by public officials who sought coverage of her appearance, including getting her reaction and describing her visit here.

The visit raised public interest in her identity. We'd have been subject to criticism if we hadn't tried to find out, and printed what we knew.

Finding her identity wasn't difficult, once her private jet put down at the Grand Forks International Airport. Each airplane displays its registration number, much as cars display license plates. It's a simple matter to check who owns the craft. We followed up by looking at records at the airport.

The *Herald* isn't the only media outlet interested in the identity of the Angel. We've had calls from national media, some responsible and some not. It was inevitable that her name would become known.

Here at the *Herald,* we felt our credibility as the source of local news would be jeopardized if we left this story to out-of-town media. So, when we learned the identity of the Angel, we printed a story.

Our concern for the community's welfare isn't any less than it was Sunday morning, before we knew the Angel's name. Our decision to reveal it was made in full knowledge that every decision has consequences, and that we have to live with them. That's true of whatever decision the Angel makes. This is a strong community, and a committed newspaper is a part of its strength. Whatever happens next, we'll deal with it. As a newspaper and as part of the community.

Writers' Workshop

Talking Points

1) The opening paragraph quickly states the point of the editorial without a long, formal introduction. How effective is this?

2) The editorial offers the public an explanation for its journalistic actions. Why did the newspaper feel the need to explain? Why did it use this forum?

3) The editorial clearly indicates that the newspaper considers itself a part of the community. Do its actions support this belief?

Assignment Desk

1) Research the story of the Angel, Joan Kroc, and her contributions to the community. Then write an editorial criticizing the decision to publish her identity.

2) Discuss whether a newspaper should consider itself a member of the community or whether it should be an objective bystander.

A conversation with
Mike Jacobs

CHRISTOPHER SCANLAN: How did you come to write these editorials?

MIKE JACOBS: My wife and I live in a neighborhood called Riverside, which is low-lying. And as a consequence, we were evacuated early on Friday morning, April 18. We were able to get settled, and I came back to the office and worked through that night. That night the dikes failed and the rest of the town was flooded. And so that first day after the flood, the editorial, "The Day That Changed Everything" needed to be written essentially on the spot, and the editorial page editor, Tim Fought, and his wife were taken by Army National Guard vehicle from their home in the middle of the night and evacuated to Fargo.

We were critically short of staff, and I felt myself wanting, more and more, to talk to my community—*to* and *for* the community, thinking that was a really important role for me. I felt compelled to write.

We were in the University of North Dakota computer lab. We had basically deployed our resources and then I turned to the question of whether we wanted to have an editorial and what we wanted to say, and talked it over with the publisher. He's not normally involved in reading and editing editorials, although he's a former editorial writer, so he is a very good wordsmith. He read it through, made a single suggestion, that we add the material at the end about Rapid City. That was an experience many people here remembered. It turned out it was a very good example of what we hoped for for Grand Forks, because people here know that Rapid City has had a complete and successful flood recovery, so it was a good, hopeful analogy.

Susan Trausch at *The Boston Globe* says that when she begins an editorial, the first thing she does is pick up a legal pad and jot down a list of thoughts that come to her mind, almost like free association. What's your process?

I'm a very bad example. I write at one sitting and I seldom revise.

What I generally do, and I did in these instances particularly, is go outside and walk around and think through the editorial. Try to start it, imagine where it's going to end up, and how it's going to get there. It's actually a writing trick that my eighth-grade teacher told me about. She said, "Think of the story as a path. When you start out on the path, you know where you're starting and you know where you're going to end up. And you have some sort of notion about how you're going to get there. And so what I see in my mind when I do that is sort of an S curve on the page. There's the beginning and there's the end, and then there's my construction that I need to go through in order to get there.

How much of this happens at the keyboard?

A certain amount of it. One of my frustrations is that I write really great stuff in my mind, and it never comes out quite that way. I write very rapidly. I'm a very fast typist. I do some revision and I'm notorious with the copy editors, who never close the pages with my stuff on it until the last minute because they think I might call back and say, "Could we change such and such a word?"

You don't let it go in your mind?

Well, I don't generally walk around with a copy, although I sometimes do. If it's important to me and I want to think about it for a while, I do make a copy and I will go back to it. Most of my work now is written on Friday, for Sunday publication, so I have the luxury of going back to it on Saturday if I want to. Of course, that wasn't the case with most of this.

Has the editorial voice of the paper changed since these were written?

The flood changed the *Herald*'s editorial voice, and these editorials, I hope, reflect that. What I wanted to happen with these editorials was to say, "The newspaper is part of the community, and is sharing an experience with the community." Rather than, "We know what ought to be done." What's happening in these editorials is we're reacting to what's happened to us, the community.

We now use the word "we" differently. It used to be "we" meant we, who run the newspaper; we, who have done all this research; we, who have great intellects and can figure out what ought to happen. Now the word "we" means we, who live here; we, who share these challenges. What I have tried to do as an editorial writer and what I have counseled other editorial writers here to do is to make that concept live in the editorials we print.

Was there a particular moment when you realized this change was occurring?

Your understanding of your place in the world, of your place in a town, changes when the sirens are blowing and you know that it means you gotta leave. And your neighbors are scrambling in the same way that you are, and it doesn't make any difference if you're the editor of the newspaper or the teacher at the school or the electrical worker or whatever, there is a shared imperative. It just makes a difference in the way that you look at what's happening.

Is the change in the voice a change for the better?

My feeling is yes. Certainly, there is a challenge to keep the newspaper from always being a cheerleader. And believe me, that's a temptation. We've tried very hard to continue to be "critically supportive." For example, the latest dust-up in town is the city hired a contractor who has been barred from doing business in Minnesota and with the federal government for some questionable contracting practices. We basically said in our editorial, "You really ought to be a little more careful about how you investigate the background of people who want to do business here. It's critical to make timely decisions, but we need to take the time to be sure that we're making the right decision." The editorial was quite critical of the city council and of the responsible council member, particularly. But, at the same time, it was friendly to them, recognizing that this is a difficult position they're in. I guess it's the difference between waving the red flag and sort of calling attention to shortcomings in a way that leaves room to appreciate the difficulty of the position that the other guy is in.

We gained an appreciation of the humanity of people who are involved in public decision-making by watching them under the most critical of circumstances. Being cast in that role ourselves, we came to appreciate that there's a level of civility that's possible that doesn't involve wounding people in editorials. We've tried to make the tone of the editorials more common-sense, less rarefied, less intellectual. We deal less with intellectual concepts and more with the grit of how decisions have to be made. Not to say that we've abandoned principle, but we don't always run to the high ground.

When everybody's under water there is no high ground.

That's exactly right. But it's a habit of newspaper editorial writers to dash for the mountain of principle or for the little hillock of objectivity. We learned that this is not a comfortable position. In fact it's not a position that we could even get to, because we were awash with everybody else.

What are the positive aspects of this change for your paper, for your community?

The *Herald* came to realize that it is part of the community. And the community came to realize that the *Herald* is important to it. Of course we wanted to believe we were part of the community, but we were never quite sure. Even though we thought that intellectually, we learned that empirically.

Does a newspaper staff have to go through what Grand Forks went through to undergo this transformation of voice and attitude towards community and its role in it?

I hope not. We've done a lot of soul searching about how we ought to be involved in things, and we've tried lots of different stuff. Partly this is the result of having an editor who has a degree in religious studies. We were on the trail early in the whole civic journalism movement. We were early on the trail in newsroom re-organization. We've been a newspaper that's looked pretty hard at fundamental questions troubling journalism today, and I think that the only thing the flood did was confirm much of what troubled us. I mean, it gave us a way to get rid of some of the baggage that kept us from behaving in ways that we wished we could.

Such as?

Wounding public officials—the sort of disrespectful attitude we had toward human beings who happen to be public officials. That's not all gone. We still have the occasional nasty barb that's enjoyed just because it's a nasty barb. There's still the headline that is celebrated because it manages to make its point in kind of an unfriendly way.

Why do newspapers do that?

Newspaper people enjoy the language and we enjoy using the language effectively, and often we are not aware that effective use of the language can be hurtful. We often are, almost always, apart from the people that we write about. We don't very often see the consequence of our cleverness.

One thing I do now is, if somebody calls who has been offended by something that the *Herald* has printed, I ask the person responsible to talk to this person in order that the journalist involved understands that what he or she has done has given offense. Not that it's wrong necessarily, but it's important that the journalist understand the perception of the person coming to us with this grievance.

Has the experience that you and your paper have gone through since last April influenced your views on civic journalism?

It washed away the baggage that we carried around with us about how we had to be something apart from the community. One of the problems that civic journalism always has is that it is seen as getting down there and grappling. And that's somehow seen as unseemly. And that notion has pretty much been washed away.

The flood helped to sweep away the vestiges of that old thinking about how "other people" do projects and we report on them. I think that the newspaper's central importance in the community was made clear; and that having happened, it became possible for everyone to understand that there are ways that the newspaper can behave that are both civic and journalistic.

I want to ask you something about the changing voice. I was really struck by the editorial about the Angel, that you drew a line in the sand.

This is a newspaper. We are in the news business. The reason that people buy us is to get truthful, current information. They're not interested in hearing theories about why you withheld some piece of information that's of interest. I think, actually, that editorial in some ways is the most important of the editorials from the point of view of journalism, because we were able to teach people in our market something about journalism.

The immediate aftermath of our decision to print the Angel's name was very negative. We happened to be in the field with a poll and so we added that question, and 85 percent of people said we shouldn't have printed her name. But there aren't very many people in town who don't understand *why* we printed her name.

How did this editorial come to be? Who's the Angel, and what's this all about?

The Angel called the mayor of the city soon after the flood and said, "I want to do something for people who are in great need, and I will give $2,000 to every flood-affected household." The city set up a procedure to distribute the money. It turned out to be a flawed procedure, and it became quite controversial, but that's another story.

How did you establish that the Angel was Joan Kroc?

It's a clever piece of reporting. She flew into town in a Gulfstream jet. We checked the tail number on the jet against the public records. She also paid for the gas with her own credit card. The airport is city-run and so the state's open records laws applied to the gas purchase records. And so our reporter said, "I gotta see the gas purchase records," and there was Joan Kroc's receipt, with her name on it. So we didn't have any doubt that it was she. We did it because the mayor had announced that the Angel was going to be here and in fact gave the Angel a tour around town and said that the Angel would be making anonymous comments she'd like to have in the paper. Any self-respecting newspaper couldn't *not* pursue the story at that point.

I have said publicly that if the Angel wanted to be anonymous she would have come into town in a pickup truck with a gun rack. You don't fly a Gulfstream jet into the Grand Forks Airport and not expect to attract attention.

What was the reaction?

Virtually the whole front page the next day was devoted to civic leaders denouncing us. The mayor and the governor, at least one member of the U.S. Senate, and all sorts of people in Grand Forks denounced us.

Did anybody come to your defense?

The controversy blew over very, very quickly. The front page editorial basically said, "Here's the line. This is the business we're in and this is what we feel we must do. Nothing has changed our fundamental role in the community, which is providing truthful information of interest."

Let's talk a bit about "Even A Deep Well of Patience Can Run Dry." What's the story behind that one?

One of the things I did every day during the flood was leave the school in Manvel, which is 12, 15 miles away, and come into town and walk around for two hours. So that I was connected with the community. Because we were isolated geographically, I didn't want to run the risk of being isolated emotionally. So every day I came into town in the early afternoon and generally that experience was the basis of the next day's editorial. The editorial was written in the morning.

Do you think that the kind of walkabouts that you're describing should be an essential part of an editorial writer's job?

Most editorials can be written without doing that. These editorials could not have been written without doing that. This was an extremely emotional time. On any number of those walkabouts, I ended up holding on to people and sobbing. I don't want to put too fine a point on this, because there were no lives lost. I actually said this in a column: It's not Baghdad. But it was an extremely emotional experience, and it was an experience in common.

The big benefit to me of doing this was to understand that this experience was universal in this community. That everybody had suffered. And that many had suffered much more than I or much more than anyone I knew. One of the things that we tend to do when we sit in our offices is imagine that the world is happening to us and not happening to other people. I really want to fight against this notion that we have special insights. I wanted very much to be in a position to share insights that others had, that the community had, and that's what this editorial is about.

My sense is that insight is the stock in trade for the editorial writer. It sounds like you're saying you're departing from that.

I am. I don't argue that an editorial writer does not have an opportunity to develop special knowledge and that that special knowledge may lead you to a better informed opinion than other people have. But it doesn't, in my judgment, give you any special insight. Insight, it seems to me, is gained by understanding how issues play with a range of individuals. I'll use the Clinton scandals as an example.

I have a fairly strong opinion about this whole thing. But I'm really interested in hearing what other people have to say about it. How it is being perceived by the public and why they have that perception. And I want to hear that before I impose my own judgments, which are the product of a particular experience, a particular moral understanding, and a particular political perspective. I just think it's more valuable if I can broaden my perspective and that there is insight to be gained in that. I'm not unhappy about my moral, political, or educational experience. I just don't think that it's all that special. It doesn't give me any advanced wisdom.

Why did you begin the editorial, "A Cruel Blow, A Tough Recovery," with the phrase, "Good morning"?

Because it *wasn't* a good morning. I wanted to say something that said, "Look, things are normal; this is another morning; it's another day; we're going to have to deal with it." The newspaper comes out in the morning, and it's a part of people's morning routine. And I wanted to emphasize that the newspaper was there. And it was still part of the morning routine, it was still coming from the place that people called home.

Frankly, I thought it was a very powerful beginning, because it is very polite, very ordinary, and what makes it effective in my judgment, is that it is being said to people whose lives are incredibly disrupted. And it's reassuring. At least, I meant it to be reassuring.

What was your goal with the next sentence: "This is the second day after disaster."

To say the days are going to accumulate. It's behind us. We're moving on. Someday we're going to be doing the year anniversary. Actually, we're very hard at work on it today.

Was this a painful one to write?

No. I had two things to say. One is that I found that people wanted to talk about what they had lost.

Actually, this is something I learned long ago, writing obituaries. When I was publishing my own little weekly, I started doing what I called "exit interviews," interviewing prominent people in advance of their deaths. And I found that people were extraordinarily appreciative of the opportunity to talk about their lives. I have found that in the wake of a loss many people are eager to talk about a loved one who has died, eager to tell stories. This is the genius of the Irish wake. It's a way for people to talk about the person who has died. It's a way to grieve.

What we were doing as a community as this occurred was grieving. In this editorial I'm grieving in print. And I'm telling people what I have lost.

You say in that first editorial that "All of our plans and projects will be re-evaluated in light of the enormous events of April 1997—ice and water and fire."

I'd really like to re-paragraph that editorial, by the way. That piece was written very quickly and it went on to a copy editor in St. Paul. It arrived without paragraphs in it. I'm looking at the fourth paragraph: "The *Herald*'s buildings may have been among them. We can't know. Water keeps us from our usual workplace." I would have started a new paragraph at "Our notions about ourselves must also have changed." I'm embarrassed that the paragraphing is senseless.

What does the paragraph break represent to you?

The paragraph is a thought. It's a pause. It's a pause to move on to another point or another line of argument. Running thoughts together is the sign of disorganized thinking.

The other thing that's important about the paragraph is that—how should I say this? I want the editorials to speak; I hear them. And the paragraph is a place where, if you are reading it, you will pause, take a breath, and then move on. My Aunt Dorothy was blind. She was diabetic, and she lost her sight. And I used to read to her when I was a kid. And it was important to pause so that she could appreciate the cadence of the writing. I think she taught me that you just didn't spit it out all at once. So there's cadence, and the cadence is marked by the paragraphs.

What have you learned about editorial writing since you started out?

That it shouldn't be obtuse. You need to have a point and you need to get to it immediately. Editorials should have one subject, and there's no need to beat it to death. I like to write short. I like to think that an editorial should be a 300-word essay. My most frequent criticism of editorial writing at this newspaper is that the editorials are too long.

What kind of response did you get to "The Day That Changed Everything"?

It's odd. People still occasionally say, "It was so important to get that first day's paper, and I really liked your editorial."

So it spoke for an experience that was shared.

There's such a nice line: "In neighborhood after neighborhood, the water found its level, and in most, it was well above the level of our daily lives, in our homes and in our consciousness." You did it on deadline, too.

This editorial was written at a time of incredible uncertainty because we didn't know for sure whether or not our buildings had burned down. We didn't know just exactly what the extent of our own involvement in the fire was. I was probably getting close to dark. People think of natural disasters happening in cloudy, windy weather, because we're used to hurricane and tornado disasters. But the weather was beautiful. There were these just priceless April days with this wonderful spring sunshine. Spring is happening, and spring is a special time in a winter-weary place like this.

And so I was outside, and the sun was getting ready to set and, there's this peculiar light of the northern plains. It's just one of those moments when you think, "Things are different now."

In "Future is as Big a Challenge as River," what you're saying is, "We lost." It's unflinching in its honesty.

Nobody would have argued that we won, because the river did overwhelm us.

But would they need to be told they'd lost?

Maybe not. But I think that the core of this editorial is the paragraph that says, "Now, we need to hear the voice that propelled us in the days that we fought together."

These seem to be editorials that spring from the heart and mind.

This is about two weeks after the flood. I think that a lot of us coming back were struck by the miles and miles and miles of sandbag dikes that we had put up. And the disbelief that we could have worked this hard and not have won.

And the other thing is that the city was such a mess, particularly downtown. And what was happening was people were coming back to Grand Forks, often from great distances, and the first thing they did is go to their houses. And to their neighborhoods. And see how bad it was. And then they went downtown. And so what's happening here is, you know, sort of saying to people, "Yeah, it looks really bad. We really fought hard and still look what the river has given us, and now we need to fight hard again."

I made an overnight trip to Minneapolis to speak at the Minnesota AP Spring meeting. On the plane coming back was an older woman with a younger man. The woman was probably 75. The man was my age, her son. And he was holding her, saying words to the effect of, "It's going to be OK. Grand Forks is going to come back."

I remember being very powerfully impressed with his determination, his conscious preparation of his mother to see what had happened. What I'm trying to do here is kind of get my arms around the community and say, "Yeah, it's horrible, but we can make it."

I saw it as a way to listen to my own ambition about being a small-town newspaper editor, and to be able to be true to myself and the town, which is always the tension in the small town newspaper's existence. We all hate to be hectored, and so much of editorial writing is hectoring. And so you want to listen to the tone of the editorial, so that it doesn't nag.

The reason that I'm proud of these editorials is that I think that I hear in them a bigger voice than my own. Writing is a lonely experience. I hope that these editorials are in some way speaking beyond an individual's intellect, into some sort of common experience.

Lance Dickie

Finalist, Editorial Writing

Lance Dickie has been an editorial writer at *The Seattle Times* for 10 years. He was a finalist for the ASNE editorial writing prize in 1996.

He previously worked at the *Statesman Journal* in Salem, Ore., as editorial page editor, editorial writer, and reporter. He is a graduate of the University of Oregon, and has a master's degree from the University of Missouri School of Journalism.

Dickie is a past winner of the Scripps Howard Walker Stone Award for editorial writing excellence. He has been a Congressional Fellow of the American Political Science Association, a John J. McCloy Fellow of the American Council on Germany, and a Jefferson Fellow of the EastWest Center in Hawaii.

In many communities, the editorial page is one of the few forums in which local issues are given close attention. When a school district proposes compulsory drug testing for high school athletes, Dickie's editorial gives readers an important starting point for debate: necessary background and an informed point of view.

Northshore: Just say no to random drug testing

OCTOBER 1, 1997

If the Northshore School District has a compelling reason for forcing high-school athletes to urinate on command, it was not made clear to dozens of upset parents.

Those who testified at a special Monday night forum were overwhelmingly opposed to the idea; indeed, many were deeply offended by the suggestion.

Listen to the parents.

This tempest in a specimen bottle is all the more curious because Northshore is an excellent school district that successfully educates children from Kenmore, Bothell and Woodinville.

For a district that is otherwise able to articulate high standards and expectations on academics and discipline, this approach boils down to policy formation by dubious polling and dueling anecdotes.

Apparently, the only reason drug testing is being discussed is because a 1995 Supreme Court ruling says the district could get away with it.

The original case involved a rural Oregon high school whose administrators felt they had lost control of the student body, and that athletes were at the heart of a pervasive drug culture. The court decided that student athletes voluntarily surrender a measure of personal privacy and are exempt from usual Fourth Amendment protections from unreasonable searches.

Northshore officials did not suggest drug use is out of control, although no school is immune from isolated problems, and individual cases are indeed heartbreaking. No one is suggesting athletes are an overriding source of concern. No one is suggesting that Bothell and, say, Inglemoor high schools have identical discipline issues or similar management styles. So why consider a one-size-fits-all approach to drug enforcement?

A parade of parents were concerned about an erosion of constitutional freedoms, invasion of privacy, confidentiality of test results, the singling out of athletes, the potential for testing all students in extracurricular activities—those students are known to be the

least likely to have academic and discipline problems—the waste of taxpayer dollars, the expense of
drug testing for families, and the shattering of trust between the district, parents and students.

If drug testing is about elevating role models in the
school environment, parents wondered, then why not
test principals, administrators and teachers.

If Northshore is as good as its reputation, then a
more thoughtful approach is not only possible, but also
expected.

Use drug tests when behavior and performance suggest a problem in young lives. Teachers and coaches
know their students. As Justice Sandra Day O'Connor
noted in her 1995 dissent, "a suspicion-based program
would be both effective and less intrusive."

Northshore, listen to your parents.

Lessons Learned

BY LANCE DICKIE

Perhaps the only lesson lurking in the drug testing editorial is a familiar one about the value of getting out of the office.

The editorial is as much reportage as opinion. Any oomph and sis-boom-bah come from the parents who turned out on a blustery October night to speak their minds.

Attending the special forum, sitting in the gymnasium bleachers, and soaking up the passion is what made the editorial work.

The next day I read up on the court case, made a few calls, and wrote the editorial for Wednesday's paper. Most everything could have been gleaned after the fact from news coverage or over the phone. Everything but the anger, frustration, and thoughtfulness the parents brought to the discussion.

Maybe the best part of writing the editorial was a chance to wag a finger at an entire school district, and lament it was not working up to its potential.

Did the editorial make a difference? Maybe. If nothing else, it was praised in a high school English class as a fine example of the editorial craft. That was nice. District administrators eventually abandoned their bad idea. They might have read the editorial, but they listened to the parents.

The Boston Globe

Alyssa Haywoode

Finalist, Editorial Writing

Alyssa Haywoode is an editorial writer for *The Boston Globe.* She joined the editorial board in December 1996. She graduated from Harvard University in 1985 with a bachelor's degree in sociology, and from the University of Iowa's Writers' Workshop in 1992 with a master's degree in fiction writing. Prior to working for the *Globe,* she was an editorial writer at *The Des Moines Register* from 1994 to 1996, where, in addition to domestic violence, she wrote about international issues, race, and city affairs.

To highlight the continuing problem of domestic violence, Haywoode's editorial "Wil Cordero's Future" calls on the community to confront the problem of battering spouses. By using a high-profile case, she manages to address the issue of collective responsibility.

Wil Cordero's future

JULY 2, 1997

Boston needs to shoulder a grim but important task: Smother Red Sox outfielder Wil Cordero in civilization. Keep him in a town where the city's outrage over his physical abuse of his wife can make a constructive difference. Surround him with the city's fierce expectation that he will seek help and make up for the injuries he has inflicted on his family. Fully engage Cordero so that in his professional, civic, and personal life he feels the community holding him accountable.

It would be easier, and possibly more satisfying, to banish Cordero, trading him to another team in another city. But to do so would only be a sop to Boston's anger, doing little about Cordero in particular or domestic violence in general. Export Cordero and he could land in another city where the news of his domestic violence would be hazier, where people would forget to pay attention, where the community would fail to do what communities do best: create an atmosphere of intolerance for abusive behavior.

Cordero has to want to change badly enough to survive the self-criticism that personal reform takes. A vigilant Boston could be a safer place for Ana Cordero and her family, pushing Cordero along and monitoring his progress. Meanwhile, he should be kept off the field until his case is resolved or there is solid evidence of his improvement—possibly for the rest of this season.

Communities are relatively new at responding to domestic violence. Twenty years ago Massachusetts was struggling to set up temporary shelters for battered women. At that time activists complained that women who reported episodes of domestic abuse to their doctors were routinely given tranquilizers.

Mercifully, we have come a long way since then. But communities still have progress to make in responding quickly, decisively, and effectively to domestic abuse. In the Cordero case, a good next step could be converting our moral outrage into responsible moral action.

Lessons Learned

BY ALYSSA HAYWOODE

The charge that Wil Cordero, a Boston Red Sox outfielder, had attacked his wife, scraped a raw nerve in Boston. People were outraged and vocal about it.

Television news broadcasts were crowded with on-the-street interviews of people bashing Cordero. It struck me that this anger made absolute sense, but it was too easy. By itself, public outrage doesn't accomplish anything. This sparked the idea of an editorial saying that Boston, a city of impressive resources, could do more about Cordero than complain. I learned several things.

The first lesson was the importance of emotional timing. An earlier editorial had done the job of keeping up with the news. It touched on domestic violence in celebrity families and how vital it is for victims to have a safety plan. But I think the second editorial came out when public attention was at a peak, increasing the editorial impact.

The second lesson was that while it seems hokey to say that someone's personal problem requires a community response, this is, in fact, often the case. Public responses to such problems as domestic violence and drunk driving try to provide the right mix of law enforcement, incentives, disapproval, and encouragement to change.

In addition, this point was a bit counter-intuitive for the *Globe*. We have a strong, consistent stand against domestic violence that would have made it easy—and predictable—for us to join the chorus of just get rid of the bum. This editorial let us stick to our principles but catch the public's ear by coming at them from a different angle.

Making the case for city action also meant finding a concise way to show how far public responses have come. A check of *Boston Globe* clips from the 1970s produced the detail that some doctors dispensed tranquilizers to women who said that their husbands were abusive—a grim fact that today sounds like lawsuit material. Given this history, it's easy to see why today something as small as a domestic violence brochure is an important and huge step forward.

Finally, the right lead seemed crucial, hence the phrasing of smothering Cordero in civilization, language I hoped would alert the reader that this wouldn't be just another editorial stroll down a street that everybody already knew.

StarTribune

Kate Stanley

Finalist, Editorial Writing

Kate Stanley joined the *Star Tribune* as an editorial writer in 1980. She studied English literature at the University of Minnesota, where she served as editor-in-chief of the *Minnesota Daily* in 1979-80. She was a plaintiff in the *Daily*'s groundbreaking First Amendment lawsuit against the university, *Stanley vs. Magrath,* which affirmed the right of student newspapers to publish free from government restraint.

From 1990 through 1996, Stanley served as a member and vice president of the Minnesota News Council, an independent panel of journalists and laypersons devoted to resolving complaints against the media out of court. She is a current board member of the Minnesota Center for Book Arts.

Stanley's editorials for the *Star Tribune* address crime and the courts, civil and constitutional rights, medicine, ethics, and social policy.

Editorials deliver opinions. They rarely tell stories. Stanley does both in this series on dying that reports the statistics, the debates, and the individual stories, especially this moving and thought-provoking discussion of hospice care and the notion it exemplifies, that "healing need not end even when curing is impossible."

A better way to end a life

MAY 28, 1997

Becky Pansch sits at the bedside of the dying school-teacher. "So what shall we sing?" she asks. "Perhaps 'The Red River Valley'—did you sing that to your students?"

The frail woman grabs anxiously at her quilt, stares uncomprehendingly and talks a little nonsense. Pansch moves her folding piano closer to the woman's bed, and soon a silky voice fills the tiny bedroom: "From this valley they say you are going...."

The old woman's blue eyes lighten with recollection, with fascination. She relaxes, lies back with a smile. It is as though an angel has come to sing for her.

This is what Becky Pansch does for a living—carting her electronic piano from house to house, singing her heart out to dying strangers. She works for Fairview Home Care and Hospice, and she and her colleagues spend their days dropping in on dying people all over town. They offer up massage and music and medicine and consolation and company—and whatever else is necessary to make life's last days as full of grace as they can be.

What they're offering, really, is another way of dying—a way that's hard to come by in a hospital. There, dying can be painful and lonely and long. It is interpreted not as life's last act, but as a sign of failure. Death comes surging over the sandbags of medicine, snatching its gasping victims from the hands of their protectors.

That kind of calamitous death is uncommon in palliative-care programs. The nurses, home health aides, social workers, chaplains, therapists, physicians and volunteers of the hospice movement don't see death as a disaster. They believe that it's no more an enemy than birth, that resisting it can often be pointless and painful.

And they see something else that doctors sometimes can't: that healing need not end—must not end—when curing is impossible. Forsaking the medical establishment's reflexive attempts to delay death, they help patients find comfort and meaning in their last days. They reject the notion that life's end is invariably grim and grueling and silent. Quite the contrary: With suffering relieved, hospice workers say, it can be a time of great intimacy and discovery and even joy—for the dying and those who stay with them.

Dying is hard work in the best of times, and hospice workers insist no one should have to do it alone. As Sandol Stoddard, author of *The Hospice Movement,* argues, "Dying, like birthing, is a process requiring assistance. It is an event that asks us to be present for one another with heart and mind...." In short, it's an experience that calls for a midwife.

This is a philosophy that transcends place. Thus it makes sense that the term "hospice" usually refers not to a building where people go to die, but to a way of caring for the dying. Hospice workers care for patients wherever they happen to be—and most of the time, they can be well comforted at home. When pain gets out of hand or family members can't cope, patients can spend short stints at inpatient facilities. Medicare picks up most hospice costs—as long as a doctor certifies that a patient is likely to die within six months.

You'd think that such a humane and sensible approach to end-of-life care would be popular. But though the nation has more than 2,500 hospice programs, only 15 percent of the 2.4 million Americans who die every year choose to use them.

Why so few? Much of the explanation lies in the American insistence on postponing death—an attitude obviously incompatible with the notion of welcoming it. Doctors who see a terminal diagnosis as an admission of failure aren't likely to refer patients to hospice care. Patients, too, tend to think of entering a hospice program as a sign of surrender, of giving in to death rather than milking every last drop out of life.

Dr. Ronald Cranford, an ethicist and neurologist at Hennepin County Medical Center, notes another subtle stifling force: "There's money to be made in treatment," he says, "but not much money in nontreatment. Dying is not lucrative; hospice is not lucrative. It takes a little time and effort to let patients die humanely, and doctors don't have the time. It's much easier to treat patients and move on."

And the hospice movement must brook the suspicion not just of the medical establishment, but of regulators as well. Eager to ferret out fraud and abuse in the Medicare system, the U.S. Department of Health and Human Services has recently mounted an effort to recover $83 million in payments from a dozen hospices whose patients outlived the six-month benefit limit imposed by federal rules.

Predicting how long a terminally ill person will last has always been a chancy business. Even so, more than 90 percent of all hospice patients do die within the six-month "deadline"; half die within 36 days of enrollment. Going after the few who don't die as quickly as expected is coldhearted and unnecessary.

It's also counterproductive, because it threatens to scare dying patients away from the one program most likely to help them. Some hospice programs are already blaming the new regulatory crusade for a downturn in referrals. One local inpatient hospice— Midwest Community Hospice in Minneapolis—has experienced such an enrollment drop lately that it's been forced to lay off staff.

There's no sense in pinching these pennies. Hospice care, after all, is far cheaper than conventional care for the dying. A study released last year found that Medicare saves $1.52 for every dollar it spends on hospice.

But the real promise of the hospice philosophy has less to do with thriftiness than with liberation. As Hennepin County's Cranford argues, "People feel they're prisoners of medical technology, and they want an escape." Some Americans are seizing upon euthanasia as the surest exit. But most would shake off that idea if a hospice death were within reach.

Whenever they suffer—wherever they die—human beings deserve the calm and comfort of palliative care. That kind of compassionate treatment ought to be a preoccupation of medical education and of medical care. It should be a fixture in every hospital ward, in every health-insurance plan, in every government health-care policy.

Surely society has more to offer at the end of life than a ventilator or a visit with Dr. Kevorkian. Somehow, it must open the door to a third possibility: a good death.

Lessons Learned

BY KATE STANLEY

"Learning to Die" was a six-day project that consumed both the editorial and op-ed pages and took a year's worth of poking around. I think my editors were skeptical—shall we say terrified?—until the last pages were printed. I suppose that had something to do with my long unproductive stints of mulling (I called it research), my glancing regard for deadlines, and my habit of waiting till past midnight to get down to the real business of writing. They seemed unsure whether I was planning for a nervous breakdown or publication, and I can't blame them.

It all worked out in the end. One editor said we were just lucky, but I maintain there was method to the madness. It's no easy thing writing about death, after all. You can't just hop on the web and gather a few quotes. You've got to shadow doctors, visit the dying, talk to the heartbroken. You've got to read a dozen books. You have to wrestle with a few very personal angels and figure out what you think. And then you have to write, which makes all that came before look like a cinch.

I did all of this, and these are the few things I learned along the way:

▪ Don't expect to know what you're doing until you're done. The "Learning to Die" series turned out to be an exquisite example of the folly of making up your mind before you gather your facts.

The project started with a trip to Holland and a plan to write about euthanasia. But after chatting with a few Dutch doctors and returning home, it became clear that the assisted-death controversy was a tiny part of what I needed to explore. What really required attention was the messier question of how Americans die, and how they should.

▪ Don't wade when you can swim. If you really want to immerse yourself, you can't just get your feet wet. You've got to take a plunge. I wanted to talk to the dying and the people who care for them. At first I thought that might mean scheduling a few interviews. After a while it became clear that it meant letting this issue take over my life.

So I hooked up with a few doctors and a local hospice program and just started hanging around. I spent a lot of silent time in the presence of dying people and their families, just observing their experience. Only a few of the stories saw print, but all helped shape my thinking.

▪ Don't fret about breaking the rules. Convention argues against asking bold questions about delicate matters. Journalistic protocol forbids intimacy between reporter and source. But sometimes to do your job well you must ask and you must get close. I found myself asking an AIDS patient, "Are you afraid? How would you like to die?" I asked the mother of the five-year-old, "How does it feel to be losing your child?" I kissed the five-year-old on the cheek as she lay dying and cried at her funeral. These were the right things to do.

There was another way in which we broke the rules. No self-respecting editorial page devotes its space to the same subject for six days running. But we did. This was a vast project: It included six editorials and three signed columns, as well as more than a dozen columns from outside contributors. We printed scores of "death stories" from readers. We printed all sorts of literary musings on death—from Plato and Thomas More to Samuel Beckett and Seamus Heaney. I don't think our readers had ever seen anything quite like it. They seemed startled and stirred by what we gave them.

▪ Don't worry; be happy. Last year, I had the same conversation dozens of times. "What are you working on?" someone would ask.

"I'm writing about dying," I'd say.

"Oh. How depressing," the someone would respond. "How can you sleep at night?"

No one looks askance at a rabbi for being able to move on cheerfully from a funeral to a bar mitzvah—or at a doctor who signs a death certificate and then pops out for lunch. So why fuss about writers who can tell life's sad stories with dry eyes? They're doing what writers from Shakespeare to Solzhenitsyn have always done: staring truth in the face, and telling it. There's something exhilarating about doing this, and there's no disgrace in enjoying it.

▪ Writing is good practice for dying. If writing is the best job in the world, it's also the hardest. The joy comes only upon completion, and I don't find that so surprising. After all, pouring your heart onto a page is one of life's most daunting tasks. It requires putting your finger on the meaning of life. Like the other big transitions in life, it takes a bit of hard labor. Is there anyone out there who finds it easy? Well, then, let's hear about it.

Justin Davidson
Criticism

Justin Davidson is the classical music critic at *Newsday*. You could summarize his career this way: He started in news reporting, moved into music, became a composer, earned a doctorate, taught at Columbia University, then did all kinds of other things, became a free-lance writer, and is now back to newswriting. He was born in Rome in 1966. After high school he got a summer job in the Associated Press bureau there, then continued as a stringer at the AP in Boston while he majored in music at Harvard. He graduated in 1987. His plans for a career in journalism changed when he witnessed "cold, generic, impersonal" coverage of the bombing death of an AP staffer's child.

After a year's music fellowship in Paris, Davidson pursued a doctoral degree in music composition at Columbia University, and taught there. His composi-

tions have been performed in the United States and abroad. He has also supervised the European dubbed and subtitled versions of American movies, written for a European travel guide, and been editorial director of Sony Classical. He has been a free-lance contributor to the *Los Angeles Times, Slate,* and *The Washington Post,* and began contributing concert reviews to *Newsday* in 1995. He joined the staff in 1996.

Davidson lives in New York City with his wife, Ariella Budick, who holds a doctorate in art history and who also writes for *Newsday.* They have a son, Milo.

—Karen Brown Dunlap

The streamlined Vienna could use a push

MARCH 10, 1997

The Vienna Philharmonic could undoubtedly play Beethoven's Fifth and Sixth symphonies without a conductor, probably without sheet music, and possibly without sleep. You could shake the orchestra's members awake at 4 a.m. and convene a concert on the spot, and what you got would probably sound much the way it did on Friday: sleek, unblemished and lustrous.

This is an orchestra as finely calibrated and precision-tuned as any piece of million-dollar machinery. It has as many moving parts as there are notes in a score, and rarely does one malfunction. The chords all balance impeccably, the pizzicatos are always in synch. The third bassoonist knows his place in the music's hierarchy, waits patiently for 70 measures and then can judge exactly how loud, long and incisive his solitary "dup" should be.

So what do all these highly proficient specialists need a conductor for? In the case of Daniel Barenboim, not much. Barenboim did not lead the performance so much as chair the proceedings, nodding at players who didn't need to be cued and then watching benevolently as they did their thing. The result was highly competent and completely generic: an interpretation arrived at by committee.

Details that might have been bristles of energy were slicked down instead, leaving the performance glabrous and undifferentiated. Wherever the music called for an interpretive decision, the musicians opted for the obvious one, and the conductor did not override them. It would have been up to him to shake the orchestra out of its buttoned-down professionalism and remind everyone concerned that Beethoven's music can still sound revolutionary, shocking and violent, but Barenboim seemed to have no interest in doing so.

The expensive sound of the Vienna Philharmonic is one of the world's great luxuries, like the oil-and-leather smell inside a Jaguar. But Beethoven, in particular, might be livid to know that his music had been turned into just another of these sedate and civilized pleasures, or that he was part of a tradition thus preserved in aspic. In the Vienna's performance, his "Pastoral" Sixth Symphony did not evoke nature so much as a bucolic mural on a cafe wall: The birdsongs smacked of the cuckoo clock, the storm was a tempest in a beer mug.

In some cases, Barenboim's cavalier conducting vitiated the music's restless ambiguities and even undermined its structure. Take, for instance, the famous transition from the third to the fourth movements of Beethoven's Fifth, in which the timpani quietly beats out the symphony's signature rhythm as the strings create a harmonic haze, veiling both the downbeat and the key but exposing an unbearable tension. When the fourth movement arrives in a loud C-major spasm, it bursts through the scrim like a revelation, and the moment resolves the previous section even as it begins the next. Under Barenboim's baton, though, the transition merely purred innocuously like an idling car, as if biding its time until the fourth movement could get on its way.

Neither Mozart nor Bruckner fared better on the following night. Mozart's Symphony No. 29 in A major, K. 201, written when the composer was 18, sounded positively middle-aged. So, too, did Bruckner's Symphony No. 9, left incomplete when the composer died at 72, aspiring to a musical transfiguration that the Vienna burghers denied him.

Bruckner built his cathedral-like musical structure from audible building blocks—phrases that repeat, climbing the scale in an ever-intensifying sequence, until they arrive at those brassy climaxes with the power of a wrecking ball, crumble, and then begin again. In Barenboim's hands, though, the work proceeded with all the excitement of road construction.

The Vienna Philharmonic is a magnificent ensemble that the right conductor can ignite, but these concerts showed that it can also suffer from a sort of plump and clubby complacency—nothing that a few women in its ranks couldn't cure.

Writers' Workshop

Talking Points

1) Reviews, like any other form of journalism, require good reporting to support their arguments. Note the amount of reporting in this review and how it affects the tone of the review.

2) Who are the readers of these reviews? How well does the writer tailor the review to his readers? Does he use this forum to educate and inform his readers?

3) "Barenboim's cavalier conducting vitiated the music's restless ambiguities..." Using this vocabulary assumes a certain level of education among readers. Is it appropriate here?

4) The writer leaves no question about his opinion of the Vienna Philharmonic's performance. What passages most strongly convey his opinions?

Assignment Desk

1) This review uses the imagery of cars: "finely calibrated and precision-tuned," "oil-and-leather smell inside a Jaguar," "purred innocuously like an idling car." Rewrite the review using a different image to convey the same opinion.

2) Attend a classical music performance and write a review. Note how much reporting you must do before the performance and how much relies on the performance itself.

Kissin powers an
electric occasion

MARCH 29, 1997

The pianist Evgeny Kissin propelled himself stiffly onto the stage of Avery Fisher Hall on Thursday, looking rather as if his joints needed oiling. He dutifully bent his mouth into a labored and momentary smile, gave a quick jerk of his torso in lieu of a bow, and then sat at the piano where, in an instant, all his discomfort melted into power and control.

Watching the awkward young pianist plunge into music was like seeing a seal slip into water, and in the 40 mesmerizing minutes that followed, Kissin gave one of the most lissome and lyrical performances of Beethoven's Piano Concerto No. 5 that I have ever heard.

Kissin has made a specialty of playing the same concerti every other pianist does, but he is alone in his ability to make the commonplace seem rare. There was not a trill that came off as filler or a scale run that sounded formulaic in this performance, and he made the rhetorical flourishes that open the concerto so intensely poetic that by the time the first theme arrived in the orchestra, the musical argument seemed almost already complete.

In his hands, the most ephemeral details became simple, explosive devices. The piano part in the second movement opens with two notes, four-and-a-half octaves apart, and a grace note in between—a quiet, spacious gesture that both expands and delimits the middle register in which the orchestra has just presented the melody. Kissin staggered the outer two notes ever so slightly, and bridged the gulf between them in a fluid, melodic bound, as if the piano were a singer of infinite range and grace, and not the brute percussion instrument it is.

Kissin flirts with excess, but never quite surrenders his virtue. Many pianists slow down slightly at the transition to the last movement, but he pulled back the tempo as if the music were a stone in some giant's slingshot, so that the finale fired off with a crack. With any other pianist, it would have seemed overdone and mannered, but Kissin carried it off.

While he was working his wonders and looking utterly humorless, the New York Philharmonic's music director Kurt Masur seemed to be having the time of his life, beaming at the pianist with merry pride. Masur had reason to be jolly. The concert began with Beethoven's "Coriolanus" Overture, and from the manly, fist-in-palm chords of the opening to the quiet, coy pizzicatos at the end, the Philharmonic played with lucid lyricism, and, in the concerto, matched Kissin's current, spark for spark.

As Kissin and the Philharmonic neared the concerto's coda, I felt the same panic that comes from fingering the dwindling number of pages at the end of a good book, and what I really would have liked after intermission was to start the whole thing again, or at least preserve the experience by spending the rest of the evening in silence.

But no: Perhaps on the theory that one good warhorse deserves another, Masur and the Philharmonic followed Beethoven with Rimsky-Korsakov's "Scheherazade." The first half's electricity still crackled through the second, powering the suite's sea voyages, and concertmaster Glenn Dicterow played the violin solo with dapper and exotic charm.

Writers' Workshop

Talking Points

1) "The piano part in the second movement opens with two notes, four-and-a-half octaves apart, and a grace note in between—a quiet, spacious gesture that both expands and delimits the middle register in which the orchestra has just presented the melody." How does the writer use this passage and others to teach?

2) The writer, in addition to describing the sound of the performance, also describes the performers. "While he was working his wonders and looking utterly humorless, the New York Philharmonic's music director Kurt Masur seemed to be having the time of his life, beaming at the pianist with merry pride." Are these comments necessary? How do they add or detract from the review?

Assignment Desk

1) What's the average sentence length in this review? Rewrite it using shorter sentences. How does it change the effect of the review?

'Siegfried': Fantastic in every sense

APRIL 21, 1997

The Metropolitan Opera reached the third part and the 13th hour of "Der Ring des Nibelungen" on Saturday, and Wagner's operatic juggernaut slouched that much closer to doomsday. The sibling-lovers, Siegmund and Siegelinde are both dead, and their inbred son Siegfried has come of age: The sword has been passed to a new generation of Aryans. Just three more acts (plus a prelude) and Valhalla will fall.

Wagner's genius was to have created a universe in which singing is not merely a convention, but an aspect of natural law: Walkyries ride flying horses, adulterous gods sire superheroes who swig dragon's blood and take advice from birds, dwarves have the gills both to court and cheat river sprites at the bottom of the Rhine —and every one of those creatures sings. The orchestra provides atmosphere in the literal sense—music is the air they breathe. That is why these operas have to be so long: One cannot make a quick tour of an alternate universe.

I am not generally fond of fantasy or situations that drip with symbolism, but having let myself into Wagner's world on Saturday night, I had no desire to re-emerge. Director Otto Schenk, set designer Gunther Schneider-Siemssen, and lighting designer Gil Wechsler have been as thorough in recreating Wagner's cosmology as the composer was in imagining it. Their hobbit habitats and fiberglass forests are as vivid as they are familiar, the dragon has a slimy crustacean charm, and the weather atop Wotan's mountain changes spectacularly with the characters' states of mind. The gods brood, and the sky goes black. Brünnhilde is kissed out of her 30-year slumber by Siegfried, and multihued light seems to come from several different suns.

If there was rarely a dull moment on this mythic planet, the credit goes to James Levine, who presided over a performance of such kinetic musicality that the hours barreled by. Levine supported the singers with an orchestral undergirding as solid and incandescent as Brünnhilde's flaming rock, and he had a valorous cast.

Wolfgang Schmidt was the titular hero, and he sang the role magnificently, matching his magic sword Nothung for well-honed, tempered heft and playing him as a good Germanic brawler: swaggering, fearless, and not terribly bright. On occasion, Schmidt played his character's thickheadedness for laughs. In that fleeting homoerotic moment when he finds the warrior-goddess Brünnhilde asleep on her rock and lovingly removes her shield, helmet, and breastplate before discovering that she is not a man, Schmidt made much of the way Siegfried's momentary horror is sublimated into instantaneous love.

Hildegard Behrens, who sang Brünnhilde (oddly, wearing a nightgown under her armor), has recovered most of her voice but not all of her focus since being afflicted by a cold in "Die Walküre," and she was the only cast member who allowed her hour onstage to drag.

James Morris could not have been more magisterial as the Wanderer, the god Wotan in human mufti. The expert tenor Graham Clark made a real character, and not just a cartoon hunchback, out of the blacksmith-dwarf Mime, expertly regulating the dosages of kicked-dog skittishness, venality, and sympathy.

Writers' Workshop

Talking Points

1) In this review, the writer reveals himself directly: "I am not generally fond of fantasy or situations that drip with symbolism, but having let myself into Wagner's world on Saturday night, I had no desire to re-emerge." Why is this included? How does it help or hurt the review?

2) Note the alliteration in this review: "hobbit habitats and fiberglass forests." Can you find other instances of alliteration in these reviews?

3) Reviews, especially those of classical music performance, assume that readers have a certain background in the subject matter. Are these reviews accessible to most readers? How would they have to be rewritten to have a wider appeal?

Assignment Desk

1) Compare the conclusions of all these reviews. Some end with a summary about the performance, yet others end with a final comment about a specific character or event. Vary the ending of one of your reviews. Which seems more effective?

New season boasts two
Santa Fe opera productions

AUGUST 3, 1997

The Santa Fe Opera house is a brown building on a brown hill outside of town. From a distance, it is a streak of adobe that blends with the landscape, which is itself highly operatic. An afternoon storm beat its way through the area the day I arrived, and an hour before Strauss' "Arabella" began, the New Mexico sky was bisected in a theatrical stroke that would have earned a set designer an ovation.

To the east, over the Sangre de Cristo mountains, the sky still looked swollen, bruised and purple, like the remnants of a violent Act I. To the west, the curtain was going up on a second act of serenity and redemption, and the sheet of clear, lavender sky was striated with scarlet. In the middle was the base of a rainbow, more apparently solid and embraceable than any I have ever seen.

The whole extravagant arrangement looked rather like the Metropolitan Opera's production of Wagner's "Ring."

In such a setting, and because the opera house is only partially roofed and walled, set designers must either compete with the landscape or use it. The set for "Arabella" was a model of Vienna, tilted up to look like a city seen from a dipping airplane, with a backdrop of real sky beyond. Vienna brightened as night fell and New Mexico disappeared, and, at these altitudes, a chilly summer evening became a reasonable approximation of an Austrian winter night. More than a few of the blanket-wrapped audience members longed to join the cast onstage in populating all those cozy interiors. (Next year, a planned new roof will keep out the rain, but the wind will still careen through the bleachers.)

That the opera here can, at its best, be worth crossing deserts for matters to Santa Fe, a city whose center can seem populated entirely by out-of-towners from lands less rich in top-flight classical music. The opera's parking lot was filled with license plates from Texas, Colorado, Oklahoma, Nebraska, Arizona and Utah. But it is not just for affluent tourists: The bellhop at

Bishop's Lodge hotel had been to see "Semele." So had Shaylor Alley, a young wrangler at the Rancho Encantado resort.

But what happens at the opera here also gets felt in the Northeast: This year, New York City Opera is bringing in two Santa Fe productions from previous seasons (Tobias Picker's "Emmeline" and Handel's "Xerxes") and if City Opera keeps up its promised rate of new productions, more may be on the way.

City Opera could do worse than simply ship in Santa Fe's whole, handsome season—although it would have to retool some of the casts. The production of Handel's "Semele" (designed by City Opera production director John Conklin) closed off the stage from New Mexico's celebrated sky and substituted its own, an Olympian firmament that remains serene even when the gods in the plot do not. Handel knew that opera audiences must be dazzled, and while this production's gilt-trimmed look and glittering costumes (borrowed from London's Royal Opera) do their part, the singers sounded drab by comparison. Elizabeth Futral was a passable Semele, the mortal woman who aspires to romance with Jupiter, but tenor Rockwell Blake was decidedly earthbound as her chosen god.

If the singing deities of "Semele" sounded less than heavenly, there were occasional intimations of immortality in "Arabella." Strauss was always at his most empathic and perceptive when writing for women, and the first-act duet between the title character (sung by Janice Watson) and her cross-dressing sister, Zdenka (Dawn Kotoski), was a touchingly performed portrait of a neurotic sibling relationship, full of unspoken jealousy and love.

The Santa Fe Opera is fine enough to make its streaks of mediocrity maddening. The quartet of lovers in Mozart's "Cosi fan tutte" stood on three solid legs—Thomas Barrett's Guglielmo, Alwyn Mellor's Fiordiligi and Mary Ann McCormick's Dorabella—but was nearly brought down by tenor Robert Swensen, who wasn't up to the task of singing Ferrando. And this company can command enough stylish and resourceful design that the second-act set, an off-putting pile of gray rocks covered in a gelatinous green slime, was all the more mystifying.

The orchestra, an impermanent band composed of seasonal laborers, was startlingly adept at switching styles on a nightly basis. John Crosby, the company's founder, general director and Strauss specialist, elicited all sorts of velvety sounds from the pit in "Arabella." Richard Bradshaw piloted the responsive ensemble through the shoals of Peter Lieberson's score to "Ashoka's Dream."

The world premiere of "Ashoka's Dream," a Santa Fe commission, was big news here. An interview with Lieberson and librettist Douglas Penick topped the front page of *The Santa Fe New Mexican.* Two days later, the review, larded with superlatives, took up most of page 2.

"Ashoka's Dream" is a curiously cloven work. Penick's libretto, about the Indian emperor who first unified the subcontinent in a hurricane of brutality and then experienced an epiphany of peacefulness, has the inscrutable, archaic quality of Indian poetry read in translation. Director Stephen Wadsworth has set the opera's series of tableaux against the backdrop of an Indian altar, densely carved with sinuous and sedentary gods. In front of it, singers dressed in iridescent silks assume stylized positions, bending wrists and touching fingers in a graceful but puzzling sign language.

Lieberson's music, though, bears no trace of all this exoticism. Far from being saddled with faux-Buddhist meditativeness, the score is propulsive and unsettled, as changeable as the New Mexico sky. The closest it gets to overt mysticism is in its homages to Wagner— not in the style but in the way the narrative is simultaneously propelled by a febrile orchestra and slowed by solemn vocal lines.

Penick has endowed his characters with little more than silhouettes, leaving it to Lieberson to fill in states of mind with orchestral color and shading. Rarely do the people in this opera really come to grips with each other, but when they do—as when Ashoka's no. 2 wife, Triraksha, is disoriented by her husband's sudden surge of benevolence—Lieberson inserts a Verdian love duet whose beauty he truncates too soon. It is both a moving and a frustrating moment, offering a glimpse of this opera as a potential masterpiece.

The premiere's Triraksha was mezzo-soprano Lorraine Hunt, one of those priceless singers whose effect on an operatic stage is like that of a good chiropractor on a spine: She makes everything snap into alignment. In her presence, Kurt Ollmann, who sang the title role, became more murderously or transcendently intense, and the music's passions seemed to flow more freely. Whether or not "Ashoka's Dream" ever makes it to New York, it is comforting to know that Hunt will be appearing at City Opera in November in the Santa Fe production of "Xerxes."

Writers' Workshop

Talking Points

1) The writer includes comments about several operas in this review, but he only describes the plot of one, *Ashoka's Dream*. Note how he includes his comments about the performance as well as the composition in his review.

2) Note the writer's verb choice in this review: "tilted," "truncates," "snap." How do these choices affect the tone of the review?

Assignment Desk

1) The writer includes the landscape as another element in the review. Find a setting in your community and make it a character in a news story or review.

2) The writer discusses three operas in this review. How could it be rewritten to focus on just one opera?

Bringing Sibelius
in from the cold

DECEMBER 18, 1997

The composer Jean Sibelius, who was born during the middle of Brahms' career in 1865 and died in the middle of Leonard Bernstein's in 1957, remains one of the most popular and mysterious composers of the 20th century. In his own life and for decades since, he was routinely berated as a reactionary in a musically progressive era, the artistic equivalent of the old man who refuses to sell his dilapidated shack to make way for a highway. Forty years after his death, however, his music has stubbornly outlasted the fashions he ignored, and during Lincoln Center's two-week "Northern Lights" festival, it sounded newly modern.

After Sibelius' reputation broke beyond his native Finland in the 1890s, he was always a significant composer, simultaneously adored and reviled for his grand symphonic style full of horn calls and sincerity, and his melodies redolent of ancient myths. Even the critics who attacked him treated him as an important bad composer. Virgil Thomson, one of America's most influential midcentury tastemakers, devoted a chunk of his very first professional music review (for the *New York Herald Tribune*, in 1940) to the opinion that Sibelius was "vulgar, self indulgent, and provincial beyond all description." The French critic Rene Liebowitz wrote a whole book conveying on Sibelius the unquestionable distinction of being "the world's worst composer." No artist worth lavishing such invective on can be all bad.

As a composer, Sibelius assiduously avoided clichés and yet he was almost always seen through their prism. Thomson's word "provincial," for instance, tapped into the popular image of the flinty Finn ensconced in his rural sub-Arctic retreat, surrounded and inspired by pines, snow and silence. Used in 1940, when Finland was fending off Soviet invasion, the word "provincial" also meant nationalistic—a smirking nod to the fact that Sibelius had helped bring Finland into being (the country achieved independence from both Russia and

Sweden in 1917). Even today, the hero-composer's legacy looms over the small nation he helped create: For one thing, virtually every important Finnish musician who came after him was educated at Helsinki's conservatory, called the Sibelius Academy.

Lincoln Center's festival began with a high-intensity, three-concert dose of Sibelius' symphonic music, gorgeously performed by Sir Colin Davis and the London Symphony Orchestra. The three concerts, which included five symphonies, two tone poems, the violin concerto and a fistful of orchestral songs, would have been festive enough (if Sibelius' doggedly serious music can be thought of as festive). But Lincoln Center supplemented those events with a series of smaller concerts and a symposium. Capping the two weeks was a concert of contemporary Finnish music performed by the chamber group Avanti!, which seemed designed to test the ornery prediction, made by the composer Constant Lambert in 1934, that "of all contemporary music that of Sibelius seems to point forward most surely to the future."

Ah, but which future? Surely not that of the Finnish musicians who came of age in the 1970s, sloughed off their Sibelian birthright, acquired educational pedigrees in Italy, France and Germany and swore allegiance to the flag of international modernism. Their organ of dissemination was Avanti!, an ensemble founded in 1983 by the conductors Esa-Pekka Salonen (now music director of the Los Angeles Philharmonic) and Jukka-Pekka Saraste (now music director of the Toronto Symphony Orchestra). The group's youthful, cosmopolitan credo was encapsulated in its pointedly non-Finnish name, which, in Italian, is the battle cry "Forward!"

"Ours is the first generation of Finnish composers for whom Sibelius is not a problem," once said the composer and member of the Salonen-Saraste gang Magnus Lindberg, whose 1995 work "Arena 2" closed Avanti!'s concert. How ironic, then, that the group should have made its New York debut Monday as the tag end of a Sibelius festival.

In that context, Monday's concert, which took place in an Alice Tully Hall that looked about as densely populated as Finland itself, seemed like a declaration of independence. Kaaija Saariaho's "Graal Theatre," a concerto for violin and chamber ensemble, placed a solo part of grinding intensity against a stark background of pinpoint dissonances—the virtual opposite of Sibelius' plummy and popular Violin Concerto. Lindberg's "Arena 2" was as dense, bristling and urban in feel as Sibelius' symphonies are spacious and steeped in Nordic nature.

But, though the Avanti! players were very young and very good and most of the works freshly composed, the concert's pose of modernity seemed dated, burdened by a high-culture rigor that today's young American composers, at least, are glad to be able to shuck off. And there is the twist of "Northern Lights": that Sibelius' style, which once sounded like the gouty and distended aftereffect of excessive Romanticism, now seems to have acquired a prescient austerity. Sibelius was chastised for his willingness to linger on a plush, comfortable chord, for relentlessly stitching and restitching a good melodic phrase, for designing vast musical tapestries with a couple of bare ideas, for making crude and illogical jumpcuts from one passage to the next.

But now newer styles have made virtues of Sibelius' mannerisms: the sluggish chords and darting rhythms of American minimalism, the stark spiritual landscapes of the popular Estonian Arvo Part, the lushly evocative symphonic style of the young New York composer Richard Danielpour. After nearly a century in which intellectuals assumed that Sibelius' Mt. Rushmore face was gazing into the past, in New York in 1997, it now looks as though he did have his eye on the future after all—or at least on that slice of future that is our present.

Writers' Workshop

Talking Points

1) The writer includes a brief biography of Jean Sibelius in the review by using information from the lives of other composers. Why are they used as reference points? How does it affect the tone of the review?

2) "Sibelius was chastised for his willingness to linger on a plush, comfortable chord, for relentlessly stitching and restitching a good melodic phrase, for designing vast musical tapestries with a couple of bare ideas, for making crude and illogical jump cuts from one passage to the next." How effective is the imagery of sewing?

3) "Lindberg's 'Arena 2' was as dense, bristling and urban in feel as Sibelius' symphonies are spacious and steeped in Nordic nature." Note how the writer uses such contrasts to comment on performances in his reviews.

Assignment Desk

1) The writer portrays composer Jean Sibelius as misunderstood and underappreciated in his time. Choose an artist you consider worthy of greater attention and write a profile.

A conversation with
Justin Davidson

**KAREN BROWN DUNLAP: How would you de-
scribe the life of a critic?**

JUSTIN DAVIDSON: I haven't been doing it for very
long, so for me it means absorbing an enormous
amount very quickly and being able to deal with a wide
range of music. I may go to a production of Wagner's
Lohengrin at the Metropolitan Opera one night, and
then to a contemporary music concert the night after
that, and then on a Sunday afternoon go to a choral sacred music concert in a church, and then the night after
that to some kind of far-out experimental multimedia
high-tech performance.

You have to be able to readjust all of your aesthetic
criteria, because you've got to deal with each performance on its own terms. You have to concentrate, really
listen, then come up with something meaningful and
interesting to say.

The hardest review is of a pretty good, middle-of-
the-road, perfectly enjoyable concert of some warhorse
symphony that everybody's heard a million times.
What is there to say? Sometimes you have much more
to say than you can possibly get into the space that
you've been allotted, and sometimes you just wrack
your brains to say something meaningful.

Do you do stories other than reviews?

Well, when a news story related to music comes up,
I've got to report it. If there's a strike at an orchestra, or
if there's a controversy with the Vienna Philharmonic,
or if a prominent musician dies, any of those things that
come up, I've got to report that beat the way any reporter does. So there's that.

I have a record column, and there are other stories
that are music-related. I might do a sidebar or an accompanying article to another story. We did a spread on
the choreographer Mark Morris. A dance person did a
feature interview with him, but I have always found

him a very musical choreographer, so I did an accompanying essay about how he interprets music.

I'm always working on features. And some of them are larger commentaries or feature essays. Sometimes they may take other disguises. *Newsday* gives me the liberty to write things that you can't necessarily put in a pigeonhole.

I also write the interviews and process pieces that I enjoy most, the long, in-depth pieces I can really sink my teeth into.

What's your work style?

I work out of New York City where we have an office, but actually I work mostly out of my home. I get up at 6 a.m. to write my reviews, which I do several times a week. I have a baby who is six months old. He plays on the floor and I sit with him and write my review on a laptop. So far he's letting me do it. I don't know how much longer that'll last.

I file my reviews by 9 a.m. and then the workday starts. I deal with publicists and do my interviews and so on. In the evening, I go out to a concert, so there are days that start at 6 a.m. and end at midnight.

How do you decide on what to review?

I have the luxury of being able to be very selective. I cover New York City and Long Island so there're some things that I *have* to do. I have to do every new production at the Metropolitan Opera, every new production at the New York City Opera, and I have to do those on opening night. Then there are certain other events that are just so obviously important that I do them, like the Three Tenors concert at Giant Stadium.

But beyond that, I look for things that seem interesting. Because I'm a composer, I'm always interested in hearing new music. I love having to react to something that nobody has heard before, putting myself on the line to say what I think of it.

I often think of a collection of really horrible reviews that a conductor and scholar named Nicolas Slonimsky put together called *Lexicon of Musical Invective.* Some of the reviews are of pieces that now are acknowledged as great masterpieces, but critics of the past said they stank. Actually, if you read the reviews carefully, you realize some of them were quite perceptive.

Why were they wrong, then?

They were wrong because the stuff was so novel. They may have been wrong in their evaluation, but the actual reporting was quite accurate. So when I review new music, I think of that book and wonder what great masterpiece of the future I'm about to pan. It's exciting in a way. There is great potential for making a fool out of yourself.

After you select the event to cover, what is your process for the review?

I go to the event and just listen as closely as I can. Sometimes I will not start writing my review. In other words, I'll try to keep the listening experience very separate from the writing experience. At other times, the concert may get me thinking right away and then I decide to get my thoughts down before I forget.

What do you put in your notes? Do you write your impressions or reminders of what's happening?

Generally it's either sensual impressions or some issue I want to tackle. Sometimes I just describe some new and unusual music. Sometimes the issues become quite obvious. An example is the piece I wrote on the Vienna Philharmonic.

You have a beautiful lead there introducing a piece on how a great orchestra seemed "highly competent and completely generic." How did you decide on that focus, and how did you settle on that lead?

My reaction to that concert was that this is possibly the best orchestra in the world performing at an amazingly professional level. You couldn't really fault it for anything, but I found myself thinking that something was missing. And what was missing was the sense of excitement.

I don't recall taking notes at that concert. Sometimes I'll start writing the piece and then, halfway through, I'll realize what the lead is. But in this case, where I was building a whole argument around what this orchestra is about and what it does, I think I probably would've started with the lead.

Near the end of this piece you wrote, "Neither Mozart nor Bruckner fared better on the following night." And you gave some background on some of their symphonies. To what degree do you see your writing as teaching?

Well, I definitely think of teaching and writing as very much part of the same activity. Part of my experience teaching as a graduate student at Columbia University has helped me enormously as a critic. I was put in charge of two sections of this class called Music Humanities. Everybody at Columbia had to take a one-semester course in the history of Western music, so this was a required course. I was given few requirements for teaching the course. They basically said, "You've got 12 weeks. You've got 25 kids. Teach them something about what's happened in music in the last thousand years."

I thought it was a great opportunity to make myself learn and try to communicate the things I learned. In some ways the course was a verbal form of what I do now. It was taking some people with limited musical backgrounds and communicating something meaningful to them *and* doing so in a way that wouldn't bore the people who'd been studying music for years.

I imagine that the reader is similar to the student in my class. My job is to try to get somebody to read what I write. And I guess my fantasy is that somebody who really doesn't know anything about music or really isn't interested may start reading my piece because it's on the same page with something that they *are* interested in. And then, as they read, they decide to read to the end because they're having a good time and they find themselves immersed in the writing. And then when they're done with the piece, they think it was interesting and they actually learned something.

I guess that teaching experience also helped with the research that you add in your pieces.

Yes. The teaching forced me to really be prepared. I don't think that you have to have a Ph.D. to be a critic. But on the other hand, it sure helps.

In "Kissin Powers an Electric Occasion," you help readers with the use of similes. You say, "Watching the awkward young pianist plunge into music was like seeing a seal slip into water..." Do you look for opportunities to use similes or metaphors?

Oh, sure. To me it's crucial; it does more than add color. When you're dealing with something that is as abstract as music, there are two ways of talking about it. One is to get technical, which is the way a musician would. And the other is to use metaphors or similes to be equally effective. I could talk about *rubato* and *legato* and use a whole lot of Italian words. And sometimes I will use them when they're appropriate, hopefully in a way that makes people understand.

There are other challenges in reviewing Kissin. I've reviewed him a bunch of times, and, of course, it becomes difficult to try to say things in a different way. That's something a lot of writers face. If you're writing about baseball, you may be at a different game every night, but it's still baseball and you have to find a different way to describe the same actions.

Another thing about Kissin is that he is an extraordinary performer. There is something that happens when he plays. I have to get across to the reader the feeling of being in the audience and being stunned without saying, "I was stunned."

You captured that nicely in the penultimate paragraph by saying you hated to reach the end of the concert. I felt the same way about reading this piece. I hated for it to end.

Thank you.

You began your piece on the Santa Fe Opera with great description, great detail, and an explosion of color. The musician and critic became the artist. What inspired this approach?

The experience. I had never been to Santa Fe before, and I'll never forget that first drive up to the opera house. I had never seen anything like it. I think anybody who has been to that opera house will tell you that one of the wonderful things about going to the opera is the experience of just *getting* there.

In the Sante Fe piece you are critical of one singer, saying he's not up to the task. In his book, *The Critic's Power in the Performing Arts,* John Booth notes performers' concerns that they sometimes don't get a "fair break" from critics. When is it fair for a reviewer to be critical of a performer and how negative should a critic be?

I've certainly written a lot harsher things than that. But that's a really good question: How negative can you allow yourself to be? I think that you're unlikely to be more critical of an artist's performance than the artist is of himself or herself. I mean artists know when they're doing something that isn't up to their standards, and *their* standards are higher than yours, as long as we're talking about really professional, top-flight people. You're not telling them anything that surprises them.

One of the things you've got to do is keep the feelings of the performers in mind and remember that they're putting themselves on the line, and you have to have some sympathy with that.

When the review is of somebody who is just starting out and you want to know how promising the person might be, then obviously, you try to find a way to get across your impression in a way that's kind.

But the more prestigious the institution or the performer you're criticizing, the more you can afford to demand, and the more you can afford to be critical, and even nasty.

On the other hand, I also have sympathy with the guy who might shell out $500 for a pair of tickets. If I'm sitting there thinking, "This is a boring, stupid evening," well, I would want him to know that before he spends that much money to sit through it.

You've had your own compositions performed in the United States, Italy, and other places. Does it help to have the experience of being a composer and of being reviewed?

I never saw reviews of foreign performances of my music, and the performances I had in New York were not reviewed. In graduate school there was criticism from my peers and my professors and my family. More profound was the criticism from the musicians who played the pieces. That was professional criticism that I took very much to heart.

I still compose, although I haven't been doing it much because I haven't had the time. I really want to make sure that there is time for that in my life.

What was the genesis of your passion for music?

I don't know. My father was very passionate about music, but in an amateur way. He plays the piano some, but he wasn't a professional. His mother had cultivated a lot of musicians. Her social circles included many famous names. She talked about Lenny, by whom she meant Leonard Bernstein, and Volodya, and she meant Vladimir Horowitz. They were her card partners. I grew up hearing all of this lore about these people, but the names didn't mean that much to me until later.

I wonder about the confidence you need to be a critic. You have the background as a composer, and you have a Ph.D., which is unusual and gives you added knowledge and authority. In spite of that, how do critics get the confidence to stand forth and render their opinions?

It comes with the territory. You *have* to. It comes from the principal demand that's being placed on you, which is to write something people want to read. If it's going to be interesting to read, it has to be strongly expressed. Now, the danger is that you don't want to strengthen your opinions in order to make a good piece of writing, because that's dishonest.

It's so much easier to write a whole review that says, "This was great," or "This was absolutely terrible," than to write something that says, "This had some good qualities and some bad." A friend calls that the 60-40 syndrome: 60 percent of it was good and 40 percent was bad, or the other way around. That produces some pretty uninteresting writing a lot of the time, but when you *do* have mixed opinions, then you have to find a way to say them in a strong way.

As far as having opinions, though, who doesn't have opinions? I don't feel that my job as a critic is to have better opinions than the next person. I think I have the background to have informed opinions, but it's not like my opinion matters so much more than the next person's. What I do is take my opinion and turn it into a piece of writing. If I had somebody else's opinion, then I would try to turn *that* into a piece of writing. The actual opinion matters less. I'm not upset at people who read what I write and disagree with me completely.

You speak with an unusual interest in the readership. You've said several times that you need to write something that people will want to read. Is that a major concern of critics?

I think that with music criticism in particular, there is a danger in assuming that the only people who are going to read what you write are people who are already interested in classical music and who know a great deal about it. You're kind of writing to aficionados.

I am always afraid of producing the equivalent of the bridge column. I don't read the bridge column because I don't play bridge. I'm afraid of people looking at my pieces and saying, "I don't know anything about opera, therefore I'm not going to read what he has to say about it." What horrifies me is that we, as critics, might start to believe what some of the editors tell us, which is that our beat is an obscure, esoteric, specialized field that people aren't really interested in.

Well, I feel passionate about the subject matter I cover. If I can communicate some of that, then I feel like I'm really doing my job well.

What kind of responses do you get from readers?

Completely unpredictable ones—a very wide range of responses. They're hard to characterize. There are certain musicians who have their loyal followings, and if you criticize them you will undoubtedly hear from their cheerleaders. Then there is an 88-year-old woman who was born in Berlin, played the piano as a child, and grew up listening to a lot of music in her household. She now lives in Queens and is housebound. So she listens to recordings. And she wrote me once asking why I didn't cover a certain recital in Carnegie Hall. I responded and she continued communicating. Finally she told me, "I want you to know that I can't get out much, but reading what you write about music makes me feel like I'm still in touch. It keeps me connected to the music world." I really felt like I was performing a service.

Do you get much help from editors?

My editor is Peter Goodman. He hired me as a free-lancer in 1995. About that time *New York Newsday* actually had two classical music critics, one of whom had been Peter. But Peter had switched over to editing. He and I have a very smooth rhythm, a very smooth relationship.

The editing process, of course, really starts with conceiving a story. I talk to Peter about scheduling a review, or when I'm starting to think about a longer-term feature, or else a reporting assignment.

He and other editors at *Newsday* have learned to trust me, so I am now pretty much able to say, "Next week I'm planning to do this, this, and this." And then I do it and send in the stories.

Then there are other times when I call Peter and say, "I can do this or I can do this, but I can't be in two places at the same time, so what do you think?" Peter is very good because he knows a lot about the subject matter. We talk and we make some of those decisions together.

Now I'm going to ask you a really strange question. Because of your specialty, and mostly because of

your work in many fields, do you think of yourself as a journalist?

Yes, I do. The job has made me that. That's what I do. I write the stuff and it goes in the paper, and it had better satisfy all the demands of journalism. It's got to be accurate. It's got to be well-reported. It's got to be on time. The copy has to be clean. It's got to be well-written. It's got to be grammatical, and all those things. And I pride myself on my professionalism about that.

I don't think that I would be a journalist, though, if this weren't my beat. If somebody came along at the paper and said, "We've determined that there are exactly three people in Yaphank who read what you have to write about classical music and we can't afford the space anymore, and so we're gonna phase out classical music. But we would like you to stay on at the paper and write about something else," I don't know if I would. There are certainly things I would be interested in writing about, but I don't know that my commitment to writing, to being a journalist, would allow me to take just any assignment.

I'm very aware of having come into journalism backwards through music.

What advice would you give to anyone interested in becoming a critic?

Well, I think somebody who wanted to be a music critic in particular would have to keep in mind what the mission is. And the mission is to try to communicate some of the passion that you have for the field to people who may not necessarily share it and may not have the background that you do.

I encourage critics in general to remember that you are writers. John Simon spoke of someone who died recently, and he said that this person was extraordinary because he *wrote* his reviews. They were pieces of writing. They weren't just reactions to things.

The package that you deliver the information in has to be elegant and appealing. And you've got to remember that you are a *writer.* That's really important.

Stephen Hunter
Criticism

Stephen Hunter, film critic of *The Washington Post,* was born in 1946 and grew up in Evanston, Ill. His father was head of the film department at Northwestern University and his mother wrote children's books. Hunter says, "I was crummy at everything except reading." His reading included pieces by *Chicago Daily News* film critic Sam Lesner, and by age eight he wanted to be a film critic.

He graduated from the Medill School of Journalism at Northwestern and spent two years in the Army. In 1971 he began work at the Baltimore *Sun* as a copy reader. Ten years later he reached his dream of becoming a film critic. After 26 years at the *Sun,* he moved to *The Washington Post* in 1997.

Hunter has written eight novels, published a collection of his reviews, and has been a screenwriter.

The Washington Post

He's a passionate fan of the Baltimore Orioles, and likes to travel and collect guns. He's married, though separated, and has two children, ages 20 and 17.

—Karen Brown Dunlap

Speed: Missing a hook and line, it's a sinker

JUNE 13, 1997

The original *Speed* was so milled to maximum stream-line, it didn't even have a subtext. The sequel—*Speed 2: Cruise Control*—takes this concept further: It doesn't have a text.

What a reeking bag of nothingness! What empti-ness, what vaporous vapidity! What rot, stink, and whiff of mold spore! It's like an existential prank mer-rily engineered by Jean-Paul Sartre in heaven.

The director, Jan De Bont, who did both the original *Speed* and last summer's brain-dead *Twister,* has put to-gether a reputation for pyrotechnic kinetics at the tech-nical level and infantile twaddle at the emotional level. Naturally, this has made him hugely successful. But in this one he underwhelms even the lowest expectations. The kinetics aren't that good, the twaddle is off the charts and the characters seem written by monkeys on amphetamines with crayons.

At least the first *Speed* had the benefit of a premise that was both original and breathtakingly clear: A mad-man had wired a bus with a bomb that would explode if the bus's speed dropped below 50 mph. Consequently, as the vehicle careened through the worst traffic on the planet, the speedometer needle was like an electrode to the collective medulla oblongata of the American pub-lic; as it flirted with the red line, it kept you in oxygen debt, even if you didn't believe a second of it.

The sequel exchanges the bus in traffic for the 25,000-ton luxury steamer wending its piglike way through the trough of the Caribbean under azure skies. It looks like a skyscraper designed by Albert Speer floating on its side. That makes the title a joke: There's no illusion of speed whatsoever. It should have been called *Sloth.*

The only survivor from the previous cast is poor Sandra Bullock, still named Annie, still acting like the girl with a good personality that nobody wants to date. Keanu Reeves and his offbeat charm being absent, she is teamed up this time with—whatta coincidence!—yet another daredevil SWAT cop, played by that refugee from the Planet of the Handsome, Dull Men: Jason Patric. His Alex is so beautiful and inert he reminds you less of Reeves than of Michelangelo's David.

The *de rigueur* madman here is the normally reliable Willem Dafoe, an actual actor. But given no actual character to play, Dafoe falls back on what appears to be the ammonia-inhalation school of method acting. When called upon to invent a passionate expression, he appears to imagine that he's just taken a stout whiff of the old NH_3; his eyeballs and nostrils blow open to about f/1. That's it for acting.

Dafoe's character, a disgruntled former software designer for the company that designed the ship's navigational system, is that archetypal office bore, the chronic whiner, always at pains to explain why he's so right and everyone else is so wrong. ZZZZZZZZZZ. He's rigged the ship with explosives, but his prime plan is to fake the passengers and crew into abandoning the vessel by commandeering the computer system and sending false information, and then looting a jewelry cargo. This leads to numerous exciting scenes of him pounding manically at a keyboard.

He gets most of the idiots into lifeboats but a small *Poseidon Adventure*-size squad is left on board, including a couple of officers, the woman with the cleavage, the woman who is fat, the rich snooty couple with the deaf daughter and the parvenu millionaire. And, of course, the "A" kids, Alex and Annie, who immediately take charge because they've learned more about the ship in 24 hours than the professionals who run it on a daily basis.

As an action movie venue, the ship needn't have been so wretchedly wasted. In fact, in 1974, Richard Lester made the masterpiece of the ships-in-peril-on-the-sea genre in his underappreciated classic *Juggernaut* (Rent it; love it; thank me later.). But De Bont wastes an hour on drizzly rescues in the ship's dark bowels, as Patric keeps leading or pulling the unfortunate out of the water. It's really more a remake of Stallone's recent *Daylight* than any kind of sequel to *Speed.*

By the second hour, De Bont finally gets to his big number: a game of ocean vessel chicken between the big cruiser and a fuel-laden tanker at anchor in St. Maarten's harbor. Watching these giant sea turtles laboriously close on each other isn't quite the thrill he thinks it is.

He does, finally, squeeze a little adrenaline out of you when he contrives to give the big ship shore leave in that quaint harbor town. It thunders ashore like Godzilla looking for the head, crunching the tinkertoy town to toothpicks. A little later, that tanker finally goes up: a very nice explosion, thank you very much.

But in all ways, shapes, forms and meanings, *Speed 2: Cruise Control* is a titanic dud. Where is that damned iceberg when you need it?

Writers' Workshop

Talking Points

1) The writer ends three sentences in the second paragraph with exclamation points. Why? Is it effective?

2) The writer assumes a personal relationship with the reader when he recommends a second movie: "Rent it; love it; thank me later." Is this appropriate in a review?

3) The writer cites his complaints about the movie, and there are many, in a very humorous tone. What makes this review so funny?

Assignment Desk

1) Write a favorable review of *Speed 2: Cruise Control.*

Air Force One:
Pressurized ride

JULY 25, 1997

This is the one into which Clinton should have had himself inserted!

Air Force One is a pulse-pounding bull goose of a movie, but more than that, it's a $90 million endorsement of the Great Man theory of history. It's *The Rough Riders* set on a jetliner. It's president as action figure, 6 feet 2 of heroic plastic.

This prez kicks butt. He kills. He knows the operating drill on the Heckler & Koch MP5 machine pistol. He gives forthright speeches—and this is really brave! —without clearing them with the staff first! He puts the world on notice that America is back in the saddle again and there's a new sheriff in town.

Harrison Ford, in the role of this righteous galoot, can't really be said to act, because he's not really required to play a character. His President Jim Marshall, lion of the free world, Medal of Honor winner, Big Ten grad, football fan and beer drinker, is so idealized he makes Barbie's Ken look positively Dostoevskian. Ford does two things brilliantly: He never bumps into the furniture and he never lets even a whisper of campy self-awareness crack the 100-foot-high Mount Rushmore of his face. *Air Force One* is set in an irony-free zone. Ford's discipline is at its highest as he cleaves to the movie's fundamental proposition: This is not a joke. (It is, of course.)

Naturally, he's the dullest thing in the movie. But that's not bad, that's good. Who wants a neurotic intellectual or an ironist or a policy wonk at the helm when psychotic Russian nationalists have taken over the president's plane on a flight back from Moscow and are busily executing hostages as a ploy to free a demonic nationalist leader recently filched from his despot's den by a joint Spetznaz-Delta team (the movie's fabulous opening sequence)? Much better this sort of leadership: doubtless, fearless, dynamic, clever, aggressive, anachronistic, impossible and dull. But his dullness clears the way for the movie's showiest special effect: Gary Oldman.

Oldman plays the evil Ivan Korshunov, the terrorist who masterminds the skyjacking of Air Force One and then proceeds to steal not merely the gigantic flying machine itself but another and more important machine: the camera. This actor is never so good as when he is very, very bad, and *Air Force One* provides him with a platform to do a variation on a combination of Boris Godunov and Boris Badenov simultaneously. Throw in some Rasputin and some Alexander Nevsky and even some Ivan Skavinsky Skavar and you've got the whole nine yards. He would eat the furniture if it weren't all plastic and fiberglass.

Director Wolfgang Petersen controls the mayhem with his usual extreme cleverness. Like everybody in the picture, however, he's working miles beneath his head. He once made a great movie about real men in a real war, *Das Boot,* but now he's making straw movies about straw men in a straw war. But you sense the intense level of his engagement. As in his last macho confabulation, *In the Line of Fire,* so much of the cleverness is in the details.

In *Fire,* I loved the way they solved the problem of getting not a ceramic gun but a brass and lead bullet through a metal detector by hiding it in a key chain, which of course would go around the detector in a little plastic tray. In this one, his micro-genius is on display in one sequence where he follows a bad MiG pilot engaging the president's plane and then Air Force F-15s. The actor (Boris Krutonog) has maybe 25 seconds of total screen time, the bottom of his face sealed off in an oxygen mask, the top of his head capped in a plastic helmet. What's left? Eyes. Fabulous, bulging, expressive eyes that radiate the raptor's glee as he looses an air-to-air missile toward the big bird, then utter fear of doom as he watches an F-15's Sidewinder come screaming to erase him in a bright orange blot. Cool movie death!

In fact, one of the pleasant surprises of *Air Force One* is how much of it is an old-fashioned airplane movie. The modern computer morphing does no task better than rendering aircraft in flight. You never for a second tumble to the fact that you are watching electricity concocted by some arrogant kid in a Southern California computer shop: The jets, as they lace through the sky in and around the president's plane, are majestic, and one sequence where a line of F-15s lets fly a phalanx of heat-seekers leaking flame as they streak across the sky has a terrible beauty to it.

But in order to keep the odor of man-sweat, testosterone and flatulence from becoming too terribly oppressive, Petersen, abetted by scriptwriter Andrew W. Marlowe (of Washington, in fact), provides some female presence. Glenn Close is effectively steely as the vice president who manages to deal with a power play by the secretary of defense while coolly managing the war room crisis team. She cries only a little bit.

Equally impressive is Wendy Crewson as the first lady. I love her sense of flintiness, too: She upbraids a staff member for not paying attention during a speech, just like the real thing, and she has a commanding presence that never breaks down, even when the guns are pressed against her head. More idealized but also welcome is Liesel Matthews as the teenage first daughter.

In all, *Air Force One* is of a piece. It takes its absurd premise and keeps itself narrowly focused, pushing its heroic cast through obstacle after obstacle. It lacks perhaps a moment of grief for the many warriors who sacrifice their lives for the chief exec, and some of its gambits—a parachute "escape" into where, the Urals? —play well on screen but fray upon application of minimum thoughtfulness. But it's a great ride.

Writers' Workshop

Talking Points

1) Does the writer like this movie? How does he bolster his argument?

2) The opening paragraph refers to a controversy about footage of President Clinton being included in a movie without his permission. Does the joke work if the reader doesn't know the background?

3) The writer compares this movie with Westerns and other action-hero films. How does the writing reinforce the comparison?

4) Study sentence length in this review. Short sentences carry additional impact because they're used well. Find examples of effective short sentences.

Assignment Desk

1) Who are Boris Godunov, Boris Badenov, Rasputin, Alexander Nevsky, and Ivan Skavinsky Skavar? Research and discuss why naming them contributes to the tone of the review.

M: Lang's masterpiece still shocking after all these years

AUGUST 29, 1997

M is for the many nightmares it gave to me. That is, *M,* Fritz Lang's 1931 dark masterpiece, out of which sprang so much of the century's bleaker popular art and some of the earliest images of the haunting chaos that dogs us to this day.

Alas, this "restored" version may represent a heroic seven-year effort on the part of the Munich Film Archive and it may well be the best possible cut of the 66-year-old film available in years, but it still seems to be in far from pristine condition. And too many times the white subtitles are projected against a white background, their information completely lost.

So you can't see parts of it and you can't read other parts of it. My advice: Deal with it like a grown-up. The movie is somehow still necessary, and its power to disturb remains profound. On top of that, Peter Lorre's sweaty, puffy, froggy-eyed portrayal of a child murderer remains one of the most frightening images in screen history. All moist flesh and grubby, fat little fingers, infantile and pathetic yet truly monstrous at once, Lorre's character is one of the great monuments to the true squalor of evil. He is not banal in the least, but neither is he dramatic: He's a little worm with an unspeakable obsession, insane and yet a horrible reflection of the society that created him.

The film is constructed as a double manhunt. In an unnamed city (the story was based on a case in Düsseldorf, but many critics place the setting in Berlin, where *M* was filmed), a child murderer is stalking the streets. In a brilliant early montage Lang shows us the young Elsie being suavely picked up by her shadowy killer, led along streets and into the woods. There's no on-screen violence, of course, but the sense of menace is unbearably intense, particularly as Lang signifies the murderer's dementia in musical terms, having him whistle a selection from *Peer Gynt* as the demon's grip on his soul grows more fierce. Lang polishes off the sequence with two horrifying images: Elsie's ball bouncing across the grass, losing energy, and reaching stasis; and Elsie's balloon caught (as if in torment) in the suspended telephone wires.

The cops, under great pressure, mount a massive manhunt; they attack the only target they have, which is the underworld. This completely upsets the orderly nature of crime—these guys are so well organized, they even have a stolen-sandwich ring!—and so the crooks respond by attempting on their own to find the killer.

In allegorical terms, Lang seemed to be getting at the escalating conflict between the increasingly inept Weimar Republic and the increasingly efficient underground Nazi Party, and the underworld, being more merciless and better organized, is able to uncover the villain before police.

It goes further. The original name of the film was *The Murderers Among Us,* which had resonance that annoyed those thick-necked creeps in the brown shirts. It was for that reason that Lang changed the title to *M,* for murderer and for the mark of Cain that a beggar chalks on Lorre's back so that he may be identified and tracked by the beggars who are the reconnaissance unit of organized criminal interests.

And, as a narrative, the film still works brilliantly. It broke the mold before there was a mold to be broken. Lang begins by completely dispensing with the mystery elements; he reveals Lorre at about the one-third mark, so there's no whodunit. There's not even really a whydunit. Instead, it's a who's-gonna-catch-him as the two sides work frantically against each other. But even when Lang documents the final apprehension (in a brilliantly edited and timed sequence where the cops are racing to a building that the gangsters have all but commandeered as they search it), he has a surprise. That is the ironic trial of which the clammy little human mushroom, where at last he speaks for himself, declares his own insanity and the pain it's caused him and asks them who they are to judge—interesting questions to be asked in the Germany of 1931.

But the movie is, perhaps, just as interesting as a piece of film design as it is as a piece of narrative. It was the domestic high-water mark of German expressionist filmmakers, who were about to be dispersed around the world by the rise of those same Nazis, who would gain power in 1933.

German expressionism, which may have gotten to its strangest moment in 1919's *The Cabinet of Dr. Caligari,* was essentially a visual version of a treacherous universe. It was spread by this diaspora of fleeing German genius (including Lang, who went on to have a distinguished American career) and came to light in the works of Hitchcock and Welles but perhaps most notably in that movie genre known as film noir, which dominated the American screen in the late '40s.

To look at *M* is to be in the heart of the noir universe, a shadowy zone of wet streets, dark alleyways, secret places and impenetrable mysteries. It's astonishing how modern this six-decade-old piece seems, especially if one focuses on the compositions and their meanings and can see past the Victorian wardrobes worn by the citizens of a German city in 1931.

M, after all these years, is still a fabulous movie.

Writers' Workshop

Talking Points

1) The writer offers readers both a description of the plot and an interpretation of the movie's symbolism. Would it be better to read the review before you see the movie or after you see it?

2) The review offers a fairly complete description of the movie. Does it still entice the reader into wanting to see the movie, or does it deflate the reader's interest in the movie?

3) Specific details give the review more resonance. "Whistle a selection from *Peer Gynt,*" "The mark of Cain that a beggar chalks on Lorre's back." Discuss the effect of these details.

Assignment Desk

1) Who is the audience for this movie? Rewrite the review to target another audience.

2) Watch another classic film and write a review. In your review, compare film tastes of previous generations with the tastes of the 1990s.

Anastasia: A magical ride unfettered by facts

NOVEMBER 21, 1997

Little-known fact about Stalinist Russia, 1926, courtesy of *Anastasia:* There was no food but there was a surprising abundance of Maybelline eyeliner.

How else to explain the almond definition of Anastasia's vaguely Orientalized eyes in this beautiful idiot of an animated movie? She doesn't look like a Russian princess at all, but more like the teenage Cher.

Though it's from 20th Century Fox, *Anastasia* shows us a very Disney Russian Revolution, so Disney that, oops, they forgot the Communists. The movie is a dream, a peach and a lie. It works fabulously as spectacle, at least marginally as story and as history it's bunk.

Of what importance is history, you ask, if it makes my little girl smile? There's no answer to this question, really, but one must ask directors Don Bluth and Gary Goldman why they chose to call it *Anastasia* and set it in the century's central drama if they meant to completely ignore that history. They could have called it *The Missing Princess* and set it in Graustarkia, Ruritania, or on the Island of Guavabuto.

Bluth and Goldman are ex-Disney animators who left the studio in a huff in 1979 because it had abandoned the classic, voluptuous, painterly stylistics of *Snow White* and *Dumbo* for a cleaner, cheaper modern look. Since then, they've bounced from studio to studio trying to out-Disney Disney, and this is one time they may have succeeded.

On the other hand, they may have cheated.

The hardest thing to animate convincingly is human movement. But it becomes considerably easier if you trace it—and, using human beings as "live action reference," Bluth and Goldman have clearly filmed some of the film's complex action, then based their images on those sequences. So the movie is an odd hybrid: It seems animated, it has all the stylizations of animation, yet the human movement is so realistic that your brain picks up on it subconsciously, sending little signals of weirdness up to the conscious. It's continually...not annoying, so much, but noticeable.

The story is an infantilized, sanitized version of the 1956 film starring Yul Brynner and Ingrid Bergman (she won an Oscar). A White Russian finds an orphan to pass off as the only survivor of the murdered Romanov clan, making her heir to a treasure that her father, Czar Nicholas II, had hidden in Paris banks before the revolution. To qualify, she must pass muster before another surviving royal, the dowager empress. But what seems a mere scam soon proves troublesome: She may be the actual princess and the con man may be in love with her.

With Meg Ryan and John Cusack voicing the roles, Anastasia and Dimitri have been simplified from the Bergman-Brynner cosmopolitan wariness into twenty-somethings, with faces as uncomplex as Ohio cheer-leaders. It's not particularly believable, but it certainly makes box office sense.

The movie evokes the terrifying events beginning in 1916 in highly spurious form, then cuts to 1926, where the con man Dimitri is recruiting a young woman to play Anastasia in his scam. Fate throws him together with the amnesiac orphan Anya, and they journey from St. Petersburg (which was then called Leningrad, though the movie never notices) to Paris and the scrutiny of the dowager empress, along the way bedev-iled by the spirit of the Mad Monk Rasputin, who in limbo has sworn to destroy the Romanovs. (More historical absurdity: The Romanovs promoted him; it was nobles who murdered him.)

One can see the material's fascination for the animation team: great set-pieces of the lavish glories of Czarist Russia, the thrills of escape, the tenderness of young love, the mystery of the girl's identity, the melancholy of a lost world, the chance to re-create not merely "St. Petersburg" in 1926 but, more promisingly, Paris.

But there are pitfalls, too: the depressing business at Ekaterinburg in 1918 when Bolshie goons took Mr. and Mrs. Czar and all the little czars and czarinas into the cellar and spattered their brains on the bricks. Not exactly your typical musical number.

So Anastasia is peeled off from her family at the railway station and the fate of her parents and siblings is never referred to again; they're simply gone. That seems okay. But the actual revolution itself is strangely handled. It's ascribed entirely to the curse by the mad monk, who "spread unhappiness through the land." Other than a hammer and sickle on one guard's babushka, there's not a single reference to the political system that replaced Mr. and Mrs. Czar and its monumental cruelties. There's no reference whatsoever to the Romanovs' culpability in the debacle, or to the idiotic blood bath known as World War I, which made the whole thing possible and set the century up for 80 more years of conflict. The brothers Lenin, Trotsky and Stalin go unmentioned.

This creeps me way out. The museum of history is full of tragedy, cobwebs and corpses. Somehow attention must be paid to the great campaigns of death that shaped the century and haunt us to this day. To pretend it's not there, even in so innocent a vehicle as this, feels indecent, as if a reliquary is being burgled by hucksters.

But let's put that aside. As a colorful spectacle, kids under 10 will love *Anastasia,* though the very young might find the final confrontation between Anastasia and Rasputin on a Paris bridge somewhat intense, as it borrows elements from both Prince Charming's battle with the dragon in *Sleeping Beauty* and the "Night on Bald Mountain" from *Fantasia.*

The vocal performances are okay. Ryan and Cusack are incongruously American—every other Russian character speaks with an accent—but as there's no requirement for internal logic in animation, it's not bothersome. Ryan hardly registers as anything beyond generically spunky; Cusack over-registers as Cusack, so you see his own face, not Dimitri's visage, when he speaks. The musical numbers are all right but they have a '50s feel to them, a sense of the static; the numbers in such recent Disney products as *Beauty and the Beast* or *The Lion King,* driven by dazzling editing, are much better.

So here's my quote for the movie ad blurb: "*Anastasia* isn't terribly bad! In fact, it's almost all right!" 20th Century Fox advertising department, go for it!

Writers' Workshop

Talking Points

1) This review offers a primer on the discrepancy between the facts of the historical Anastasia and the movie version. How well-informed does a movie critic need to be?

2) The review undercuts the frustration with the lack of historical accuracy by its sarcastic tone: "Oops, they forgot the Communists." Why does the writer offer his critique using this technique?

3) The review adopts the language of cartoons: Bolshie goons, Mr. and Mrs. Czar. What is the effect?

4) Who is the audience for this review? How would the tone change for a different audience?

Assignment Desk

1) Watch the animated version of *Anastasia* and the 1956 version with Yul Brynner and Ingrid Bergman. Then write a review comparing the two.

The Sweet Hereafter:
A cry of hope

DECEMBER 25, 1997

Here's one way to look at it: Man is a meaning-seeking creature.

Pitiful being, he cannot accept the random cruelty of the universe. That is his biggest failing, the source of his unhappiness and possibly of his nobility as well. He paws through disasters with but one question for God: Why? And God never answers.

He certainly doesn't answer in Atom Egoyan's superb *The Sweet Hereafter,* which watches a mad, vain scrambler seeking to impart his own meaning on someone else's terrifying disaster. As derived from the intense Russell Banks novel, the story follows lawyer Mitchell Stephens (Ian Holm) on his peregrinations through a western Canadian town where a school bus has recently fallen through the ice, drowning 14 children and leaving an enamel of grief as blinding as the snow that blankets the place.

This lawyer: greedhead or pilgrim of pain?

This town: victim of horrid coincidence or of God's vengeance?

This story: remembered myth or spontaneous occurrence?

The answer to the questions is: All of the above. And one more thing is certain, and that is uncertainty. The movie is of the mode called postmodernism, which no one understands but everyone recognizes. To borrow from Kurt Vonnegut, its story has come unstuck in time, and though the narrative materials are eventually clarified, we seem to drift for a period between now and then, here and there. Some people can't handle this willed ambiguity and grow restless, if not anxious, in the absence of a clear chronology. But as in *The English Patient,* the chronological looseness is part of the pleasure of the piece, which magically reassembles in the last reel into something strong, lucid and compellingly powerful.

Basically, its "now" appears to be a plane ride in which Stephens returns, in defeat, from his trip. As he tells the story to his seat-mate, a friend of his daughter, the whole story emerges in bright and tragic vignettes, seen from a dozen perspectives, revealing the heart of the observer.

It turns out that in one sense, it's the most old-fashioned of narrative archetypes, the small-town story. Sam Dent, as the place is named, picturesque in the Canadian Rockies, soon reveals itself to be another in the form revealed by Grace Metalious all those years earlier in *Peyton Place,* a caldron of promiscuity, alcoholism, even some terrifying sexual child abuse.

In his recollection, as he bobs about the town in support of his lawsuits against the school board, the county that maintains the road and hires the driver, even the bus manufacturer, in search of a villain, any villain, Stephens encounters instead human weakness and culpability in all its forms. A was sleeping with B, C was molesting his daughter, D was cheating on her husband and on and on.

On top of this, Egoyan adds something that Banks never thought of. That's an overlay of myth, as he impresses Robert Browning's "The Pied Piper of Hamelin Town" on the events as if to ask the question, that eternal question: Who took the children? Who was the piper? Why did the portal in the mountain—an actual portal in the ice at the bottom of the mountain in the movie's most shattering scene—why did the portal open up and why did they disappear? As the saying goes: You've got to pay the piper. Why didn't the townspeople pay the piper?

But the final ambiguity is the lawyer himself. As it advances, the film makes clear he's not merely in search of wealth (though he may be), but driven by the need to impose meaning. He wants to inflict punishment on them. Them? Oh, you know: Them, they, the unknown agents of all destruction, workers for Lucifer, corporate, municipal or ecclesiastical, as the case may be. For he is also a parent in mourning: He once loved his daughter, Zoe, so much that he went beyond taboo and attempted to save her life with an emergency tracheotomy, taking upon himself the moral weight of cutting into his own daughter's flesh. Zoe is among the lost, not in this accident, but in another, larger accident called society.

Zoe phones him, wheedles for money, pretends to be his old Zoe, but she is clearly of that subset of living dead, the hopelessly addicted, her soul crippled with lust for heroin, her immune system finally overcome. We realize that the lawyer has gone west seeking meaning in the larger society of a town of lost children in hope of finding meaning in his own lost child.

Of course, it's hopeless. One can, after all, never know the reasons and the meanings. But there's something so human in the attempt that the movie, despite the crushing weight of the pain it contains, ultimately feels hopeful. The sweet hereafter of the title is that zone of wisdom where we ultimately come to accept the unacceptable and in some provisional, broken way, go on living.

Writers' Workshop

Talking Points

1) This review starts with a short, direct sentence and offers others through the article. What tone is set by the first sentence? How is the tone maintained throughout the review?

2) This review gives readers an interpretation of the film, a way of processing the information in the movie. Does this make the review essential reading for those who want to see the movie?

3) The review discusses timeless themes of hope and the search for life's meaning. Is it the discussion of those themes or the discussion of the narrative plot that would lure moviegoers?

Assignment Desk

1) Rewrite this review commenting solely on the narrative of the film. How does it affect the appeal to moviegoers?

A conversation with
Stephen Hunter

KAREN BROWN DUNLAP: You've been a film critic for about 17 years. How have the films changed, and how has your writing changed? Let's start with the films.

STEPHEN HUNTER: Well, one of the things I've seen is the death of certain genres. In my early years as a film critic, the Friday afternoon ritual was to go to some multiplex and see the latest movie in which teen-agers were slaughtered by a guy in a hockey mask. That was the height of the slasher movie craze. I think I saw more teen-agers die than any man this side of Roger Ebert.

There was a great deal of outrage about these films, and it was one of the things we were always hearing when we wrote about them. But one of the fascinations of the American film industry for someone who covers it is the sense that popular formulas wear out, and they're replaced by other popular formulas. You could just feel the slasher formula losing energy with each successive year, and now it's been years and years since I've seen a slasher film.

Another change is that the merchandising of movies has become much more sophisticated. What you see more and more is movies that are elaborate orchestrations of multimedia product movement. You see movies that have enormous tie-in deals with fast-food restaurants, and toy chains, and things like that.

So what you have is movies that aren't movies. They're simply the most visible part of an enormously complex marketing scheme. All these marketing schemes are planned on the idea that the movie is going to be a success, and so it's always both edifying and horrifying to watch a hundred-million-dollar-campaign disappear in a day when the movie fails to attract the audience.

How does that affect the quality of films?

It's certainly poisoning the sense of innocence. There's almost never a chance to discover anything anymore. Somehow, that sense of discovery is lost because these things are so overproduced and overorchestrated, and so hell-bent on squeezing the last penny out of the most obscure market possible.

What about your writing? Has it changed over the years?

You know, I'm an instinctive writer. I'm an unself-conscious writer. I will honestly say to you, the writing doesn't feel any different to me now. The process feels very much the same when I wrote a piece yesterday as it did when I wrote my first film review. There's a period of 17 years in between, yet the energy feels very much the same.

One presumes, one hopes, one prays, that with wisdom and experience you reach higher levels, that you do get better, and yet, when I look at pieces that I wrote years ago, they seem to me to be pretty good. And when I look at a piece I wrote yesterday, I think, "Boy, that sucks."

So I can't make a claim that the stuff has gotten better. I'm much more aware of a general arc in a career. I understand that by the weird chemistry or physics of talent there are some months when the movies are particularly fascinating, and stimulating, and juicy, when I'm better.

You're always better when you get movies that are fun to write about, that challenge and provoke you. Anyone could be a great movie critic if all they had to do was write about movies that provoked them. But, as a professional movie critic, you have to write about everything.

In preparing for an interview like this, the wise thing for me to do was read a book about film criticism. And of course, I did that, and found out that you didn't write the book, but you *did* write the chapter. The text is *The Complete Book of Feature Writing* and the chapter is "Becoming a Film Critic." In your chapter you wrote that film critics have the best job in America. That was about seven years ago. Do you still believe that?

Absolutely and totally. It's odd that you should read this. I just raised this issue today because of a magazine piece by a very good film critic that just seethes with self-pity and a sense of victimhood. It was the lament of a late middle-aged man that the movies are not as good as they were when he was a kid, and that he, as a critic, has become irrelevant, and that the movies are being made for other kinds of people, and they no longer speak to him.

We all feel that way sometimes, and when you get a bad run of movies, it can be really depressing. But another part of me is just screaming, "You have the best damned job in America." I mean, these are fabulous jobs, great jobs, and they provide access into very interesting worlds.

I venture to say most journalists, particularly most movie critics, have some sort of attention deficit disorder woven into their personality, and one of the great things about the movies is that there's always a new one next Friday. You're constantly being stimulated with new ranges of experience, new ranges of performance, new ranges of visual splendor, some of it good, some of it bad, some of it banal, some of it very mediocre.

I want to keep the part of me open that gets a kick out of really bad movies, and I still want to take movies apart with a pick ax, with a great deal of panache, and aggression, and bravura style, if I can. I want to keep myself excited.

So I do. The very long answer to a very short question is, yes, I do still really enjoy being a movie critic.

What is the journalistic purpose of film criticism? What do you hope to achieve in your writing?

That's a very good question, but it's almost too broad a question for me to answer because I don't think in those terms. In a sense, what you're doing is asking a front line soldier to talk about the aims of the war. And all he wants to do is get a good night's sleep and not get killed. I'm trying to write between 12 and 20 inches of good, vivid, provocative copy two to four times a week, depending on the week.

Here are a few thoughts, though. I think one of the things that a film critic brings to a newspaper is a personality. The film critic, the columnist, the drama critic are permitted the luxury of a personality. And we give a paper its charm, or we take away from it.

It seems to me people don't have intimate relationships with reporters, because the reporter's voice is more objective, or, if he's a feature writer, he's usually not covering a beat. But those of us like myself, or Tom Shales, or Lloyd Rose, or Rita Kempley, who cover specific beats as daily critics, become very important to our readers, specifically for people who care about our beats passionately.

I always take it as the highest compliment when I get a letter that says, "Dear Steve," instead of "Dear Mr. Hunter." That person, A, probably doesn't want something from me, and B, thinks of me as a friend. And so I think one of the things that movie critics do is they give the paper its personality.

I also think there's an intellectual responsibility for the paper to take covering popular culture seriously, a responsibility to stay in contact with what's happening, and to chronicle the play of ideas through public culture.

One of the things a critic does is look for meaning to apply to phenomena. The critic can do this by looking at the past, looking at the present, or the future, but it is important to provide a context in which movies can be situated.

And I think there's a consumer obligation to moviegoers and to parents to keep an eye on what's going on. They may disagree with my interpretations or judgments on a specific movie, but I'm hoping to sell them some idea of the shape of the industry, the shape of the season, the concerns of the season, and let them enjoy the confidence of knowing that professionals are looking at them.

What does it take to be a critic?

Well, it takes some things that you can't get. You have them, or you don't have them. The critic has to have some amount of writing ability, a great work ethic, and the willingness to work hard, to work fast, and to work clean.

When I say "clean," I mean copy that's cleanly conceptualized and cleanly delivered, and doesn't need to be broken down and reassembled at great length, copy that's highly professional and is very close to being publishable exactly as it is. If the ideas are clear, the writing will be clear, and the piece will be clear, and that's what I'm striving for.

The main thing is, the critic has to work hard. I don't like critics who see themselves as little, precious, special souls who are too delicate for the rough and tumble of the actual world. I'm a great believer that if you have any talent, you treat it roughly. That is, you work.

What's your work life like?

Well, I think people think it's a lot more glamorous than it is. It is a workplace situation, and it has all the frustrations and banalities of the workplace.

Now, I've been very fortunate at both the *Post* and in the latter part of my *Sun* career to enjoy what might be called the freedom of a senior correspondent. They've always understood that what they will get from me is the necessary number of pieces, well-written and on time; and I hope they're not interested in a little perfect attendance record pupil who shows up with a shoe shine and an apple for the teacher every morning at 8:30.

I can't give them that.

The movie critic lifestyle is kind of incoherent. I work on books at night, and I usually don't get up real early. I get to the office around the lunch hour. I like to spend my office time writing. The *only* thing I like to do in the office is write. I'm always behind on expense accounts, and I sometimes don't open my mail for weeks, and I almost never return phone calls.

But what I like to do is write. My friend, Henry Allen, our great feature writer, said to me, "You know, you're the most efficient man on the *Post,* because all you do is write. You never open your mail. You never clean your desk. You come in and write and then you go home."

I go to the movies two or three nights a week. I see a lot of movies in the morning, at the various theaters in Washington. Sometimes I see them in the afternoon. Sometimes I work five nights in a row. It's a very fluid lifestyle.

Talk a little bit about your winning pieces. You didn't really like *Speed II*. That came across strongly.

Earlier in this conversation you talked about reviewing bad movies. Is it easier to write about a bad movie?

It's easier to write about the extremes than it is about the bland middle. And yet I feel that the most important thing a film critic does is write about the bland middle. You'll notice when there's a movie that's a big critical hit, everybody becomes a movie critic. All the op-ed pages have pieces, George Will and Richard Cohen will write about it; everyone will find a way to write about it.

To some degree, that's true of really monstrously bad films, particularly when they are overly hyped and overly sold and overly advertised, and everybody is aware of them, and anticipating them.

Most films are in between: they offer some pleasures and they offer some pains. You find yourself looking for some novel way of dealing with issues you've dealt with a hundred times before. That's the mark of a great film critic, being able to write those stories well.

You're not doing your job if you're only writing about great movies. I don't like elitist critics who will only write about movies that are on their own exalted level. I'm a great believer in jumping into the mud of popular culture.

The tone of the review of *Speed II* is very different from your other reviews.

One of the things I think a critic has to have, particularly a critic who writes a lot, is a variety of voices. It's one of the things I take some pride in, because I think it's not appropriate to review entirely different movies in the same voice.

Speed II is a really rotten movie. It just doesn't work on so many different levels, and it's so self-important and misconfigured, and it was so heavily hyped, I just relished the chance of writing about that movie, because I knew I could really have a good time. And if I had a good time, then most of my readers would have a good time.

What are your guidelines about burying a movie?

Well, let's look at the two *Speeds* as a perfect example. The first movie was a genre movie. It was very clean, powerfully done, and it delivered on the promise of the genre. You give them your seven bucks, and they'll take your mind away from you for two hours, and send you out of the movie exhausted, yet happy.

And so there seems to be what might be called the integrity of craftsmanship in that movie. They're trying very hard. And I've got to give them credit for trying, and for executing.

Speed II, on the other hand, smacked of cynicism in the sense that everybody in it wanted to be somewhere else, and they were all doing it because the first movie had made so much money. The level of passion and engagement and conviction was much, much lower.

And so I felt justified in driving a nail into its heart, because I perceived a kind of cynicism there, a kind of crassness that struck me as inappropriate.

In your review of *Air Force One* you seemed to show the joy of simply watching a movie. It's a more personal side of journalism. Several times you say, "I loved" certain aspects.

Well, I think it's a technique that can be overused or underused. It has to be done consciously and controlled. Too many movie reviews are too personal. I think readers particularly pick up when the movie review ceases to be about the movie, and becomes about the reviewer.

When I use the first person, it signifies two things: One, I've thought about it, and I'm doing it at that specific time because I want to emphasize something that might not be as strongly expressed were I not to personalize it. And two, I think it signifies my comfort level.

I don't feel uncomfortable referring to myself. I think I went 10 years at the *Sun* before I used the first person. And I still do it fairly sparingly.

Your reviews of *M* and *Anastasia* each include interesting history. How much research do you have to put into your pieces?

Well, it depends a lot on the movie. I didn't see how I could do *M* without pretty thoroughly looking into it, because it was, after all, a historical document, and it comes from a certain specific time and place in movie and European history. So I did a lot of background reading on it.

I don't think I did a great deal of research on *Anastasia,* because I know a little bit about the Russian revolution, and I have strong feelings about the Soviet Union.

Let me ask about your audience. Toward the end of your review of *Anastasia,* you write, "This creeps me way out." Why do you use an expression like that, and how do you see your audience?

I used that expression because it seemed to me to catch exactly the awkwardness that I felt. But the real reason I used it is because someone had used that in a discussion. I was in the process of getting a novel ready for publication, and I had a little sequence in it. The editor, Bill Thomas of Doubleday, said, "This creeps me out."

I'd never heard that phrase before, and one of the things a writer does is treasure little phrases, and carry them around like quarters, and look for a place to spend them. And once I heard that phrase, I knew I would spend it soon, and it was probably a week or two before I had an opportunity to say that.

Now, you asked about audience. Do I think of audience? Well, not in the sense that I'm trying to please an audience, or not in the sense that I'm pandering to an audience. I'm just sort of operating on an assumption that if the piece is well-written and vivid, the audience will appreciate it.

My idealized audience is the most old-fashioned kind, which is a literate, ironic, informed audience. I hope they get what I'm talking about. I take on faith that that audience is out there rather than trying to write a piece and dumb it down or smart it up for a certain audience.

When I was in my courtship dance with the *Post,* I knew there was some concern that I was too old, and that I couldn't reach a younger audience. If you look at my work, you'll see it assumes a certain cultural heritage, and it's probably the cultural heritage of people my age who know who Humphrey Bogart is, and know who the Three Stooges are, and remember John F. Kennedy, and know who won World War II, and have read Ernest Hemingway, and know the difference between the Dodgers and the Mets, because all those things are important to me.

And you could say to me, "Gee, those are irrelevant to today's younger audience or today's ethnic audiences." And that point would be entirely, completely true. I would have no defense. Basically, what I'm selling is who I am.

You have a really nice approach in telling the plot of *The Sweet Hereafter*. How do you determine what to tell without telling too much?

That's a key technical question to writing a movie review. I've always believed that people were more interested in characters and situations than plots, and I think a reviewer who oversynopsizes is doing no service. I try to evoke the movie rather than retell it. And I think in terms of plot synopsis, less is always better.

In "Becoming a Film Critic," you wrote about six qualities of films that a reviewer should consider. They are: performance, movie effects, the auteur's, or director's, voice, photography, pace, and ideas. Do you still use those six qualities as a guide?

The article derived from a speech I'd given in which I tell a story about how I started writing reviews at the *Sun*. I had seen a movie, and when I left that movie, I was very puzzled and baffled by it. I remember thinking very explicitly maybe I wouldn't be such a good movie critic, because I wouldn't know what to say about that movie.

The next day in the office, our film critic was fired by our publisher, and the editor of the section came to me and said, "I know you've been dying to do this job. Have you seen..."—and he named the movie I had seen the night before. The movie was *Southern Comfort*, directed by Walter Hill. He said, "Could you write a piece on that?" And I said, "Uh, yeah."

And so what I had to do was sit there on the spot and invent a way of reviewing the movie. I wrote out six areas that should be considered, and I used that as my fall-back structure.

When you write a review, you'll see that of those six qualities, one or two are usually predominant. They're the ones that are the most provocative and the most interesting. So much of the review will touch on those aspects.

Over the years, I've gotten to the point where I do that reflexively or subconsciously. Something in the movie will suggest itself to me as being the crucial factor. It may be the story. It may be what I take to be the directing. It may be a certain performance. You just never know going in what it's going to be.

You mentioned that you do other types of writing. You've written novels and articles. How did you get started in that and how does that help you?

Well, in a certain odd way I was born into it. I had two goals. One was to write novels, and the other was to be a film critic. It never occurred to me that there was any reason to pick one over the other. Maybe the lesson of my career is it's really good to have very specific goals. I wanted to write the kinds of novels I write, and I wanted to write the kind of film pieces I write.

I joke with people. I say, "My two best lengths are 800 words and 140,000 words." I can't write anything in between. In fact, I had an offer from a Washington think tank to write a piece that was 6,000 words long, and I said to myself, "I don't know 6,000 words about anything. I don't have 6,000 words of wisdom in me." Six thousand words seems much harder to me than 140,000 words.

The novel writing satisfies one of my needs to create stories. And the publication of the novels validated me in ways that I would not have otherwise been validated. I have a sense that, had I not published the novels, I would not have become a film critic.

Tell me a little bit about your novels.

They are—I guess the generic term is "thrillers." I guess they reflect my mindset. They're male-oriented novels. They're usually about some professional in the field of security or the military who's put in some crisis and has got to rely on certain specific skills, both intellectual and physical, in order to solve a problem.

The character I've created, and now have written four books about, is named Bob Lee Swagger. He's from Arkansas, and he's a former Marine sniper in Vietnam, where he was very successful, and where he was also grievously wounded. He came back suffering all the nightmares of post-combat stress syndrome.

He just doesn't sound much like a guy from Illinois.

No. I couldn't write a novel about *my* life. I've got to project the issues of my life into some fantasy mechanism. The only thing I can hope is that somewhere out there, there's an ex-Marine sniper who'll write a great novel about being the film critic of *The Washington Post.*

Is there any other advice that you'd give to a person who is either a film critic or who wants to become one?

Well, the lesson of my career is to get inside the culture somehow, and once you're inside, it's much easier to move laterally than it is to come in cold. I mean, I would not have gotten that job on the *Sun* had I not been there for 10 years, and done reasonably well, and established a reputation. And I would not have gotten the job at the *Post* had I not been at the *Sun* for 16 years, and done well, and established some kind of reputation.

So my counsel to would-be film critics is, the first thing you should do is master the fundamental journalistic skills. If you have to start on a paper as a copy reader, or as a layout man, or as a copy boy, you can do that. And once you're in the culture, possibilities will open up. You'll hear about things. You'll meet people. There will be chances to do this, that, and the other thing. And the next thing you have to do is you just can't give up on your dream.

The Boston Globe

Gail Caldwell

Finalist, Criticism

Gail Caldwell is the chief book critic for *The Boston Globe,* where she has been a staff writer and reviewer since 1985. From 1991 to 1995, she was the *Globe'*s book editor. She has twice been a finalist for the Pulitzer Prize in criticism. Her reviews and essays have also appeared in the *Village Voice, The Washington Post,* the *Atlanta Constitution,* and other publications. She is a nominator for the *Irish Times* Fiction Prize and has served several times on the fiction jury for the Pulitzer Prize. She holds a master's degree from the University of Texas, where she was an instructor in American Studies until 1981.

Like any good journalist, a reviewer acts as a guide for the reader, directing us to information and insights that make our lives richer. Gail Caldwell's book reviews take her readers deeper into today's books while exploring the machinations of the literary marketplace. In this illuminating look at best-seller *Cold Mountain,* she retraces the steps contemporary authors take on paths made by yesterday's writers and helps us understand why they are so successful.

Textbook example of
a literary whirlwind

NOVEMBER 25, 1997

Yes, Miss Scarlett, war is hell—except in the Land of
Art, where unmitigated slaughter can take on the pri-
mal allure of Hieronymus Bosch and the exalted di-
mensions of myth. Charles Frazier knows this, and
apparently his publisher knew it, too: Within a month
of its publication date this summer, *Cold Mountain* had
hit *The New York Times* bestseller list; six weeks later,
it was in No. 1 position, and *Atlantic Monthly Press*
had 500,000 copies in print. The Civil War saga about
a wounded Confederate soldier's journey homeward is
Frazier's first novel, but that didn't stop (or even diminish) grandiloquent comparisons to Homer, Faulkner, and Cormac McCarthy. Still, the early literary
groundswell about *Cold Mountain* was mostly a populist phenomenon, driven by booksellers and word-
of-mouth recommendations, only picked up by the
national media when the book hit six-digit sales. And
then, on Nov. 18, *Cold Mountain* won the National
Book Award for fiction—beating out four more established contenders, among them Don DeLillo's gargantuan *Underworld* and Cynthia Ozick's eminently
literary *The Puttermesser Papers.*

This is the kind of marketing-cum-art spectacle that
publishers adore, where the spin is self-perpetuating
and the second book contract is itself a thing of wonder. Like the parents of the septuplets in Iowa, Charles
Frazier is all set for the time being. In the brave new
world of multimillion-dollar advances and mega-
publishing, such legends are the bait that feeds the
shark, which, after all, must keep moving lest it die:
Three years ago, it was John Berendt's *Midnight in the
Garden of Good and Evil* (never mind the movie); a
decade earlier, it was Umberto Eco's *The Name of the
Rose* (never mind that no one actually read it). Less in-
sanely successful, but more literary, have been Donna
Tartt's *The Secret History* and this year's contribution
to Eastern chic, Arundhati Roy's *The God of Small
Things.* The buzz blueprint looks roughly like this:

Undiscovered, mildly literary author—who secretly believes book will never be published—brings battered manuscript to attention of agent. Agent recognizes sex/violence/intrigue wrapped within quick-lit milieu; by end of day, a bidding war has already begun paving the way to Hollywood.

Well, fair enough; Melville should have been so lucky. But *Cold Mountain* is really *Bridges of Madison County* bumping into *The Odyssey,* and that brilliant marriage of formula—epic pop, where the timeless themes of war and exile are tempered by love letters and hog butchering—has made the book a hit. It's a little bit of Yee-ha lit, with its heart and ambition in Odysseus's journey homeward, its deep emotionality in the grit and texture of the Carolina mountains at the end of the Civil War. Charles Frazier has taken his love of the classics, his memories of a great-great-uncle (from whom his protagonist, Inman, is roughly imagined), and transformed them into a great and baggy monster of endless calamity, corn grits, and the tender promise of home. If you can feel the shadow of horror just over your shoulder in *Cold Mountain,* you can also smell the honeysuckle vine that has to be just around the bend.

DEVOURING SHAMELESSLY

I devoured *Cold Mountain* shamelessly, often returning to it at the end of a day of more austere reading with a kind of perverse glee: Who would Inman murder on the road tonight, I wondered; would Ada, his long-suffering Penelope, get those winter cabbages in the ground before first frost? The novel unfolds in alternating chapters: Wounded at Petersburg, soul-sick of war, Inman has become a deserter, climbing out a window of the hospital and beginning the long walk home to Cold Mountain. Waiting there, or so he hopes, is Ada Monroe—daughter of a high-falutin' preacher (he named his horse Ralph and his cow Waldo, after Emerson), herself versed in the Greek poets, "educated beyond the point considered wise for females." With her father now dead, most of this knowledge has proved useless to running a farm. When we first meet her, Ada is scrambling under the bushes looking for an egg to eat—beat up by a rooster, and as pathetic as

Scarlett O'Hara before she cut down those drapes to make a dress.

Such helplessness will not last: Enter Ruby, a scrappy little thing who can plow all day, reshingle the smokehouse, and tell you where in the woods to find goldenseal. (She also killed that damn rooster, on the day Ada met her.) When Ruby moves in to help run the farm, Ada reads to her from Dickens and Homer; Ruby delivers her own oral narrative, which includes spirit voices, Cherokee teachers, a drunken father who fiddles beautifully while all the South burns. She was self-sufficient by about age 7, and she passes this independence of spirit on to her new partner; Ada's may be the true transformation in *Cold Mountain,* but the presence of Ruby is as rich and compelling as anything in the novel.

Our Odysseus, meanwhile, has become the reluctant pugilist on his way back to Ithaca. *Cold Mountain* presents itself as an antiwar novel: the battles take place offstage, in Inman's memory, and there is nothing redemptive about one drop of blood spilled therein. (When news of the war reaches Ada, it's delivered in vainglorious idiocies by women trying to bear up.) But Inman has to kill a lot of guys to survive in his role as pacifist hero: bounty hunters, the nefarious Guard looking for deserters—few are a match for the scythe or LeMat's pistol Inman wields to fend off the inevitable evil stranger on the road. With its picaresque detours and often mock-heroic struggles, *Cold Mountain* bears the same equivocal message as Homer's monument, decrying war and yet bound to its bloodshed, cherishing the idea of peace by swimming through carnage to get there. This is an obvious irony, but its pop-culture charm is more subterranean: You get the feel-good premise of honor and mayhem both, with the armchair frisson of violence cloaked in the higher consciousness of human virtue.

The parallels to *The Odyssey* provide a kick of allusive pleasure, from the blind prophet at the beginning of *Cold Mountain* to versions of Calypso and Odysseus's loyal swineherd (here, she cooks him a goat and sends him on his way). Lots of caves abound, as do animal sacrifices; for the more pacific crowd, there are the somewhat less barbarous metaphors visited upon crows, herons, bears, and ducks. Frazier's deliverance of the natural world, in fact, is one of the near-palpable joys of *Cold Mountain;* between its chicken and dumplings and its gorgeous, step-by-step geography, it offers passages as enveloping as a feather-down comforter. This bedrock realism may be the real sustenance of *Cold Mountain,* and what has made it the darling of mass culture and highbrow juries alike. Paying homage to a structure—the epic poem—as old as written history itself, with its fictional premises couched within the parameters of the 19th-century novel, the book is everything the au courant modern novel no longer wishes to be.

IS IT LITERATURE?

In other words, it's irresistible, but is it literature? I didn't weep at the end of *Cold Mountain,* like a lot of people confess to doing; a few ducks floating about symbolically in an earlier pond tipped me off to the tears that lay ahead. I was nonetheless drawn relentlessly back into its elaborately imagined world, where yet another dawn signaled Inman's faltering pilgrimage and Ada's blooming strength—where war was wrong and love was good, and, God willing, where the phoenix again would rise.

But the implicit covenant of literature is that it offer something beyond its own story line: outlasting, for instance, the creaky, homespun narration of *Cold Mountain* and the precisely romantic arc of its hero homeward bound. The novel is momentous and unforgettable in the same way a terrific Disney movie can be: Certain scenes are in your mind forever, whether you want them there or not. What it doesn't give you is any greater authorial wisdom, anything more enduring than its own heartrending tale—two lovers rent by war and separation, waiting to be united in Athena's endless night. Homer offered as much 3,000 years ago, when he gave us one of the cornerstones of Western lit guised within the yearning and lamentation of Odysseus and Penelope. Ain't no amount of cold biscuits and tragic consequence gonna improve on that.

Lessons Learned

BY GAIL CALDWELL

When Charles Frazier's *Cold Mountain* came from the rear and won the National Book Award, I decided to write a somewhat tart appraisal of the novel and its gargantuan popular appeal. What I hadn't counted on was having my deadline compressed from a matter of days to several hours. The essay was due Wednesday evening. Monday morning my phone rang. The section editor had a dangerously sweet tone in his voice. How was the piece coming? (I hadn't begun.) There had been a space change at the last minute, he confessed; our choice was to go for broke or to hold the piece. Was there any way I could do it today...say, by 2 p.m.? I had four hours.

As staff book critic, I rarely work under the same starting pistol as the newsroom. That morning, I traveled into that white chamber of deadline pressure where adrenaline and caffeine reign. I tried to remember everything I knew about Homer's *The Odyssey* (which *Cold Mountain* sought to emulate), got the latest publishing stats on the novel's sale, and—most important—tried to get out of my own way.

The rest, in retrospect, came pretty easily; I was finished by 1 p.m. I've always been a fairly shy person with an analytical mind and a big mouth—an idiosyncratic mix that makes me well-suited to my job. (Some of this is a result of my having grown up in a small town in Texas, where I read all the time, and where nobody paid much mind to what I thought about what I'd read.) But one of the things I've learned over the years is that an honest critic has to interpret her own emotions and intuitive responses to the work in question: If a novel makes you weep with despair, is it because it's *Madame Bovary* or just that you're a sentimental fool? I've spent days of my life with *Middlemarch* or *To the Lighthouse* in my lap, where the light changed in the room and the entire afternoon receded behind the novel: This is what art does, and is supposed to do, and our response to it is part of its genius. You can critically appraise a novel or play from here to kingdom come, but if you're not also willing to read *yourself*—the effect the work had on you—then your own writing will lack the life and voice that good critical discourse requires.

I'm not talking about self-referential or first-person writing, though there is a place for that, used sparingly and with great consideration. I'm talking about the domain between authority and thoughtful acknowledgment where I believe the critic must reside to do her job. Like most journalists or reviewers, I've had people ask me if it doesn't terrify me, knowing that I'm writing for tens or hundreds of thousands of people. While a part of me is always conscious of the numbers, the fact is that the argument I construct while writing is usually far more private than that: The only presence in the room with me is the novel itself.

When I wrote the *Cold Mountain* piece, I wanted to get at the novel's tremendous pop-culture allure, but also dismantle some of the overblown rhetoric about the book's literary merits. This wasn't Faulkner, but Charles Frazier was enjoying such a high ride for a reason, even if it was as simple as the smell of bacon or the memories of home. The next day, after my piece had appeared, I got a written phone message, taken by a *Globe* intern, from an anonymous and irate reader who was clearly a Frazier loyalist. "Your piece this morning was arrogant, provincial, and narrow-minded," the message read. "Like most New Englanders, you think you know more than you do. This world is a lot wider than your little corner of it."

"Honey," I wanted to say, "it's even worse than you think. I spent the first 30 years of my life in Texas." I kept the message to remind myself of some of the tenets of good criticism: Be respectful, and be fair. Don't be afraid to make people mad. Tell the truth. If you tell it well enough, you're likely to get a rise out of somebody.

Two ways to read, three ways to write

BY ROY PETER CLARK

I've been thinking about reading and writing as a professional for almost 30 years. I've taught storytelling to journalists for more than 20. But it has only been in the last few months that I've learned the most important lesson for those who want to write well.

The lesson is this: There are only two ways of reading. And there are only three ways of writing.

My teacher is a woman I've never met. Her name is Louise Rosenblatt. She is retired and living near Princeton, N.J. In the 1930s she began teaching literature to high school students, and eventually taught at New York University. As a scholar, she not only studied great works of literature, but she also was curious about the different ways her students read works like Shakespeare's *Hamlet* or *Romeo and Juliet.*

She realized early what is now a commonplace: that reading is a transaction in which each reader brings his or her own biography, experiences, prejudices, knowledge, ignorance to the text. The writer may create the text, but the reader makes it a story.

Rosenblatt defines two kinds of reading, which she describes as "the efferent" and "the aesthetic." Excuse the technical language for a moment; we'll be getting to journalism soon. The word efferent means to "carry away from." The reader carries away information, things that have some potential utility. Rosenblatt believes, rightly, that most of journalism falls into this category.

- A new restaurant opens in town.
- The city passes a new tax on property.
- Four new movies open this week.
- A new drug for AIDS is being tested.

In each case, the reader has something to learn, to carry away from the story, to use in his or her personal life, perhaps to pass it on to another. It should be obvious that, whatever the reader brings to the text, the writer can help the reader carry something away. The writing must be clear and comprehensible, and not call attention to itself.

But much of the reading we do is also "aesthetic," which is to say that it is rendered artfully. When we read *Hamlet,* the purpose is not to find our way to Elsinore, or to learn how to dig a grave, or how to poison the tip of a sword. We still read or see *Hamlet* because it is an experience. A virtual reality. It seeks not to *inform* us, but to *form* us.

In the United States, and in other cultures, there is a long tradition of storytelling in newspapers:

- Three men, thought lost, are rescued at sea.
- A woman is murdered in her house, and although many neighbors hear the screams, no one calls the police.
- A dolphin rescues a dog.
- A woman's hearing is restored in an experimental operation.

This kind of news cries out for stories, not articles. Stories are told through scenes. They have characters who speak with dialogue. Details excite the senses, making the experience more real. Stories also have settings, places characters inhabit. We can see things from another's point of view.

Richard Zahler of *The Seattle Times* makes a helpful distinction:

"When we write for information, we depend on the traditional Five Ws: Who, What, Where, When, and Why. But when we write for story, when we thaw out those articles, Who becomes Character; What becomes Plot; Where becomes Setting; When becomes Chronology; Why becomes Motivation."

Let's get back to Louise Rosenblatt's distinction, which she made in 1938 in a book titled *Literature as Exploration.* But this time, I'll use language suggested by my former student, now a successful journalist, Darrell Fears. He talks about language that Points You There and language that Puts You There.

Consider this list of contrasts:

Pointing you there	**Putting you there**
What is useful	What is experienced
What is carried away	An event in time
What is learned	A journey
What happens after	What happens during
The civic	The literary
The poison label	The poem

Rosenblatt explains this last distinction. Let's say you swallow some poison and need to find the antidote on the bottle. When you read it, you are looking for specific information that can save your life. You don't expect metaphor or alliteration. You will notice the words only if the antidote is badly written, creating the "static" that leads to miscommunication.

But we expect a poem to be literary, to use language that calls attention to itself even as it conveys a higher meaning.

So let's say Hurricane Chip is headed for St. Petersburg. I am desperate for information: Should I evacuate? When? Where? What should I bring with me? What about my dog, Rex?

But after the hurricane has hit, and more than 100,000 people are evacuated, and 37 have been killed, and hundreds are homeless, I am looking for more than information. I am looking for story. I want to share an experience with my fellow citizens. Nothing does this better than story.

Now let's illustrate the distinction with two pieces from the *St. Petersburg Times* about education. The first is a standard announcement:

> The League of Women Voters of the St. Petersburg area will hold a forum from 7 to 8:30 tonight on controlled school choice, which would allow parents to choose from any school in their attendance zone. The forum will be at the St. Petersburg Main Library, 3745 Ninth Ave. N. Speakers will be Linda Benware, administrator on special assignment-choice programs, and Gabrielle Davis, education committee from the league. For information, call 896-5197.

The writer includes most of the Ws in this announcement. We know Who, What, Where, and When. Why is implied: School choice is an important issue. The writer expects this information might be useful, that it might mobilize the reader. You can drive to the library. Or call the information number. Perhaps the paragraph could be improved by simplifying the technical language (such as "controlled school choice" or "attendance zone").

Tom French, a writer at the *St. Petersburg Times,* spent a year reporting at Largo (Fla.) High School and another year writing the story of six students trying to survive American education in the 1990s. In the following scene, a group of struggling students play "show and tell," usually a game for kindergarten students:

> The biggest presentation of the day comes from Mickey. His real name is Steve, but he won't let anyone call him that. For as long as the kids in the pod can remember, he has always wanted to be known by the name of his hero, Mickey Mouse. This is not a joke. Mickey has a sense of humor about it, but underneath, he is dead serious.
>
> He shows the others his Mickey Mouse harmonica, and his Mickey Mouse cap. And his Mickey Mouse doll, and his Mickey Mouse toothbrush container, and his Mickey Mouse earring. He would have brought his Mickey Mouse underwear, he says, but he doesn't think they'd really want to see it.
>
> "Anything and everything, I've got it."
>
> He shows them a clipping of a newspaper photo that shows a cow with spots naturally shaped like Mickey Mouse's head. According to Mickey, the people who owned the cow have already sold it to Disney.
>
> "They got like a million bucks for that cow," he says.
>
> The other kids are stunned by the sheer number and diversity of the souvenirs. Especially the Mickey Mouse fishing bobber.
>
> "No way," says another kid, staring at the bobber. "Where would you get that?"
>
> Mickey smiles.

"I don't reveal my sources," he says.

Mrs. O'Donnell asks him how the fascination began. It started a while back, Mickey says, when he had quit school for a time and was at home by himself. He was depressed. He was lonely. He felt like a failure. Then he found Mickey Mouse.

"I couldn't make friends or nothing," he says, "and it's like this was my friend, who would never tell me I was a loser...he never argues back."

A girl nearby raises her hand. "He can never talk to you, either," she says. "Have you thought of that?"

"I don't care," says Mickey. "He never tells me that I'm wrong."

When he says this, the rest of the class grows uncomfortably quiet. Some of the kids are studying Mickey with amazement. Others are fighting not to laugh. Finally someone breaks the silence.

"Is your house, like, Pee-Wee's Playhouse?" says one of the girls.

Mickey stands there with an uncertain smile, looking out at the faces of his classmates. He could take their reactions two ways. Maybe he's made a hit and they're just laughing at the oddness of his obsession. Or maybe they think he really is a loser, confirming his worst suspicions.

Before it goes any further, Mrs. O'Donnell steps in. Politely she thanks Mickey for his presentation and moves on. A few seats down, among a group of kids who refuse to take show-and-tell seriously, always blowing it off, a boy holds up a can of diet Coke he's been drinking.

"This is my can," he says with a smirk. "You can recycle it and get money for it."

"This is my pen," says the boy beside him, playing along. "It flies."

With that, he pulls the pen back and flips it into the air. It sails across the room in a graceful arc, tumbling lengthwise end over end...

This kind of writing depends on intensive reporting that comes, first and foremost, from access. Tom French had to sit in that classroom for many days, before this incident came to light. He is there on another day when the students in the class learn that none of them lives with both birth parents. Stories can be reconstructed from people's memories, but nothing is better than an eyewitness account—where the reporter is the eyewitness.

When we think about the two ways of reading, and the two ways of writing, it is helpful to think about a spectrum—a scale of 1 to 10. The announcement about the school choice meeting is almost pure information: it scores a 1 or 2. The scene about Mickey Mouse is straight narrative: it scores a 9 or 10.

So what might a "5" look like, something in the middle of the scale? Perhaps a historical account in the biography of a famous person, such as this passage from a book on American inventors:

> De Forest's love of analogy also appears in the poetry he frequently wrote, a selection from which he included in his autobiography. His use of metaphor seems to have emerged unconsciously and spontaneously. For instance, when observing under a microscope the flow of minute particles between electrodes in his wireless detector, he imagined...

This passage contains some information, but also helps us envision a scene of a creative man looking into a microscope.

One question remains: What do I mean in my title when I say there are two ways of reading and three ways of writing? The first two ways of reading and writing should be obvious by now. We read and write for information. We read and write for story. Language points us there. Language puts us there.

So what is the third way: reading and writing for both information *and* story.

Journalists often write articles that have story elements and vice versa. Moreover, we have some tricks of the trade that help us do this. The first is the anecdote, a word often confused with "antidote"—unless we say that the anecdote is an antidote to the poison of dull writing.

The anecdote is a tiny story within a story, "a short account of some interesting or humorous incident." The word comes from the Greek meaning "previously unpublished," suggesting some little secret piece of history or biography. So Chip Scanlan, now director of Poynter's writing program, tells us that the grieving mother of a girl missing for years leaves the front porch light on for her, and places a piece of tape over the light switch so it cannot be accidently turned off. The story tells us about eternal grief, but the anecdote shows us.

Don Fry, my fellow writing coach, suggests a story structure in which anecdotes can be used as gold coins. "Imagine yourself walking along a path through the forest when you come upon a gold coin. You pick it up and put it in your pocket. You walk another mile, and find another coin. Another mile, another coin. Even though you're tired, you keep walking until the coins run out." In the same way, a reader will more likely move through an informational story if he or she is rewarded with a gold coin, a tiny bit of story that intensifies the experience of reading.

So an article can be mostly informational and be brightened by embedded stories. Or it can work the other way around. The story can begin with an experience, a narrative, rendered so artfully that we can see it, hear it, smell it. Bill Blundell, now-retired reporter for *The Wall Street Journal,* once wrote this lead to a story about the disappearing cowboy:

> The lariat whirls as the man on horseback separates a calf from the herd. Suddenly, the loop snakes around the calf's rear legs and tightens. Wrapping a turn of rope around the saddle horn, the rider drags the hapless animal to his crew.
>
> The flanker whips the calf onto its back, and the medicine man inoculates the animal. Amid blood, dust and bawling, the calf is dehorned with a coring tool, branded in an acrid cloud of smoke from burning hair and flesh, earmarked with a penknife in the ranch's unique pattern and castrated. It is all over in one minute.

Fascinating story. But why are we reading this scene? What's the point? What is the context? So what? It turns out there are few real cowboys left in an era of cowboy hype. And the author communicates this in a passage called the nut paragraph, or "nut graph" for short:

> Finally, there is a little band of men like Jim Miller. Their boots are old and cracked. They still know as second nature the ways of horse and cow, the look of sunrise over empty land—and the hazards, sheer drudgery and rock-bottom pay that go with perhaps the most over-romanticized of American jobs. There are very few of these men left. "Most of the real cowboys I know," says Mr. Miller, "have been dead for a while."

Another story begins with a man making himself a Spam sandwich, even though he swore that if he ever survived World War II, where he ate so much of the stuff, he would never eat Spam again. But why read about Spam? Check the fourth paragraph: "Spam lives, believe it or not. The Hormel company sold 91 million pounds of it last year, making Spam America's most popular canned meat."

The narrative can slow down, or even stop, for a bit of background or explanation. Think of this structure as the moving train, a reader's journey created by the writer's narrative line. Every so often, the train slows down or even makes a whistle stop, during which the reporter may speak directly to the reader to explain, or offer history, or provide context or background.

So we've learned that stories can brighten information, and that information can enrich stories.

One other tool to bring information and narrative together is a story form I call the "hourglass." This form works well when there is breaking news combined with narrative chronology. The top of the hourglass looks like the old inverted pyramid, but is shorter in duration—perhaps four or five paragraphs. So we learn that a man shot a police officer in the leg, ran into a house, held a boy hostage for eight hours, surrendered without harming the boy, and was finally arrested. What follows is a transition, called the "turn." "Police and witnesses gave the following account of the dramatic incident." What follows is a retelling of events in chronological order, with many more details than a standard story would allow.

Readers now have a choice. They can read the top and quit, or, if interested can linger down in the story.

If any of these ideas serve you well, say a prayer of thanks for the contributions of Professor Louise Rosenblatt.

This article originally appeared in Workbench: The Bulletin of The National Writers' Workshop, Vol. 4, Winter 1998, published by The Poynter Institute.

Annual bibliography

BY DAVID SHEDDEN

WRITING AND REPORTING BOOKS 1997

Adams, Paul. *Writing Right for Today's Media.* Chicago: Nelson-Hall, 1997.

Baskette, Floyd K., Jack Z. Sissors, and Brian S. Brooks. *The Art of Editing.* 6th edition. Boston: Allyn and Bacon, 1997.

Blake, Gary, and Robert W. Bly. *The Elements of Copywriting.* New York: Macmillan, 1997.

Blum, Deborah, and Mary Knudson, eds. *A Field Guide for Science Writers.* New York: Oxford University Press, 1997.

Bolker, Joan, ed. *The Writer's Home Companion.* New York: Henry Holt, 1997.

Bonime, Andrew, and Ken Pohlman. *Writing for New Media.* New York: John Wiley & Sons, 1997.

Bowles, Dorothy A., and Diane L. Borden. *Creative Editing for Print Media.* Belmont, Calif.: Wadsworth, 1997.

Burack, Sylvia K., ed. *The Writer's Handbook.* Boston: The Writer, Inc., 1997.

Gach, Gary. *Writers.Net: Every Writer's Essential Guide to Online Resources and Opportunities.* Rocklin, Calif.: Prima Publishing, 1997.

Gutkind, Lee. *The Art of Creative Non-Fiction.* New York: John Wiley & Sons, 1997.

Harrington, Walt. *Intimate Journalism: The Art and Craft of Reporting Everyday Life.* Thousand Oaks, Calif.: Sage Publications, 1997.

Hennessy, Brendan. *Writing Feature Articles.* 3rd edition. Oxford: Heineman, 1997.

Holm, Kirsten C., ed. *1997 Writer's Market.* Cincinnati, Ohio: Writer's Digest Books, 1997.

Levin, Michael. *Writer's Internet Sourcebook.* San Francisco: No Starch Press, 1997.

Maloy, Timothy K. *The Writer's Internet Handbook.* Lakewood, N.J.: Watson-Guptill, 1997.

Mencher, Melvin. *News Reporting and Writing.* 7th edition. Madison, Wis.: Brown & Benchmark, 1997.

—. *The Sayings of Chairman Mel.* The Poynter Papers: No. 9, St. Petersburg, Fla.: The Poynter Institute, 1997.

Mutchler, John C., ed. *The American Directory of Writer's Guidelines.* Fresno, Calif.: Quill Driver Books, 1997.

Pitts, Beverley J., et al. *The Process of Media Writing.* Boston: Allyn and Bacon, 1997.

Rich, Carole. *Writing and Reporting News: A Coaching Method.* 2nd edition. Belmont, Calif.: Wadsworth, 1997.

Scanlan, Christopher, ed. *Best Newspaper Writing 1997.* St. Petersburg, Fla.: The Poynter Institute.

Sloan, W. David, and Cheryl S. Wray. *Masterpieces of Reporting.* Northport, Ala.: Vision Press, 1997.

Sloan, W. David, Cheryl S. Wray, and C. Joanne Sloan. *Great Editorials: Masterpieces of Opinion Writing.* Northport, Ala.: Vision Press, 1997.

Wells, Gordon. *The Magazine Writer's Handbook.* London: Allison & Busby, 1997.

CLASSICS

Atchity, Kenneth. *A Writer's Time: A Guide to the Creative Process, from Vision through Revision.* New York: Norton, 1986.

Berg, A. Scott. *Max Perkins: Editor of Genius.* New York: Dutton, 1978.

Bernstein, Theodore M. *The Careful Writer: A Modern Guide to English Usage.* New York: Atheneum Press, 1965.

Biagi, Shirley. *Interviews That Work: A Practical Guide for Journalists.* 2nd edition. Belmont, Calif.: Wadsworth, 1992.

Blundell, William E. *The Art and Craft of Feature Writing: Based on The Wall Street Journal.* New York: New American Library, 1988.

Brady, John. *The Craft of Interviewing.* New York: Vintage Books, 1977.

Brande, Dorothea. *Becoming a Writer.* Los Angeles: J. P. Tarcher; Boston: distributed by Harcourt Brace, reprint of 1934 edition, 1981.

Brown, Karen, Roy Peter Clark, Don Fry, and Christopher Scanlan, eds. *Best Newspaper Writing.* St. Petersburg, Fla.: The Poynter Institute. Published annually since 1979.

Cappon, Rene J. *The Word: An Associated Press Guide to Good News Writing.* New York: The Associated Press, 1982.

Clark, Roy Peter. *Free to Write: A Journalist Teaches Young Writers.* Portsmouth, N.H.: Heinemann Educational Books, 1986.

Clark, Roy Peter, and Don Fry. *Coaching Writers: The Essential Guide for Editors and Reporters.* New York: St. Martin's Press, 1992.

Dillard, Annie. *The Writing Life.* New York: Harper and Row, 1989.

Downie, Leonard, Jr. *The New Muckrakers.* New York: NAL-Dutton, 1978.

Elbow, Peter. *Writing With Power: Techniques for Mastering the Writing Process.* New York: Oxford University Press, 1981.

Follett, Wilson. *Modern American Usage: A Guide.* London: Longmans, 1986.

Franklin, Jon. *Writing for Story: Craft Secrets of Dramatic Nonfiction.* New York: Atheneum, 1986.

Goldstein, Norm, ed. *The Associated Press Stylebook and Libel Manual.* 27th edition. Reading, Mass.: Addison-Wesley, 1992.

Gross, Gerald, ed. *Editors on Editing: An Inside View of What Editors Really Do.* New York: Harper & Row, 1985.

Howarth, William L., ed. *The John McPhee Reader.* New York: Farrar, Straus and Giroux, 1990.

Hugo, Richard. *The Triggering Town: Lectures & Essays on Poetry & Writing.* New York: Norton, 1992.

Mencher, Melvin. *News Reporting and Writing.* 5th edition. Dubuque, Iowa: William C. Brown, 1991.

Metzler, Ken. *Creative Interviewing: The Writer's Guide to Gathering Information by Asking Questions.* 2nd edition. Englewood Cliffs, N.J.: Prentice Hall, 1989.

Mitford, Jessica. *Poison Penmanship: The Gentle Art of Muckraking.* New York: Knopf, 1979.

Murray, Donald. *Shoptalk: Learning to Write With Writers.* Portsmouth, N.H.: Boynton/Cook, 1990.

—. *Writing for Your Readers.* Old Saybrook, Conn.: Globe Pequot Press, 1992.

Plimpton, George. *Writers at Work: The Paris Review Interviews.* Series. New York: Viking, 1992.

Ross, Lillian. *Reporting.* New York: Dodd, 1981.

Scanlan, Christopher, ed. *How I Wrote the Story.* Providence Journal Company, 1986.

Sims, Norman, ed. *Literary Journalism in the Twentieth Century.* New York: Oxford University Press, 1990.

Snyder, Louis L., and Richard B. Morris, eds. *A Treasury of Great Reporting.* New York: Simon & Schuster, 1962.

Stafford, William, and Donald Hall, eds. *Writing the Australian Crawl: View on the Writer's Vocation.* Ann Arbor, Mich.: University of Michigan Press, 1978.

Strunk, William, Jr., and E. B. White. *The Elements of Style.* 3rd edition. New York: Macmillan, 1979.

Talese, Gay. *Fame & Obscurity.* New York: Ivy Books, 1971.

Wardlow, Elwood M., ed. *Effective Writing and Editing: A Guidebook for Newspapers.* Reston, Va.: American Press Institute, 1985.

White, E. B. *Essays of E. B. White.* New York: Harper & Row, 1977.

Witt, Leonard. *The Complete Book of Feature Writing.* Cincinnati, Ohio: Writer's Digest Books, 1991.

Wolfe, Tom. *The New Journalism.* New York: Harper & Row, 1973.

Zinsser, William. *On Writing Well.* 4th edition. New York: Harper & Row, 1990.

—. *Writing to Learn.* New York: Harper & Row, 1988.

ARTICLES 1997

Brown, Karen F. "How the Best Writers Do It." *Quill,* June 1997, pp. 11–14.

Davis, Nancy M. "Honor Thy Copy Editors And They'll Help You Regain the Faith of Readers." *Presstime,* November 1997, pp. 49–54.

Fry, Don. "Creating Quiet Corners in a Noisy Profession." *The American Editor,* July/August 1997, p. 25.

Hart, Jack. "Why Worry About Words?" *Editor & Publisher,* Feb. 1, 1997, p. 13.

Kieran, Matthew. "News Reporting and the Ideological Presumption." *Journal of Communication,* Spring 1997, pp. 79–96.

Killenberg, G. Michael, and Robert Dardenne. "Instruction in News Reporting as Community-Focused Journalism." *J&MC Educator,* Spring 1997, pp. 52–58.

Kirtz, Bill. "Writing Advice to Woo Readers." *Quill,* June 1997, p. 7.

LaRocque, Paula. "Good Writing Springs from Keen Observations, Use of Our Intellects." *Quill,* July/August 1997, p. 35.

McGrath, Kevin. "Consult Your Compass Before Starting to Write." *The American Editor,* September 1997, p. 26.

Morris, Mackie. "Word Warriors." *Communicator,* August 1997, p. 63.

Potter, Deborah. "The Write Stuff." *Communicator,* September 1997, pp. 121–122.

Smith, Edward J. "Professional and Academic Levels of a Mass Media Writing Course." *J&MC Educator,* Spring 1997, pp. 59–65.

Walton, Tom. "We Need to Watch Our Language." *The American Editor,* July/August 1997, pp. 14, 16.

Weinberg, Steve. "The Reporter in the Novel." *Columbia Journalism Review,* November/December 1997, pp. 17–18.

Wiist, W. Michael. "Seeking a Coaching Style of Teaching News Writing." *J&MC Educator,* Winter 1997, pp. 68–74.

Willis, Jim. "Risky Business: Science and Journalism." *Presstime,* December 1997, p. 71.